The book of Numbers must be one of the least read books in the Bible simply because the title "Numbers" unfortunately sounds rather boring. The book is really about the Israelites' journey through the desert and their journey from slavery to nationhood as the people of God. Dr Modine's detailed knowledge of the Old Testament is demonstrated in this helpful commentary. He helps to bring this book alive and brings out lessons which we can apply to discipleship today.

Neville Bartle, DMiss
Former missionary to Papua New Guinea

Mitchel Modine brings out the dynamic spirit of the book of Numbers to challenge readers to pause and think deeper in order to capture its truths and their current relevance.

Jason Valeriano Hallig, PhD
Professor, Asia Graduate School of Theology, Philippines

Asia Bible Commentary Series

NUMBERS

Asia Bible Commentary Series

NUMBERS

Mitchel Modine

General Editor
Federico G. Villanueva

Old Testament Consulting Editors
Yohanna Katanacho, Tim Meadowcroft, Joseph Shao

New Testament Consulting Editors
Steve Chang, Andrew Spurgeon, Brian Wintle

© 2018 by Mitchel Modine

Published 2018 by Langham Global Library
An imprint of Langham Publishing
www.langhampublishing.org

Langham Publishing and its imprints are a ministry of Langham Partnership

Langham Partnership
PO Box 296, Carlisle, Cumbria CA3 9WZ, UK
www.langham.org

Published in partnership with Asia Theological Association

ATA
QCC PO Box 1454 – 1154, Manila, Philippines
www.ataasia.com

ISBNs:
978-1-78368-414-4 Print
978-1-78368-415-1 ePub
978-1-78368-417-5 PDF

Mitchel Modine has asserted his right under the Copyright, Designs, and Patents Act, 1988 to be identified as the Author of this work.

All rights reserved. No part of this publication may be reproduced, stored in a retrieval system, or transmitted in any form or by any means, electronic, mechanical, photocopying, recording, or otherwise, without the prior written permission of the publisher or the Copyright Licensing Agency.

Unless otherwise stated, Scripture quotations are from the New International Version, copyright © 2011. Used by permission. All rights reserved.

British Library Cataloguing in Publication Data
A catalogue record for this book is available from the British Library.

ISBN: 978-1-78368-414-4

Cover & Book Design: projectluz.com

Langham Partnership actively supports theological dialogue and an author's right to publish but does not necessarily endorse the views and opinions set forth and works referenced within this publication or guarantee its technical and grammatical correctness. Langham Partnership does not accept any responsibility or liability to persons or property as a consequence of the reading, use, or interpretation of its published content.

To Reynaldo "Raning" De Castro (1941–2017),
who counted for more than he ever thought he did.

CONTENTS

Commentary

Series Preface	xi
Author's Preface	xiii
Acknowledgments	xv
List of Abbreviations	xvii
Introduction	1
Commentary on Numbers 1–36	9
Bibliography	191

Topics

The Importance of Symbols in Christianity: Reflections from the Philippine Context	16
Sacred Fire in Papua New Guinea	23
Blessing and Cursing in Tribal Societies	47
Can God Speak through the Buddha?	71
Sabbath Observance	85
The Red Heifer and Eschatology	104
Balaam the Shaman	121
Can God Speak through a Pig?	128
Marriage of Daughters in Nagaland, India	188

SERIES PREFACE

In recent years, we have witnessed one of the greatest shifts in the history of world Christianity. It used to be that the majority of Christians lived in the West, but Christians are now evenly distributed around the globe. This shift has implications for the task of interpreting the Bible from within our respective contexts, which is in line with the growing realization that every theology is contextual. Thus, the questions that we bring into our reading of the Bible will be shaped by our present realities as well as our historical and social locations. There is a need therefore to interpret the Bible for our own contexts.

The Asia Bible Commentary Series addresses this need. In line with the mission of the Asia Theological Association Publications, we have gathered evangelical Bible scholars working among Asians to write commentaries on each book of the Bible. The mission is to "produce resources that are biblical, pastoral, contextual, missional, and prophetic for pastors, Christian leaders, cross-cultural workers, and students in Asia." Although the Bible can be studied for different reasons, we believe that it is given primarily for the edification of the Body of Christ (2 Tim 3:16–17). The ABCS is designed to help pastors in their sermon preparation, cell group leaders or lay leaders in their Bible study groups, Christian students in their study of the Bible, and Christians in general in their efforts to apply the Bible in their respective contexts.

Each commentary begins with an introduction that provides general information about the book's author and original context, summarizes the main message or theme of the book, and outlines its potential relevance to a particular Asian context. The introduction is followed by an exposition that combines exegesis and application. Here, we seek to speak to and empower Christians in Asia by using our own stories, parables, poems, and other cultural resources as we expound the Bible.

The Bible is actually Asian in that it comes from ancient West Asia, and there are many similarities between the world of the Bible and traditional Asian cultures. But there are also many differences that we need to explore in some depth. That is why the commentaries also include articles or topics in which we bring specific issues in Asian church, social, and religious contexts into dialogue with relevant issues in the Bible. We do not seek to resolve every tension that emerges but rather to allow the text to illumine the context and vice versa, acknowledging that we do not have all the answers to every mystery.

Numbers

May the Holy Spirit, who inspired the writers of the Bible, bring light to the hearts and minds of all who use these materials, to the glory of God and to the building up of the churches!

Federico G. Villanueva

General Editor

AUTHOR'S PREFACE

When the invitation to write the volume on Numbers for the Asia Bible Commentary Series first came to me, I was in the final stages of writing the volume on 1–2 Chronicles for a series published by my denominational publishing house in the United States of America. Previously, I also had the privilege of contributing parts of the second volume on the prophet Jeremiah for this same denominational series. Thus I have now completed commentaries on books in each of the three divisions of the Old Testament, according to the Hebrew reckoning: Prophet (Jeremiah), Writings (1–2 Chronicles), and Torah (Numbers).

The two latter volumes required me to stretch as a scholar into areas with which I was not familiar. I received the assignment for Jeremiah because my editor for the previous series and I had both written our doctoral theses on Jeremiah at the same institution, under the same mentor, precisely twenty years apart. In addition, as most people familiar with the Old Testament are aware, Chronicles and Numbers tend to rank among the "boring" books, whose content seemingly offers little of interest to the scholarly reader, much less to those who interact with the Bible on a casual or devotional level. Nearly one-third of 1 Chronicles, in terms of the number of chapters, is taken up with genealogies. Numbers, so far as I knew, concerned itself with lists of this and lists of that, along with various obscure laws for sacrifices and whatnot.

Yet by studying these books extensively in preparation for the commentaries, I discovered a wealth of material that contributed to my understanding of the thought-world of ancient Israel. In the case of Chronicles, I learned a great deal about the concerns of Persian-Period Judah. Studying Numbers led me to a deeper awareness of the monarchical period in which, according to the theory that still holds large command of the field, the book received its final form.

More than that, however, through my deep study of these "boring" books, God's Holy Spirit revealed to me insights that I never expected to find. At several points during the writing of the present volume, I was brought to my feet, overwhelmed by a sense of wonder at the holiness of God. I do hope that this sense of amazement will communicate well to the readers of this commentary. I further hope that God will be able to use my work to raise the "boring" book of Numbers back to its rightful place – not leaving it relegated to a place of secondary importance amongst more "interesting" works such as Genesis or Romans. May God inspire the readers of Numbers and of this commentary, just as God inspired the writers of Numbers and the writer of this commentary, with eyes trained toward God's glory alone.

ACKNOWLEDGMENTS

Many thanks to Dr. Bruce Nicholls, who first approached me on the steps of Malaysia Bible Seminary in June 2012 with the opportunity to write this volume. Thank you also to Dr. Federico Villanueva who, taking the mantle of leadership after Dr. Nicholls, encouraged me along the way without showing any trace of impatience as the project drew on and on. I also appreciate the labors of the blind editors, who provided many helpful comments, along with a few challenging ones. Finally, I wish to thank three people who provided some of the stories used for contextualization purposes. Neville Bartle served for many years as a Nazarene missionary to Papua New Guinea and Fiji. In addition, Tsutu Thurr and Achichita Thupitor gave me insight into their tribal wedding practices in Nagaland, India.

I also wish to extend my gratitude to the leadership of Asia-Pacific Nazarene Theological Seminary in Taytay, Rizal, Philippines for the opportunity to work with many talented students from around the world. Chief among all humans who deserve my thanks stands my wife, Marnie De Castro Modine. She helped me in ways I cannot express with sundry bits of information regarding Asian culture and Filipino culture in particular. She gave me this assistance mostly without knowing that she was doing so, as I typically framed my questions without specific reference to Numbers, the Old Testament, the Bible, or teaching.

Above all, as usual, I give thanks to Almighty God, who inspired the biblical writers and continues to inspire biblical readers. I offer this volume in response to the many ways in which God's grace has been showered upon me. I dedicate this volume in loving memory of my father-in-law, who passed to his eternal reward while this volume was in its initial editing stages.

Mitchel Modine

Asia-Pacific Nazarene Theological Seminary

Taytay, Rizal, Philippines

LIST OF ABBREVIATIONS

BOOKS OF THE BIBLE

Old Testament
Gen, Exod, Lev, Num, Deut, Josh, Judg, Ruth, 1–2 Sam, 1–2 Kgs, 1–2 Chr, Ezra, Neh, Esth, Job, Ps/Pss, Prov, Eccl, Song, Isa, Jer, Lam, Ezek, Dan, Hos, Joel, Amos, Obad, Jonah, Mic, Nah, Hab, Zeph, Hag, Zech, Mal

New Testament
Matt, Mark, Luke, John, Acts, Rom, 1–2 Cor, Gal, Eph, Phil, Col, 1–2 Thess, 1–2 Tim, Titus, Phlm, Heb, Jas, 1–2 Pet, 1–2–3 John, Jude, Rev

BIBLE TEXTS AND VERSIONS

Divisions of the canon
NT	New Testament
OT	Old Testament

Ancient texts and versions
LXX	Septuagint
MT	Masoretic Text

Modern versions
AT	Author's Translations
ESV	English Standard Version
KJV	King James Version
NASB	New American Standard Bible
NIV	New International Version
NJPS	*Tanakh: The Holy Scriptures: The New JPS Translation*
NLT	New Living Translation
NRSV	New Revised Standard Version

Journals, Reference Works, and Series
ANE	Ancient Near East
BHS	Biblia Hebraiaca Stuttgartensia

INTRODUCTION

Upon reading the thirty-six chapters of the book of Numbers, one discovers that it has the wrong title, for it is not really about enumerating things at all. True enough, there is a census of the army at the beginning of the book, and there is another census of the tribes about two-thirds of the way through. However, apart from these two accounts, there are few references to numbers in the rest of the book. There is a reference to the sequential ordering of sacrifices brought for the tabernacle (see ch. 7), another for the number of the spies sent into the land (see chs. 13–14), and another identifying that a fellow named Zelophehad had five daughters but no sons (see chs. 27, 36). Yet these accounts are few and far between, thereby rendering the title "Numbers" rather strange.

The title "Numbers" comes from the Septuagint translation, created sometime in the second century BC. This Greek title is *Arithmoi*, "Numbers," which the editors undoubtedly used because of the first story, the counting of the army. The Hebrew titles for the first five books of the Bible (the Pentateuch, or the Torah) all come from the first verses of the books. Thus Genesis is called, *bereshit* ("In [the] beginning"), and Leviticus is called, *vayyiqra* ("And [the LORD] called"), after their first words. The Hebrew titles of Exodus and Deuteronomy, respectively *shemoth* ("names") and *d^ebarim* ("words"), are the second words in the Hebrew texts, the first in both cases being, "And these [are]." The Hebrew title of Numbers, *bemidbar*, means, "In the Desert," and is the fifth word in the Hebrew text. Because almost the entire book is set within the wilderness between Mount Sinai and the Promised Land, this Hebrew title seems far more appropriate to the content of the book.

The titles of the books, of course, do not have theological importance. Nevertheless, a better English title for the book of Numbers might be: "Journey with God in the Desert." James S. Diamond agrees with such a designation: "The narrative sections [of Numbers] . . . tell of a people adrift in the desert, adrift physically and spiritually."[1]

This commentary on Numbers assumes the Hebrew title, organizing the material under three large headings, each of which describes a stage of the journey and begins and ends at major waypoints along the route. A waypoint is a stopping point along a journey, and in stories about traveling, the reader often finds that significant events take place at such waypoints. Though one

---

1. James S. Diamond, *Stringing the Pearls: How to Read the Daily Torah Portion* (New York: Jewish Publication Society, 2008), 158.

must not discount significant events that take place along the way, the stopping places often seem more important, for reaching each of these places represents a significant achievement in the larger journey.

Part One, labelled "At Mount Sinai," runs from 1:1–10:10. The Israelites have been camped at this most important mountain since Exodus 19:1, and so leaving it behind marks a significant step in their journey from the land of slavery to the land of promise. The Israelites leave the area of Sinai in chapter 10.

The commentary then follows them as they follow the Ark of the Covenant and the presence of God in the fire (at night) or cloud (by day). They go from one mountain to another, Sinai to Hor (10:11–21:3). On or near this mountain, two of the three great leaders of the Exodus – Aaron and Miriam, Moses' older siblings – die. Their deaths foreshadow the judgment recorded in Deuteronomy 1:35: "Not one from this evil generation shall see the good land I swore to give your ancestors." The reasons for this are complicated, and the commentary will deal with them in due course.

The final stage of the journey recorded in the book of Numbers moves from Mount Hor to the Plains of Moab (21:4–36:13). The Plains of Moab will be the literary setting for the book of Deuteronomy, which represents itself as three final speeches of Moses prior to the Israelites' entry into the Promised Land. Moses will not be able to join them in this entry, and an interesting contrast between Numbers and Deuteronomy explains why this is the case. (See the commentary on 20:1–13.)

PREVIOUS SCHOLARSHIP ON THE BOOK OF NUMBERS

Numbers is considered the fourth book of the Pentateuch, an organizational framework that has been shaped by a particular scholarly consensus for more than a hundred years. Popularized, though not invented, by the famous German scholar Julius Wellhausen (d. 1918), this theory posits that the Pentateuch was made up of four more or less independently created sources, which editors brought together around the time of the Babylonian Exile. Wellhausen refined an earlier theory of Karl Heinrich Graf (d. 1869), which attributed the writing of the Pentateuch to four anonymous sources of tradition, compiled sometime near the Babylonian Exile (586–539 BC). Scholarship subsequent to Wellhausen has refined and expanded this theory to a great extent, even to the point of questioning the existence of one or another of the sources, extending the theory into the book of Joshua (or all the way to

Introduction

2 Kgs),[2] or deleting Deuteronomy to create the Tetrateuch of Genesis through Numbers. Yet the underlying thought of the theory remains intact.

Scholars identified the four sources that come together in the Pentateuch with the letters J, E, P, and D.[3] J stands for Jahwist (pronounced "Yahwist," as the letter J makes a y-sound in German) and was produced just after the division of the kingdoms by someone connected to the royal palace in Jerusalem. E, or "Elohist," responded to J about 850 BC and supported the interests of the Levitical priesthood. Levites eventually joined J and E together, elevating the character of Moses in the process. The elevation of Moses has influence on the book of Numbers, particularly in the various times in which Moses' leadership is called into question (see, for example, ch. 12). The P, or Priestly document, also pays close attention to the Levites, in particular the descendants of Aaron. The rebellion of Korah (Num 16–17) specifically directed itself against the prominence of the Aaronide line amongst the Levites. Finally, the D, or Deuteronomistic document, came into being as the law book was supposedly "found" – but more likely created – during the reign of Josiah (2 Kgs 22:8), and it includes at least the core of Deuteronomy 12–26. (Because this document is completely contained within Deuteronomy, some cut this book out of the theory.) A redactor (called R) brought all this together sometime during the exile, and some identify this redactor with Ezra, though that is a matter of dispute.

As one might expect, the book of Leviticus is dominated by the Priestly document. However, there is also a significant amount of P material in the book of Numbers, which makes sense when one considers the emphases on order and proper religious behavior throughout this book. We will consider some of these ideas in this commentary, in particular the cleansing of the tabernacle. Though such rites may sound strange to contemporary readers, this ancient text can help us bear witness when we take into account the differences between our societies, not only in culture but also in time.

The title "Pentateuch" simply means "five books," which comes into English from Latin and into Latin from Greek. This term preserves the organic connections that appear between and among these five books, without needing

---

2. A recent summary of scholarship may be found in Thomas B. Dozeman, Thomas Romer, and Konrad Schmid, eds., *Pentateuch, Hexateuch, or Enneateuch: Identifying Literary Works in Genesis through Kings,* vol. 8, Ancient Israel and Its Literature series (Atlanta: Society of Biblical Literature, 2011).

3. I am indebted for the following summary to Brian Arthur Brown, "A Diagram of Sources of the Pentateuch," accessed February 1, 2017, http://www.brianarthurbrown.com/files/A%20Diagram%20of%20Sources%20of%20the%20Pentateuch.pdf.

the figure of Moses as the "glue." Yet the "Pentateuch" designation does not consider the relationship between the book of Deuteronomy and the books that follow it. In simple terms, the books of Joshua, Judges, 1–2 Samuel, and 1–2 Kings recount the story of Israel's history in a way that is infused with the theology of the book of Deuteronomy. Thus if Deuteronomy stands at the head of Joshua through 2 Kings, then perhaps it does not belong at the end of the grouping of Genesis through Numbers. Including Deuteronomy with the historical books that follow it (a collection of books that is referred to as the Former Prophets in the Hebrew ordering) leaves Genesis, Exodus, Leviticus, and Numbers as the "Tetrateuch," or "Four Books." Indeed, Wellhausen did this when he ascribed Deuteronomy almost exclusively to his D source.

Finally, the designation of Genesis through Deuteronomy as "the Books of the Law" has both advantages and disadvantages. The primary advantage to this designation is that it describes well the content of these books, without having recourse either to the figure of Moses or to literary theories that group material together. However, this designation has two glaring disadvantages as well. First, the English word "law" is only partially acceptable as a translation for the Hebrew term *torah*, which can refer to the concept of law in general and to specific laws like the Third Commandment ("Do not take the name of the LORD your God in vain"). Yet *torah* also has a much broader significance, reaching into concepts covered by English words such as "lifestyle," "teaching," "instruction," and the like. Moreover, actual legal material forms a rather small proportion of the Torah. True enough, one may find 613 commandments, both positive and negative, in the Torah. However, considered against the entirety of Genesis through Deuteronomy, this is a paltry sum. Indeed, the majority of these 613 laws occur in Exodus through Deuteronomy, thus creating a different version of the Tetrateuch than that described above.

Second, the Christian reader often finds this material, frankly speaking, rather boring. While this reaction is understandable, one should avoid the temptation toward supersessionism, which is the idea that God replaced Judaism and Jewish law because they were too focused on law rather than grace. As the above comments show, even a book with lots of legal material (such as Numbers) should not be considered as a book of law – much less the entire Old Testament or Jewish religion as a whole.

Admittedly, the laws may be difficult to understand, primarily because modern Christian readers are outsiders to the cultural context in which the laws belong. The twentieth-century anthropologist Mary Douglas provides some help in this regard, particularly in her approach to laws regarding ritual

Introduction

cleanness and purity. She writes: "No particular set of classifying symbols can be understood in isolation, but there can be hope of making sense of them in relation to the total structure of classifications in the culture in question."[4] In other words, taking the laws of the book of Numbers as a window into the culture of ancient Israel reveals the intimate relationship the laws have with the culture. Examination of the culture then illuminates the deeper significance of the laws. Understanding this deeper significance of the laws helps the interpreter build bridges between ancient and modern societies, which is, after all, the stated aim of careful biblical interpretation. Thus the laws, though difficult to understand, are far from boring. The interpreter does the church a great disservice when she/he skips over the legal material of the Old Testament because it is difficult to understand or, worse, tries to interpret the laws with a half-understood or ill-conceived notion of the relationship between the Testaments.

READING NUMBERS IN ANCIENT AND MODERN ASIAN CONTEXTS

In many ways, Asian readers of the Bible are much closer to the Bible's original cultural context than Western readers since the Bible came from Western Asia. Admittedly, the historical circumstances are wildly different and confusing – the two often lead to misinterpretation.[5] More importantly, many of the cultural norms visible in the Bible seem quite similar to cultural norms in Asia. The caution here is that the population of modern Asian countries, especially megacities like Tokyo, Manila, or Mumbai, is quite mixed in terms of ethnic and cultural background. While the Exodus and wilderness wandering generation of Israelites may have had some mixture of different cultures as well (see the commentary on 11:1–9), final judgment on this question lacks sufficient evidence.

"With God in the Desert" has many important lessons for our Christian life. It describes God taking a rabble of refugees, who are fleeing from genocide and oppression in Egypt, and forming them into a nation. In Egypt, each person had simply been a slave with a number. This is also the case in Asia,

---

4. Mary Douglas, *Purity and Danger: An Analysis of the Concepts of Pollution and Taboo*, reprint (London: Routledge & Paul, 2001), vii.
5. As, for example, with Palestinian readers' identification with the displaced Canaanites. This may or may not be based in a misidentification of the modern state of Israel with the wandering Israelites in the desert. See below the discussion of Numbers 33:50–56 for more on this idea.

where, awash in a sea of people, individuals often find their personal identities melded into the crowd, valued only for the work they can contribute. In the book of Numbers, the Israelites are organized into tribes and extended family communities. They are identified as a people on a journey, and God is visibly traveling with them. Though God promises to bless them in chapter 6, many times, like us, they miss out on God's blessing because of their lack of faith or their grumbling and quarreling. If we listen carefully with open hearts, we will hear God speaking to us and teaching us about how we should walk and talk so that we can live under God's smile rather than God's frown.

In some ways, Asians who read Numbers may find more connections than Western readers because many features of so-called "traditional" societies are still quite prevalent in Asia, at least in some form. When our reading of the Bible interacts with our own cultural background in this way, we can generate many interesting insights. For example, one of the topics included in the commentary has to do with marriage and the clan system of Nagaland, India. If the residents of this place were specifically to follow the junction laid upon the daughters of Zelophehad (see Num 36:6), then daughters would marry within their own clans. However, marriage within one's clan is an abomination in Nagaland. Therefore, some interpretation is necessary in order to discover how this text should be applied. On the one hand, one could adopt the earlier story of Zelophehad's daughters (ch. 27), which does not include this specific instruction. On the other hand, one could set aside this instruction as applying to a specific situation rather than applicable for all time. I do not feel that the often-heard distinction between the "timely" and the "timeless," or between the historically conditioned material and the universally valid material, is helpful. Instead, one should view all of the material in the Bible as culturally conditioned. The Bible was written in Israel during ancient times rather than Egypt, Greece, the modern-day Philippines, or Nagaland, and we need to take these differences in society seriously as we read the text.

One of the main goals of reading and interpretation, which are essentially the same activity, is to draw analogies between the ancient context that produced the Bible and the modern contexts in which its interpreters function. The evangelical view that the Bible is the inspired Word of God – however one understands that term – makes these analogies necessary. It will not do to ignore the differences between the cultures and the wide span of history that has passed since the writing of the Bible. However, those differences should not present an insurmountable barrier to understanding the Bible, even if our understanding is always provisional and subject to constant renegotiation.

Introduction

Thus, for example, the issue of Sabbath observance has importance in both ancient and modern contexts. The principle is important – setting aside one day in seven to pay attention to the things of God. However, the specific day is irrelevant. It makes no difference if one worships God on Sunday, Saturday, or even Tuesday. For that matter, Christians simply do not observe Sabbath in the same way that Jews do. First, Sunday (the typical day) is not a day of rest, especially for pastors and other ministers. Second, the Christian day of worship is not indexed to Sabbath, the seventh day of the week, but rather to a weekly remembrance of Jesus' resurrection on the Lord's Day, the first day of the week.

It seems that errors of interpretation, such as associating the red heifer (19:1–10) with the doctrine of the end-times, often stem from interpreters departing from the basic principles that they have established to guide their interpretation. Chief among these principles is to study texts within their contexts, both literary and historical. Simply put, any interpretation which relies on things not stated in the text should be received with suspicion. To use an example from outside the book of Numbers, some interpreters suggest that the family of Naomi – her husband, Elimelech, and her two sons, Mahlon and Chilion – die in Moab because God punished them for having left Judah. However, nothing in the text makes this claim, nor even suggests that this might be the case. Hence, an interpretation based on this claim runs into immediate problems. Such an interpretation should not immediately be judged as incorrect, but neither should it be accepted as correct without careful thought.

By contrast, the strategy of "reading against the text" is quite different. One may, and many interpreters do, disagree with the logical connections the text itself makes, or question the assumptions on which the story is based. We may consider the story of Zelophehad's daughters (chs. 27 and 36) for an example. The assumption of male dominance lies behind both texts, but especially the tribal elders' claim in chapter 36 that they may lose their inheritance if the case is dealt with in what they perceive as "the wrong way." One may conclude that, since an extra stipulation is laid on the women, chapter 27 represents a more female-friendly version, while chapter 36 is more patriarchal.[6] On the other hand, one may "read against the text" and conclude that patriarchal concerns

---

6. I concluded thus in a recent paper: Mitchel Modine, "Zelophehad Had," (paper presented at Research Seminar, Asia-Pacific Nazarene Theological Seminary, Taytay, Rizal, April 17, 2017), 8.

about land transfer and inheritance underlie both texts, even though they each express this concern in slightly different ways.

THE DATE OF NUMBERS

In general terms, I follow the scholarly consensus that the book of Numbers is composed of material that comes from a wide variety of historical eras. Though it reached its final form relatively late in Israel's history – perhaps around the time of the Babylonian Exile or a little later – some of the earlier material originated much earlier. The different historical contexts of particular texts within Numbers, which are often difficult to pin down, have implications for later debates within the Israelite community. For example, the commentary on Numbers 12:1–2 indicates that the dispute between Aaron, Miriam, and Moses may reflect disagreements between Northern and Southern priests after the Northern Kingdom was destroyed around 721 BC (see also Num 7:1–11). The final editors of Numbers then assembled all of this together, because it held some measure of authority for them and their tradition. Though their understanding of textual authority was certainly different than modern evangelical notions of biblical authority, nevertheless they are somewhat similar. The commentary that follows will recognize the interplay of possible different historical contexts for the material, which ultimately came together in the final form of Numbers – thus creating another historical context.

In summary, the ancient and modern contexts of the Bible are alike in some ways and very different in other ways. For that matter, even the society that produced the Bible experienced a tremendous amount of change and development. Thus the material that came together as the book of Numbers seems to speak to very different historical contexts (see 12:1–16 as an example of a story which may reflect later disputes in the community). In other words, evangelicals largely agree that the Bible continues to have relevance for later periods of history, both within ancient Israel itself and within modern Asian societies. This hermeneutical principle will inform much of what follows.

NUMBERS 1:1–10:10
AT MOUNT SINAI

The first major section of the book sees the people staying around Mount Sinai. There is reason enough to read the Pentateuch as a more or less continuous story, which means that the people have been here since Exodus 19, including the whole of the book of Leviticus. They will not leave here until Numbers 10:11. While this represents a large literary block – most of the Pentateuch in terms of number of chapters at any rate – Numbers 10:11 says that the Israelites left just after two years of camping near Sinai. These were a productive two years!

1:1–4:49 PRELIMINARY MATTERS, OR SETTING THE SCENE

The first four chapters introduce the main characters and set the story in its larger context. Mostly, the story here establishes the number of people able to fight in battle and the number of people able to serve God in the tabernacle. These two groups of people will be extremely important in the rest of the story, and even if there is some critical difficulty with the numbers given (see below), the larger point remains intact.

1:1–54 Census of the Army

The book of Numbers begins, like all good stories, in the middle of things. As the story of the journey with God in the desert begins, the people are camped around Mount Sinai, where they have been since Exodus 19. Like all journeys, this particular one has a goal: entry into the Promised Land. In order to make that possible, Moses and Aaron have to count the military forces that are available. So this story looks back to the Exodus from Egypt and the giving of the law at Mount Sinai and also forward to the conquest of the land, which the book of Joshua takes as its main subject.

As noted above, this census is the first one identified in the book of Numbers. The second one comes in 26:1–65, which I will address when I come to that portion of the commentary. One of Jesus' parables in the Gospel of Luke provides a parallel to this story. In Luke 14:31–32, Jesus teaches about counting one's resources before going out to war. The account in Numbers 1 does not suggest that the census of the army was meant to determine whether the land could be conquered, the idea of counting resources is the same.

1:1–3 Initial Command

Verses 1–3 describe the setting and the initial command of God to Moses and Aaron. As noted above, the Israelites will stay at Mount Sinai for roughly the first third of the book, as they will not leave until 10:11. Moreover, the setting of the entire book of Numbers is outside the Promised Land, except when Moses sends spies into the land of Canaan very briefly in 13:21–24. Other than these four verses, the literary setting is in the wilderness.

God orders Moses and Aaron to "Take a census of the whole Israelite community by their clans and families, listing every man by name, one by one" (v. 2). Males twenty years old and above were available to go to war, which is similar to the age requirements observed in the post-exilic period for Levites to become priests (see 2 Chr 31:17, and certain Talmudic sources). Finally, the army is to be counted "according to their divisions" (v. 3), a phrase that suggests the formulation of the battle plan. Though it will fall to the book of Joshua to describe the actual invasion and conquest of the Holy Land, the Israelites make preparations before leaving Mount Sinai.

1:4–16 The Assistants

In verses 4–16, the Lord continues the instruction, indicating that Moses and Aaron will have one representative from each tribe to assist them in the counting. Though the final tally is quite large (see v. 46), God sends only these fourteen to do the work. By contrast, counting the population of a modern nation requires the assistance of several million census takers (in the case of the United States, at least). The results, according to some, are often quite inaccurate, which has led to calls for statistical sampling to be used instead of a precise head count.

1:17–19 Beginning the Census

Having received their instructions, Moses, Aaron, and the twelve leaders then set about their work in verses 17–19. The narrator informs us again (v. 18) that the census took place on the first day of the second month. It seems unlikely that Moses, Aaron, and the twelve leaders could accomplish the job of counting so many people in one day. Indeed, though the reader sees no more time indications throughout the rest of the chapter, the next reference confirms this suspicion. For the next time reference tells us that the Israelites leave Sinai "On the twentieth day of the second month of the second year" (10:11). Allowing for time to arrange the companies in their march, which is the topic of chapter 2, the fourteen census takers have more than two weeks to complete their work.

1:20–46 Census Details

The next twenty-seven verses (vv. 20–46) detail the numbers of soldiers counted in the census. Twenty-four verses are devoted to the twelve tribes (two each), and then the final three verses summarize the count of the soldiers. Within the count of the tribes, the reader finds a generally unified scheme. First, the tribe is mentioned, followed by the phrase, "All the men twenty years old or more who were able to serve in the army were listed by name, one by one, according to the records of their clans and families" (v. 20). The NIV translators translate this formula consistently, though there is some variation in the Hebrew original. The regularity of expression exhibited in this chapter will appear again in the reports of sacrifices given by representatives of the tribes in chapter 7. The differences between the tribal reports in the Hebrew original do not significantly affect the meaning of the passages. They hold interest, however, because of what they might say regarding the freedom available within the liturgical structure.

Many Western interpreters have suggested that the number of soldiers, 603,550 according to verse 46, is legendary. Eryl Davies, for example, writes: "The vast population presupposed . . . could hardly have found subsistence in the desert for any length of time."[1] J. Maxwell Miller and John H. Hayes are more specific. Citing the similar number in Exodus 12:37 ("about six hundred thousand men on foot, besides women and children"), they write: "This number plus their wives and children along with the mixed multitude said to accompany them would have totaled some two and a half million. Marching ten abreast, the numbers would have formed a line over 150 miles long and would have required eight or nine days to march past any fixed point."[2]

However, for many readers, both Western and Asian, the accuracy of the number is important. This is an example of what the psychologist Leon Festinger has called "cognitive dissonance."[3] In simple terms, cognitive

---

1. Earl W. Davies, *Numbers,* New Century Bible Commentary (Grand Rapids: Eerdmans, 1995), 14.
2. J. Maxwell Miller and John H. Hayes, *A History of Ancient Israel and Judah,* 2nd ed. (Louisville: Westminster John Knox, 2006), 72.
3. Leon Festinger, *A Theory of Cognitive Dissonance* (Stanford: Stanford University Press, 1957).

dissonance arises when a person encounters two facts that contradict each other, neither of which the person is willing to deny. Thus, here we have the fact of the biblical number contradicted by the lack of archaeological evidence. It seems that three options present themselves.

First, one could deny the archaeological evidence or question its validity. For example, one may suggest that the archaeological evidence of these three million plus people simply has not yet been found. This strategy seems unsatisfying, however, for at least two reasons. Explaining the matter in this way confronts yet another factual reality: throughout history, there have been many attempts to discover clear and convincing archaeological evidence for the claims the Bible makes. However, one must discern the motivation behind these attempts. Because they are based predominantly in an attempt to prove that the Bible is true, this raises the question of whether the Bible's claims can, or even need to be, proven. In addition, attempts such as these misunderstand the nature of archaeology to begin with. Archaeology, particularly Syro-Palestinian archaeology,[4] serves to help us understand the society of ancient Israel and its contemporaries in the ancient world. This is all it can do. In other words, archaeology is incapable of proving or disproving the Bible.

The second option goes the other way: denying the claims of the Bible because they do not conform to the archaeological record. Denying the claims of the Bible is an unacceptable option for many evangelicals. However, many scholars, pastors, and other readers – Christian, Jewish, and non-religious – have accepted this option. Marek Dospěl summarizes the situation: "Biblical scholars of the last 35 years or so thus split into two camps of thought: historical minimalism and historical maximalism. The minimalists would argue that most of the Hebrew Bible has little value for the study of history because it is made up of prose fiction, folk tales, legends and theological treatises, while the maximalists would defend the Bible's claims regarding the early history of ancient Israel."[5]

Regardless of the position one takes on this question – minimalism or maximalism – ignoring the debate is irresponsible, even if we acknowledge that attempts to prove the Bible are misguided from the outset. Such attempts

---

[4]. This is the preferred scholarly term for the branch of archaeological science that deals with the general area and the general time periods in which the Bible, among other things, came to be.
[5]. Marek Dospěl, "Who Tells the Truth-the Bible or Archaeology?" Biblical Archaeology Society, May 15, 2017 (accessed May 16, 2017), http://www.biblicalarchaeology.org/daily/archaeology-today/biblical-archaeology-topics/truth-bible-or-archaeology.

follow the Western Enlightenment's quest for sources and sure foundations of belief rather than the Bible. In other words, faith must not be brought as a sacrifice upon the altar of proof, for this elevates science – specifically, archaeological science – over faith. To put the matter differently, while one should not advocate a stubborn belief in something for which there is no evidence – or, in this case, for which the only available evidence is opposed to the belief – subjecting faith to proof makes science the final arbiter of truth, a problematic position for evangelicals.

The third option refuses easy attempts to resolve the cognitive dissonance. This means that the archaeological record's contradiction of the Bible simply does not pose an issue for faith. In other words, if truth means only what can be proved, then the Bible is not true. Since Christians, and evangelicals in particular, believe that the Bible is true and cannot depart from this claim, then truth must mean more than what we can prove through this or that scientific method. Moreover, scientific methods themselves are constantly undergoing revision, so not even science reaches something resembling universally valid truth. In terms of the numbers in the book of Numbers, it seems best to consider the numbers as an incidental detail. The most important claim to affirm is that the people – no matter their number – are with God in the desert. For it is in this place, according to the narrative, that God desires to be in relationship with them.

1:47–54 *The Levites*

Verses 47–54 report that the census of fighting men does not include the Levites. This may indicate the influence of the Priestly document on Numbers (see the Introduction). The main responsibility given to the Levites is to take care of "the tabernacle of the covenant" (v. 50). God instructs Moses that they are also to pay attention to the furnishings in the tabernacle, most prominently, the Ark of the Covenant. Though the ark does not appear here, various stories in the Old Testament detail what happens when anyone other than the Levites take care of it, and in any other than the proper manner. The most striking story appears in two versions, 2 Samuel 6 and 1 Chronicles 13. In these stories, the ark is on its way to Jerusalem at the orders of King David. A man named Uzzah, apparently trying to protect the ark from falling, reaches out to steady it. However, God does not appreciate Uzzah's efforts, and strikes him dead for touching the ark without authorization. No such fireworks attend the instruction here. God does not give a warning or go into detail about improper behavior, but instructs that only the Levites may touch the ark and that laymen who come near it will be put to death (v. 51).

The chapter ends with the narrator's short note that the Israelites did everything that God had commanded (v. 54). Interestingly, only one command was given in the chapter: to count the warriors twenty years of age and older. To be sure, a negative corollary accompanied it – namely, that Moses should not count the Levites. God gives a second indirect command to Moses: that he should put the Levites in charge of the tabernacle. Rather than reporting God's instruction as a positive command to the Levites ("You shall do it"), the narrator describes what the Levites are to do ("They shall do it"). Most likely, this indirect command, where God commands Moses to command the Levites, identifies Moses as the lawgiver who is invested with this authority from God. This text recognizes that God's commands can be given in myriad ways. One of those ways is through God's chosen intermediary or intermediaries – in this case, Moses.

2:1–34 Arrangement of the Companies

After the census of the army, Moses and Aaron arranged the soldiers for the invasion of the Promised Land. The interpreter may see that this arrangement does not give insight into military strategy but has theological significance. Considering this material in light of the larger biblical story, this description of the tribes – and, in particular, the placement of the Ark of the Covenant in the center – indicates the centrality of God's presence in the life of the community.

This is an important theological theme throughout the book of Numbers. In the same way that the cross and the empty tomb are central symbols in Christianity, so the Ark of the Covenant and the tabernacle are central symbols for Judaism. True enough, the Ark of the Covenant will later fade out of history. Eric H. Cline notes: "the last time the ark was definitely seen by anyone was when Solomon placed it within the Holy of Holies inside the Temple in Jerusalem during the tenth century B.C."[6]

For much of Israel's history, in fact until the time of King David, the ark – which symbolized God's presence – was kept in the temporary shelter of the tabernacle (see 2 Sam 7 for David's initial thoughts about building the Temple). One might wonder how "temporary" this "temporary" shelter was, owing to the length of time that passed from the construction of the tabernacle

---

6. Eric H. Cline, *From Eden to Exile: Unraveling Mysteries of the Bible* (Washington, DC: National Geographic Society, 2006), 127–128.

(detailed in Exod 25–40) to the construction of the permanent dwelling in the Temple. The question of language aside, however, the idea that God had a permanent residence in the Temple, as opposed to the mobile residence of the tabernacle, which was the point of the collapsible structure, tended in the direction of domesticating God. God in the tabernacle was a God on the move; God in the Temple was a God at rest (see, for a few examples: Pss 33:14; 74:7; 76:2; 84:1; 132:7).[7]

Christianity faces a similar temptation to domesticate or tame God. The most important symbol of Christianity is the cross of Jesus, yet the cross cannot be separated from the empty tomb without causing harm. From a Protestant perspective, this is the problem with the symbol of the crucifix. While the suffering of Jesus is of inexhaustible importance for bringing humanity back into right relationship with God, Jesus does not remain on the cross for all eternity. This is why the empty tomb is so important: God is on the move! As the angel said to the women who first came to the tomb, "I know that you are looking for Jesus who has been crucified. He is not here, He has risen, just as He said" (Matt 28:6; see also Matt 26:32).

2:1–2 Introduction of the Arrangement of the Tribes

The first two verses introduce the arrangement of the tribes. As one may see repeatedly throughout the book of Numbers, Moses and Aaron act according to the direct command of God. This will be the case throughout Moses' life, who – except for one instance – follows God without turning to the right hand or to the left (see Josh 1:7).

Two things stand out regarding the arrangement of the tribes. First, God instructs the soldiers to "camp facing the tent of meeting on every side" (v. 2), indicating the centrality of worship even at this early stage of Israel's existence. Of course, for all the soldiers to face the tent of meeting, the tent of meeting must be in the center of the camp. Moreover, the Ark of the Covenant must always be in the center of the tent of meeting. The ark symbolized God's presence with the people, which reinforces the idea that this book is really about Israel's journey with God in the desert.

---

7. Psalm 90:1 is quite different, suggesting that the Lord has been Israel's "dwelling place throughout all generations." This idea is much closer to Numbers than to the other references in the Psalms.

THE IMPORTANCE OF SYMBOLS IN CHRISTIANITY: REFLECTIONS FROM THE PHILIPPINE CONTEXT

Symbols are very important in religion. Symbols take the forms of both symbolic objects and symbolic actions. Many Protestants, in their zeal to dissociate themselves with practices which they perceive to be abusive, have tended to discard all symbols. This is unfortunate. While an improperly understood symbol can be mistakenly elevated, this does not mean that all symbols should be thrown out.

In Manila, Philippines, on Maundy Thursday, millions of Roman Catholics make a procession from all points of mega Manila to the Church of Our Lady of Good Voyage in Antipolo City in Rizal province. This procession is called the *Alay Lakad*, or "walk offering." Many people may join this procession out of a sense of obligation, yet an equally significant number join this procession out of a sense of genuine devotion to Jesus. One must truly decide matters of the heart with compassion and humility.

In 2016, I joined in the procession, accompanied by another professor and a handful of students from our Protestant seminary. Two particular experiences on our march stand out in my memory. First, we were carrying a small cross along with us. At one point, when it was my turn to carry the cross, a Filipino man approached me with a handkerchief in his hand. He wiped our cross with his handkerchief, and then touched it to his face. This is a common practice, which Filipino Catholics also do with statues of Jesus or the saints. It struck me that the man had done this without realizing that, technically speaking, it would have been a violation of his theology, since the cross was not a proper crucifix and the minister carrying it was not a Catholic. Nevertheless, I thought it was a positive, ecumenical experience, and I felt privileged to have shared in this unknown man's devotion to Jesus.

The second experience during the walk was also significant, but in a negative way. As we processed around the traffic circle called Tikling – just a few meters from our seminary – I noticed some Protestant protestors standing on the side of the road, holding a giant banner with a critical message about the practice of *alay lakad*. I do not remember the specific words, but it said something to the effect that the people joining the march were sinful and in need of repentance. Moreover, the message indicated that repentance and forgiveness could not be found in the *alay lakad* or in any other Catholic practice. Just down the road, our Protestant seminary students were passing out free water to

> the participants. While disagreeing on a point of theology or practice is legitimate, it is a risky proposition to judge another person, especially another Christian, as sinful.
>
> The next week, as I reflected on our experience, an American missionary who used to be in the Philippines but now lives elsewhere in Asia told me that he objected to us joining the *alay lakad*. I asked him why, and he said, "Because these people can only see this as earning merit before God." While this sentiment reflects a common Protestant critique of much of Roman Catholic pageantry, it falls into the same trap as the protestors – not to mention the cultural superiority inherent in the missionary's dismissive comment. How can we judge what is in another person's mind and soul? The discarding of all symbolism, whether objects or actions, has impoverished Protestant Christianity. Symbolic objects and symbolic actions have a place, even though they are sometimes elevated to an overly high level of importance.

The second clear implication of the placement of the tent of meeting in the center of the camp, with all the tribes facing it, makes a profound statement about the centrality of worship in the Judeo–Christian tradition. God's presence in the middle of the camp exemplifies the idea that God is God-with-us. The worship of God is the primary activity of humanity, as the Westminster Confession of Faith proclaims: "The chief end of man is to glorify God and to enjoy him forever."

2:3–24 *The Order of Marching*

The tribes arrange themselves among the four points of the compass, with the tribe of Levi and the tent of meeting in the middle. It is important to note that there are thirteen tribes numbered in this chapter, even though they usually number twelve. First, the Levites are "replaced" among the tribes by breaking up the tribe of Joseph into two tribes named after his sons Ephraim and Manasseh. Second, in the historical record, the specific names the tribes called themselves were somewhat fluid. However, the number twelve is consistent throughout Israel's history. Why, then, does the number appear here to be thirteen? The simple answer is that the Levites, who are in control of the tent of meeting and all the holy objects contained therein, were of a different character than the other tribes. The other tribes would receive inheritances of land within what would become Israel following the conquest, whereas the Levites would not.

2:3–9 Tribes on the East

In any event, the tribes placed on the east side of the tent of meeting, toward the rising sun, were the tribes of Judah, Issachar, and Zebulun. One should notice throughout this chapter that the numbers given for the individual tribes, the total number of soldiers in the three tribes in each group, and the names of the leaders of each tribe, are the same as those given in chapter 1. These first three tribes were to "set out first" when the Israelites begin to march (v. 9). This functional equation of "east" and "front" is found also in the words for directions in the biblical Hebrew language: the word *qdm* means both "east" and "front." The orientation of the march, then, once the Israelites get around to leaving Sinai in Numbers 10, is toward the east. Eventually the whole operation will turn the opposite direction, for under Joshua, the Israelites will march across the Jordan River from east to west. The position of the Ark of the Covenant, however, will not change, because it is in the middle, which reinforces the above discussion about the centrality of worship and God's presence in the lives of Israel and our lives today. Indeed, so long as God is in the middle, we can go forward in almost any direction – even when we do not know which way to turn, which is usually the case.

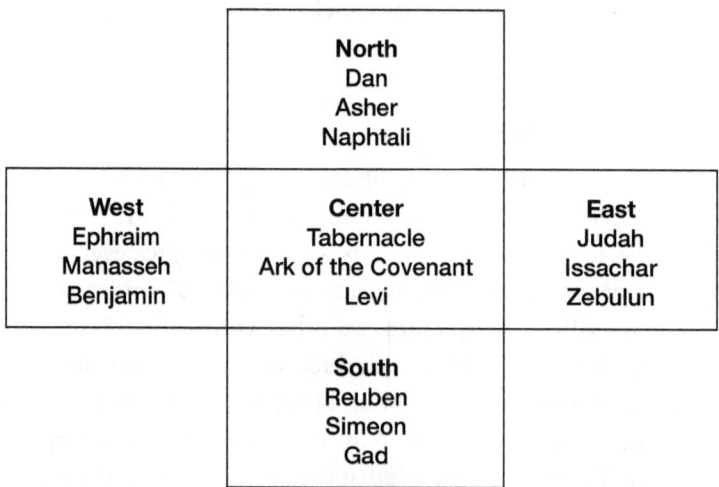

Figure 1. The Arrangement of the Tribes for the March

2:10–16 Tribes on the South

Moving in a clockwise direction, the arrangement next comes to the tribes on the south (see Figure 1). This group is composed of Reuben, Simeon, and Gad. Reuben and Gad are particularly noteworthy here, since these two tribes will settle on the eastern side of the Jordan River. Though they do not technically reside in the Promised Land, they are still an important part of the people, as chapter 32 (especially v. 23) will make clear later on. Simeon is also significant in that, in the later course of history, this tribe will more or less become merged with the tribe of Judah. Miller and Hayes remark: "Even Simeon, while attributed independent status in the twelve-tribe scheme, is subsumed under Judah for all practical purposes in the tribal allotments."[8]

2:17 Levites in the Middle

Verse 17 notes again that the Levites march by themselves. As noted above, this is because they will not take a directly active role in the conquest, instead giving attention to the tent of meeting and the holy objects. In 1:53, God gave the Levites charge of the tent of meeting so that God's wrath would not fall upon Israel. Chapter 2 does not repeat this idea, but the centrality of the Levites, because of the centrality of the tent of meeting and especially the Ark of the Covenant, lies beyond question. This arrangement involves a bit of shifting around in preparation for the march. The eastern group, being in front, leaves first. This is fine insofar as the movement is toward the east, which it is for the most part until the Israelites make their great turn toward Canaan (see above). The southern tribes, however, must move from the right side of the Levites to march in front of them. Finally, the Levites set out third, leaving two groups, or six tribes, to fall in behind. This arrangement does keep the Levites in the middle, which emphasizes the centrality of worship and worship-related materials during Israel's lifetime, especially during this time of journeying with God in the desert.

2:18–24 Tribes on the West

Setting out third in the military marches (see v. 24) – or fourth if setting out with the tribe of Levi for non-military purposes – are the tribes on the west. The tribe of Ephraim leads them, named for one of the two sons of Joseph, whose tribes replaced the tribe of Judah amongst the twelve. Manasseh and Benjamin join them. Manasseh will later be divided and join Reuben and Gad

---

8. Miller and Hayes, *History of Ancient Israel*, 94.

as settlers on the eastern side of the Jordan River. Benjamin ultimately proves to be a great deal of trouble in the history of Israel. It is the smallest tribe in terms of tribal allotment, and in Judges 20, the rest of the tribes goes to war with the Benjaminites and nearly obliterate them. Later in Israel's history, the tribe of Benjamin will produce two men by the name of Saul. One of these will start out good and turn bad – the first legitimate king of Israel, who eventually goes insane. The second will start out bad and turn good – the apostle Paul, who began by persecuting the followers of Jesus (who in Acts 9 are called "followers of the Way") and ended up being one of the greatest advocates for Jesus in the history of the world.

2:25–31 Tribes on the North
The tribes stationed on the north bring up the rear of the march. This group is comprised of Dan, Asher, and Naphtali. Later in history, the tribe of Dan will first settle in the south but later migrate to the north, taking the city of Laish and renaming it for themselves. Here, in the site known as Tel (an Arabic word meaning "mound") Dan, archaeologists discovered in 1993 what many thought was clear external evidence of the Davidic monarchy. Though some have later doubted the significance of the Dan Stele, as it came to be called, it was a significant find, since prior to then, there had been no evidence, disputed or otherwise, for the existence of the Davidic line outside of the Bible.

2:32–34 Summary
The chapter concludes with a summary statement, noting that the total of all the warriors is the same given at the end of chapter 1: 603,550, not including the Levites, since they would not go to war. Both chapters 1 and 2 end with a note that the Israelites carried out the instructions that Moses gave them without deviating from it. Though this will not always be the case, so far, everything is as it should be.

3:1–51 and 4:1–49 Genealogy of the Levites

Chapters three and four continue to discuss the Levites and their unique role within the camp of Israel, so this commentary will discuss these chapters together. At several points throughout the books of Genesis through Deuteronomy, God commands that the Levites should not receive a tribal inheritance among the Israelites. In exchange, they receive the role of caring for the holy things of God and, among other things, the tithes from the rest of the Israelites' land should go to support them.⁹

This commentary will divide chapter 3 as follows: introductory and concluding material (vv. 1–20), followed by more specific treatment of three main lines of Levitical genealogy (vv. 21–39), concluding with God's declaration that the Levites belong to him (vv. 40–52). As a whole, chapters three and four seem quite intermixed as to their material, with the focus moving back and forth among the Gershonites, the Kohathites, and the Merarites. To avoid unnecessary confusion, the commentary will not attempt to collect all of the material related to each of these three major clans together, as this would result in a commentary that stumbles around chapters 3 and 4 in a haphazard manner. Rather, the commentary will simply move through the chapters sequentially, noting when the topic shifts back and forth.

3:1–4 Nadab and Abihu Offer Strange Fire

These first four verses summarize a story that appears in longer form in Leviticus 10. Verse 3 states simply the importance of the sons of Aaron. The Levites are already set apart as the ones responsible for the holy objects, ritual purity, and so forth. However, the Aaronides are particularly significant Levites, for they are ordained to be priests forever before God. Thus, one must be cautious in using the term "Levitical priesthood." It would perhaps be better to say, "priesthood," or "Israelite priesthood," since every priest (*kohen*) was a Levite, but not all Levites were priests.

Christians do not practice hereditary priesthood, especially in light of the fact that Roman Catholicism forbids priests to marry and have children. Though this stricture has been inconsistently enforced throughout history, this official dogma draws a definite distinction between Christianity and the ancient Israelite religion. The situation is somewhat different in Protestant traditions. Protestantism has a great legacy of multi-generational leaders, though this is not built into the structure by God's command. In other words, the child of a priest/minister may herself or himself become a priest/minister, but she/he is not compelled to do so – unless by God's particular command. Moreover, the children of priests/ministers are not the only individuals who are allowed to become priests/ministers. In some cases, the transfer from parent (usually father) to child (usually son) can lead to abuses of power. Such a practice should only be done after careful reflection. Emile Durkheim, a French sociologist,

---

9. In Numbers, one may find these claims in 18:23–24.

makes the following illuminating comment: "the heredity of the professions was very often the rule even when the law did not insist upon it."[10] Durkheim concludes that heredity in the transfer of a profession is a mark of a lower level of societal development.

This passage also makes an interesting summary note about Nadab and Abihu, the first- and second-born sons of Aaron. As noted above, Leviticus 10 offers a fuller statement about the sin of the sons. Leviticus 10:1 says that Nadab and Abihu offered "unauthorized fire" on the Lord's altar, using the same Hebrew word as found in Numbers 3:4. It is not at all clear what made this fire strange or unauthorized. The point is that they did something wrong, and the Lord did not tolerate it. Ironically, Nadab and Abihu's names are important here. Nadab means "offering," and Abihu means "he is my father." It is both interesting and unfortunate that children so named should bring their father Aaron to such grief by offering something that leads the Lord to kill them.

A larger issue here is the replacement of older sons by younger sons, a common theme in the Old Testament. Thus Abel, in effect, replaced Cain because his sacrifice was honored while his brothers were not. (Abel was then replaced by Seth after Cain killed Abel, apparently out of jealousy.) Many other examples could be recorded, but in the Numbers passage, the younger sons, Eleazar and Ithamar, replace their older brothers, who were unfaithful. Thus, even though Nadab and Abihu sinned – and the nature of their sin is difficult to understand – the line of Aaron's sons was undiminished.

---

10. Emile Durkheim, *The Division of Labor in Society*, trans. W. D. Halls, reprint (New York: Free Press, 1997), 249.

SACRED FIRE IN PAPUA NEW GUINEA[1]

In Papua New Guinea, some of the tribal peoples used to make a distinction between different kinds of fire. Regular fire used in the house was not considered sacred, and women used it for secular purposes such as cooking. On the other hand, some men who served as diviners could not eat food cooked by women. Their food needed to be specially prepared on a separate, sacred fire in their own homes. They could not let their fire go out, if at all possible. If the fire did go out, relighting it was not a simple matter of going next door – or sending an assistant next door – to borrow from the fire that the women used. (In this society, the people did not make use of matches, lighters, or other such technology.) Instead, the men had to restart the fire from scratch. They would use dry wood and split pieces of bamboo, rubbed together to produce heat and fire by friction.

While it is a risky procedure to compare societies, it is interesting that the book of Leviticus also orders Israelite priests not to let the fire go out in the tabernacle or the Temple (Lev 6:12–13). The Levites were given the charge to take great care with the things of God. Nadab and Abihu, in this text, offer unauthorized fire. Perhaps their fire had gone out, and they restored it from an improper source. In any event, what they did was incorrect, and they were accordingly punished for their infraction. In the same way, all those who worship God are to show great concern for the things of God. The Levites in Israel and the diviners in Papua New Guinea must not allow their physical fire to go out. In the same way, we must not allow our metaphorical fires to go out. It remains unclear what was unauthorized about Nadab and Abihu's fire, but it offended God, perhaps in a similar way to the Papua New Guinean diviner eating food that had not been cooked with sacred fire.

---

1. The following is a summary of a private communication with Neville Bartle.

3:5–13 Summary of the Levites' Duties

Verses 5–13 give a kind of introduction, summarizing the areas in which God has commanded the Levites to serve. Only the Levites are to approach the tabernacle. Anyone else who dares approach it suffers the death penalty. Thus, the Levites are very important as those who represent God before the people and the people before God. Doubtless, a text such as this has led to a kind of arrogance on the part of members of the clergy, and indeed such a high view of ordained ministers led, in part, to the Protestant Reformation, with one of its key doctrines being the priesthood of all believers. This is the idea that all believers can have direct access to God without needing a priest as an intermediary. This liberating theological concept has, unfortunately, become a bit of an obstacle as some people think that clergy and ordination are unnecessary. Although every believer has access to God on her/his own, clergy have a special calling from God, hopefully good training, and usually more comprehensive knowledge of the Bible, church history, and theology than most lay people. Though clergy members are by no means always correct, like experts in any field, they are much more likely to discern questions pertaining to their field with wise insight than those who have not obtained the same level of training.

3:14–20 Command to Count the Levites

The final verses in this introductory section (vv. 14–20) give the Lord's command to complete a census of the Levite males from one month old upward. This numbering is different than that encountered in chapter 1, where the final tally – 603,550 – was the total number of males in the twelve tribes (Ephraim and Manasseh replacing Levi and Joseph in the counting) who were able to pick up a sword and fight. Of course, one-month-old babies would not be able to assume priestly or other Levitical duties. Yet this accounting reveals that the only distinction among the Levites is where someone might be called to serve. In other words, there are Levites who are sons of Aaron and Levites who are not sons of Aaron. The former were to serve in offering the sacrifices at the tent of meeting or the tabernacle, while the latter were to serve in various other supporting roles. All Levite males were to serve in some capacity. This echoes the Protestant doctrine of the priesthood of all believers, by which the reformers maintained not only that all could access God, but also that all would have a role to play in God's service. In modern terms, one might say that God calls all persons into ministry, but some are called into the ministry of "priestly" service (notice that the word "priestly" should be understood in its broadest possible sense, not referring only to Catholic priests).

3:21–26 Gershonite Clan

Beginning with verses 21–26 about the Gershonite clan, the text specifically describes where each clan will march with respect to the tabernacle. Previous passages have made clear that the Levites are to march in the center of all the tribes, with the tabernacle and the Ark of the Covenant. However, the specificity here lends further uniqueness to the Levitical clans. Chapter 2 outlines the battle arrangement for the twelve tribes according to who should march on the east, south, west, and north, identifying a principal tribe among each group of three (Judah on the east, Reuben on the south, Ephraim on the west, and Dan on the north) and indicating that other tribes should march next to the principal tribe. The instructions do not divide the tribes into clans. Yet here in chapter 3, the "Gershonite clans were to camp on the west, behind the tabernacle" (3:23). In contrast with chapter 2, the westernmost clan appears first in the list here, perhaps because of the comparatively more important task given to the Gershonites, which was the responsibility for the tabernacle itself – though not, of course, for the service inside it.

3:27–32 Kohathite Clan

Verses 27–32 discuss the Kohathites. Divided into four clans – the Amramites, the Izharites, the Hebronites, and the Uzzielites – the descendants of Kohath marched on the south side of the tabernacle. The MT says that there were 8,600 Kohathites. One manuscript of the LXX disagrees, giving the number 8,300. The NIV follows the MT. In addition, the MT has singular pronouns in two instances, whereas other versions have plural. The first instance, "everything related to their use," in verse 31 of the LXX refers to the responsibilities of the Kohathites, which are listed earlier in the verse: the ark, the table, the lampstand, the altars, the sanctuary vessels, and the screen. The MT translates this same verse as, "All this was his service," referring to Kohath and his descendants. It seems best here to agree with the Septuagint versions rather than the MT.

The second instance is found in verse 32, where the discussion relates to the appointment of Eleazar, the son of Aaron, as the chairman, so to speak, of the joint chiefs of staff. The MT uses the singular: "chief over the chiefs of Levi," whereas the Septuagint reads: "Levites." Again, the Septuagint is to be preferred. A general principle of textual criticism maintains that the more difficult reading should be preferred to alternatives when there is a confusing original. In both of these cases, the reading as it stands in the MT is more difficult, and – the Septuagint alternatives apparently tried to lessen the confusion. P. Kyle McCarter colorfully corrects the usual principle of preferring the more difficult reading. He writes, "The more difficult reading is not to be preferred when it is garbage."[11] While "garbage" might be an overly strong term, there is no justification for the use of the singular in the first of these cases. In the second case, one might perhaps reach for the principle of metonymy, by which one representative of a group stands for the group as a whole. Yet this seems unsatisfactory, especially since it makes an additional layer of interpretation necessary for modern readers.

3:33–37 Merarite Clan

Verses 33–37 describe the clan of the Merarites, who are to be encamped on the north side of the tabernacle. These 6,200 men were responsible for all manner of physical equipment related to the shrine. Some manuscripts give a slightly different spelling of Abihail in verse 35 (Abihel), though this does not affect the meaning of the passage. There is a seeming monotony to the tasks assigned to the Merarites, who maintain such things as the pegs for the tent of meeting.

The Apostle Paul, in his first letter to the Christians in Corinth, maintained that "not many . . . were influential; not many were of noble birth. But God chose the foolish things of the world to shame the wise . . . God chose the lowly things of this world and the despised things – and the things that are not – to nullify the things that are" (1 Cor 1:26–28). Walter Rauschenbusch praised apparently "lowly" service in God's work: "The actual results of his work proved to Jesus that his success was to be with the simple-minded, and not with the pundit class. He accepted the fact with a thrill of joy, and praised God for making it so . . . In bringing in a new order of things, God had to use plain people to get leverage."[12] Thus today, and through history, the overwhelming majority of ministers labor in obscurity, with no official recognition or public fame. The eighth century traditional Irish hymn, "Be Thou My Vision," comes to mind in the present context. Even the lowliest task – or the task that seems lowliest in terms of how the world reckons lowliness and loftiness – has eternal significance. According to this hymn, the fact that Jesus exists is enough to sustain the soul throughout a lifetime of selfless service, such as minding

---

11. P. Kyle McCarter, *Textual Criticism: Recovering the Text of the Hebrew Bible* (Philadelphia: Fortress, 1986), 17.
12. Walter Rauschenbusch, *The Social Principles of Jesus* (New York: The International Committee of Young Men's Christian Associations, 1916), 45.

one tent peg for twenty years,[13] or serving as the pastor of a small church in a small town in the province. The third stanza holds particular significance:

> Riches I heed not, nor man's empty praise,
> Thou mine inheritance, now and always;
> Thou and Thou only, first in my heart,
> High King of Heaven, my Treasure Thou art.[14]

3:38–39 Total of the Levites

Verses 38–39 indicate that the total number of Levite males was 22,000, a figure that refers to those serving or those who would eventually serve once they became old enough. God set the tribe of Levi – and the sons of Aaron in particular – apart to serve him throughout all generations, with the accompanying idea that there would always be those who were called and qualified to serve; Israel would never lack Levites and priests throughout all its generations.

3:40–51 The Levites Belong to God

In verses 40–51, the Lord declares that the Levites belong to him rather than the firstborn of all the Israelites. The reader may compare this text with Exodus 13:1–2, in which the Lord commands: "The first offspring of every womb among the Israelites belongs to me, whether human or animal." Here, however, the Levites serve a different kind of representative function. Throughout the history of Israel, the Levites served as God's representatives before the people and also as the people's representatives before God, but here their particular role is especially significant. In many ancient societies, the firstborn of the flocks or herds was dedicated to the deity or deities whom the people of those societies worshipped, and this dedication was expressed by killing a firstborn animal. Some societies, Carthage in particular, were known to dedicate firstborn children – especially sons – by killing them as an offering to the god or goddess.

The Torah explicitly forbids child sacrifice in a number of places (for example, Lev 18:1; 20:3; Deut 12:30–31; 18:10), perhaps indicating that some Israelites thought child sacrifice was legitimate. The primary example of this line of reasoning is Jephthah, who sacrifices his daughter to the Lord in Judges 11:30–39. Most striking in this episode, aside from the willingness of the daughter to accept what was decreed for her, is the game-of-chance aspect to

---

13. I owe this observation to Dr. Floyd Cunningham, long-time Academic Dean of Asia-Pacific Nazarene Theological Seminary.
14. "Be Thou My Vision," trans. Mary E. Berne, in *Sing to the Lord*, reprint (Kansas City: Lillenas Publishing), no. 460, stanza 3.

the episode: Jephthah vowed that whatever first came out of his house to greet him after he returned from his victory of the Ammonites would be sacrificed to the Lord. Given that a judge did this, one must not dismiss this as a simple aberration or oddity in Israelite worship. In the main, however, child sacrifice was not widely practiced in Israel. Moreover, the practice often receives a dismissive response (see Mic 6) or outright condemnation, as with the wicked kings, Ahaz (2 Kgs 16) and Manasseh (2 Kgs 21, though see 2 Chr 33:10–20 and the deuterocanonical "Prayer of Manasseh" on the latter's repentance).

The substitution of the Levites for the firstborn of the Israelites does not mean that the Levites were to be killed. Instead, they were to be dedicated to the Lord for all time for service. This idea is supported by the fact that the Levites' cattle are included as a substitute for the firstborn of the cattle of Israel. While the numbers of the cattle are not given in this text, the number of firstborn males is 22,273. These men, having been spared from dedication by death, have the potential to become dedicated servants of the Lord, just like the Levites were.

4:1–20 *The Kohathites and Their Duties*

Moving into chapter four, verses 1–20 discuss the Kohathites and their duties. God gives this particular clan charge over the most holy things, or the things in the Holy of Holies. These items, especially "the ark of the covenant law" (v. 5), indicated in a tangible way the presence of God among the people. There are three special considerations to this charge. First, these "holy" things did not represent God himself. The Old Testament frequently criticizes other peoples who employ statues of their gods in worship. The biblical writers call these statues "idols" in order to make the critique clear. Though the other peoples believed that their gods and goddesses allowed the statues to be faithful representations – thus not the deities themselves – Israel was very different. The holy objects had no connection to the identity of the Lord.

Second, the Israelites expend great effort in caring for these holy objects. Thus the Kohathites are charged with wrapping the ark of the testimony in the veil, which is normally used to separate the Holy of Holies from the remainder of the tabernacle. Blue and red cloths, as well as coverings of goatskin, are used to protect the holy items.

Third, the holy items are to be carried on poles just like the ark. Moreover, the Kohathites are barred from entering the holy space until the sons of Aaron have covered the holy objects. Although the Kohathites carry the holy objects, they must not touch the objects themselves, on penalty of death.

Many, perhaps most, modern Christians have a similarly high view of the sacred nature of religious objects. For example, one of my former students from India informed me that, in his context, one must not place a Bible underneath a stack of other books on one's desk. As a Westerner, I had not come across this idea before. In my estimation, treating the Bible in this way was not to disrespect it; for me, it was simply a matter of space. (Yet after my student told me about this practice, it raised my awareness, and I now make an effort not to stack things on top of Bibles.) By contrast, while I write many notes in the margins of books I read, I very rarely make notes, highlights, or other marks in my paper copies of the Bible. Many similar things could be said about church buildings and objects used in worship (even things like guitars, amplifiers, and altar benches), raising a potential criticism of church-planting strategies that do not take into account the importance of holy space. Though the death penalty may no longer apply – at least, in most contexts – to the mishandling of holy objects, the issue remains important.

4:21–28 Another Census of the Levites

The census takings of the Levitical clans listed in 4:21–28 number the clans differently. In chapter 3, the numbers of men from one month old were counted, but here only the men from thirty to fifty years old were counted. In other words, the previous census determined how many potential workers there were, whereas this census determined how many actual workers there are. Elsewhere in Numbers (8:23–26), the age range is from twenty-five to fifty. The different age ranges for service likely reflect different traditions, from different times or places, regarding how old Levites should be. Like the numbers of the tribes themselves, the accuracy and consistency of these age ranges is not significant. What is most important is that God designated the Levites to serve as a perpetual order of ministry in Israel. While hereditary service is not widely practiced in Christianity – or in contemporary Judaism – it was a key feature for the earliest Israelites and this history is important to the book of Numbers. A final note in this section is that the Gershonites are to serve "under the direction of Ithamar son of Aaron, the priest" (v. 28). This makes an important distinction between Levites and priests. Though both are Levites, only the sons of Aaron are to serve as priests.

4:29–33 Duties of the Merarites

Verses 29–33 describe the duties of the Merarites, the third of the three clans of Levites. Whereas the Kohathites are assigned to holy objects, the Merarites seem to be assigned to a much lower task, involving the tent pegs, cords, and other assorted materials that kept the tabernacle in place, so that the rest of the Levites and the sons of Aaron could perform their duties. However, viewing the duty of the Merarites as lower is a grave mistake. For in the physical dimension, the Holy of Holies could not be marked off within the tent of meeting if the tent itself were not marked off from the world. In the desert, the floor of the tent was probably desert sand, so some religious distinction would need to be made between "this sand," or the sand which was marked off as part of the holy shrine, and "that sand," or the sand which was outside the tent. If the Merarites failed to do their duty, the holy place could not be defined and, therefore, the sons of Aaron would have nowhere to go in order to make intercession for the people.

4:34–45 Restating the Numbers

In verses 34–45, the text revisits each of the clans to repeat their respective numbers. The order is slightly different, beginning with the Kohathites (vv. 34–37), then the Gershonites (vv. 38–41), and ending with the Merarites (vv. 42–45). In chapter 3, the order began with the Gershonites (3:21–26), then the Kohathites (3:27–32), and also ended with the Merarites (3:33–37). The final section (vv. 46–49) gives a summary of all the material in chapters 3 through 4. The numbers in chapter 4 are different than the previous listings in chapter 3, because this section only considers those who are between the ages of thirty and fifty – or, in other words, those who are qualified for service in, around, and for the tabernacle (see above commentary on vv. 21–28). It is unclear why the final form of the text separates the duties of the various clans from their numbers, though this probably reflects the assembling of the different source material. In any event, this section reports that 2,750 of the 8,600 Kohathites meet the age range of between thirty and fifty, which amounts to about 32 percent. For the Gerhsonites, 2,630 of their 7,500 meet this age range, which amounts to 35 percent. For the Merarites 3,200 out of 6,200 fall within this age range, which amounts to 52 percent. These percentages may explain why the order is different between chapters 3 and 4. In chapter 4, the order is given in ascending order, based on the percentage of males aged between thirty and fifty.

4:46–49 *Summaries of Chapters 3–4*

Verses 46–49 summarize the two chapters devoted to the census of the Levites. The total number of those eligible to serve the tabernacle between thirty and fifty years of age was 8,580, which represents about 1 percent of the total population of fighting men listed at the ends of chapters 1 and 2. Although these numbers, according to Western interpreters, are probably legendary, the minuscule population of Levites relative to the general population sounds a striking note with regard to the theory and practice of ordination.

The Levites were the only ones authorized to serve in God's tabernacle. In the course of time, the tabernacle and its successor, the Temple, eventually would no longer exist. One wonders if the special place of the Levites thus ended with the destruction of the Temple – for the tabernacle was not destroyed, but replaced by more permanent structures: first in 586 BC, then forever in 70 AD. (Forever, that is, unless the hoped-for "Third Temple," the building that will be a sign of the end of the end times, will be a physical building.) For in Jewish communities today, though sons and daughters of rabbis may or may not become rabbis themselves, they are not required to do so, nor is it necessary for a potential rabbi to have rabbis in his/her family ancestry in order to qualify. Thus, modern Jewish practice is similar to Christian practice on this point.

Christian practice, for much of history, naturally precluded the possibility of an heredity priesthood since, at least ideally, priests were commanded to be celibate and thus could not have children who could potentially succeed them. Among Protestants, especially Protestant evangelicals, the notion of a "call to ministry," or the experience of God's summoning into the ministry, has become all-important. These call experiences take multiple forms, but there is often a sense of compulsion. Though the Levites were called to compulsory service, there is no notion in the Old Testament of anyone but a Levite being fit for this service. In fact, the offering of sacrifices and other religious activities by non-Levites brings them in for severe criticism and sometimes-divine punishment, most notably in the case of King Saul, who was not a Levite, but came from the tribe of Benjamin. By contrast, in New Testament times, a later Saul, also called Paul, did great religious service for Jesus Christ, yet he was not a Levite but was also from the tribe of Benjamin. In the book of Numbers, the Levites serve a particular function – and this is the only function they fulfill. Moreover, they are the only ones who may fulfill this particular function in the service of God and God's tabernacle.

5:1–6:27 THE LAWS OF THE LORD ARE PERFECT

The laws in the Torah are found within the books of Exodus through Deuteronomy. In chapters 5 and 6 we come to the first of several sections in the book of Numbers that deal with legal matters rather than narrative. Included in this section are notions of ritual uncleanness, personal injury, jealousy, vows, and blessings. These laws give a good view into ancient Israelite society, and they also have importance for present-day ethics and action.

5:1–4 Uncleanness

These verses introduce a lengthy bit of legal material, where God instructs Moses to have the people put offensive matter "outside the camp" (v. 3). This characteristic phrase highlights the important idea that inside the camp is the presence of God, and so it has to be kept ritually clean. This idea also occurs at various points in Leviticus. Specifically relevant for comparative purposes is Leviticus 13:45–46: "Anyone with such a defiling disease must wear torn clothes, let their hair be unkempt, cover the lower part of their face and cry out, 'Unclean! Unclean!' As long as they have the disease they remain unclean. They must live alone; they must live outside the camp."

According to Mary Douglas, cleanness was never merely a utilitarian matter of physical cleanliness or keeping away germs. Specifically with regard to Israel, it was a matter of keeping God's blessing intact. God cannot tolerate uncleanness or ritual pollution; therefore, any such pollution, once it is found, must be removed from the camp. Douglas writes: "This much reiterated idea of physical completeness is also worked out in the social sphere and particularly in the warriors' camp . . . The army could not win without the blessing and to keep the blessing in the camp they had to be specially holy."[15]

Therefore, when God tells Moses in verses 1–4 that uncleanness must be removed from the camp, it is a serious matter. The specific uncleanness referred to here has to do with leprosy, which could refer to a number of skin diseases (see also Lev 13). The camp could not be defiled because God dwelled in the midst of it. This also reflects the overall theme of the book: the people's journey with God in the desert.

However, the interpreter must remember that the Israelites' compliance did not stem from fear, as so-called "advanced" researchers thought about so-called "primitive" societies as late as the nineteenth century. Douglas gives a strikingly different interpretation: "anthropologists who have ventured further

---

15. Douglas, *Purity and Danger*, 52.

into these primitive cultures find little trace of fear . . . So primitive religious fear, together with the idea that it blocks the functioning of the mind, seems to be a false trail for understanding these religions. Hygiene, by contrast, turns out to be an excellent route, so long as we can follow it with some self-knowledge."[16] Along these lines, one should say not that the Israelites were afraid of God or afraid of uncleanness, but rather that they knew that uncleanness and God could not abide in the same place. The presence of God, as Douglas notes, was key to the blessing under which they were operating, so they had to do whatever was necessary to ensure that the blessing stayed with them. For this reason, as the text says, the Israelites were careful to do everything that Moses told them: not because they were afraid of God, but because they wanted to make the camp an acceptable living space for the presence of God, without which they could not hope to prosper in their undertakings.

Modern interpreters of this passage should avoid equating ritual impurity with moral impurity. While one should not simply set all of this legal material aside as pertaining only to the ancient society, one must recognize the difficulties that come with applying this material in modern contexts. Moreover, for Christians, it is important to note that, by the time of the New Testament, the laws on ritual impurity had been taken to an extreme by such persons as the Pharisees and Sadducees – the main opponents of Jesus in the Gospels – and had thus becomes ends in themselves. One might recall the discussion of the symbolism of the Ark of the Covenant above, wherein the abuse of a particular symbol does not invalidate the use of a particular symbol. In the same way, with legal material, one may look for an underlying principle in the quest for justice between persons, especially in terms of care for the oppressed and the poor. There is biblical support for this principle, particularly in the Israelite prophets, who were the first recorded persons to question abuses of ritual observances of the law.

5:5–10 Personal Injury and Restitution

The legal material continues with basic rules for confessing sin and making restitution. These two stages have different requirements based on the conditions of the case. Because of the conditions associated with the restitution, this text seems to be a good concrete example of the difference between what Albrecht

---

16. Ibid., 1–2.

Alt calls "apodictic" and "casuistic" law.[17] Apodictic laws are given in the form, "You shall do x" or, negatively, "You shall not do x." The Ten Commandments are the clearest examples of apodictic laws in the OT. Apodictic laws allow for no conditions; instead, they issue more or less universal commands: do this always or do not do this ever. In the present text, the apodictic law holds that when the sinner, whether male or female, recognizes that he or she has done something contrary to the law, he or she must confess his or her sin. One finds here no mitigation or condition. According to this text, no possible conditions might soften the person's guilt or make confession unnecessary.

When it comes to restitution (vv. 7b–10), however, conditions do in fact apply. Verse 7 indicates that the offender must make full restitution for the offense and add an extra one-fifth besides. The text is not clear on this point, but the extra fifth may serve for what many legal systems call "punitive damages," or an amount of restitution that is above the amount of the original injury. These extra damages intend, as their name implies, to punish the offender. This applies whether the injury is a physical one – so that the offender is paying, say, the medical bills of the injured party – or a monetary one, as in the case of theft or fraud. Again, the law gives no specific information as to the nature of the offense. It seems, rather, that this law could apply to any number of cases. This is, in fact, a key characteristic of casuistic law: the facts of the case determine the resolution of the case.

In this instance, something seems to be missing. The gap comes between verses 7 and 8. Verse 7, as noted, suggests that the offender must pay to the victim 120 percent of the value of whatever was stolen, destroyed, damaged, or otherwise offended. This suggests a property violation of some kind. However, verse 8 says that the offender should pay restitution to the Lord for the priest if the offended party does not have a next-of-kin. This restitution implies homicide as the crime in question. The text has leapt over, so it would seem, a stipulation that, in case the victim died, the restitution should go to the next of kin.

However, a solution to this apparent problem readily presents itself. No reader should expect the biblical laws to be fully complete; rather they are an abridgement. As Samuel Greengus notes: "The biblical law collections, even when considered *in toto*, fall short of including all of the legal areas operative

---

17. Albrecht Alt, "The Origins of Israelite Law," in *Essays in Old Testament History and Religion* (New York: Doubleday, 1967), 101–171.

in ancient Israelite society."[18] Clearly, therefore, a level or two has dropped out of this text in the course of its transmission. Perhaps most important to note is that in no case is the offender to go free without penalty. Thus, at the end of the day, this reinforces the apodictic character of the law pertaining to confession and restitution. Even if there is no human to pay the restitution to, the offender still must pay restitution to God before restoring himself or herself to full membership in the community.

5:11–31 Ritual for Jealous Husbands

This text is easily the most bizarre in the entire book of Numbers. On the one hand, the bizarreness of this text can lead and – in the history of scholarship, particularly over the last fifty years or so – has led to various attempts to explain away this text. For example, one could dismiss this text as an anomaly, since this is the only description of such an ordeal, and the Bible contains no record of anyone ever taking the steps detailed here. By contrast, records do exist for the case of the marriage of a brother to the wife of his deceased older brother (Deut 25:5–6). Similarly, the case in Genesis 38 also represents an apparently anomalous case since the child of Tamar belongs to her father-in-law and not to the dead man. Ruth 4 is also a record of an anomalous case, since Boaz is considered the father of Obed. One may assume that most of the time situations like this were resolved according to the law. Given that these two cases are the only ones mentioned, the reader should probably understand them as unusual exceptions. In Genesis 38, Onan refused to do his duty; in Ruth 4, the dead Mahlon had no brothers who could do this duty. Even still, both cases demonstrate the law's practical application. The case of the daughters of Zelophehad may be another example of exceptions made to this law (see commentary on Num 27:1–11; 36:1–12 below). No such practical application of the law in Numbers 5 exists, leaving the reader almost completely in the realm of speculation.

Lacking specific evidence for the carrying out of this ordeal, one might attempt to compare this text with other texts having to do with adultery. However, such a procedure has its problems, since this text may not deal with adultery after all, but instead only with the suspicion of adultery. Eve Levavi Feinstein provides a representative example of this treatment, for she notes that this text "relates a ritual for determining the innocence or guilt of

---

18. Samuel Greengus, "Biblical and ANE Law," in *Anchor Bible Dictionary*, vol. 4, ed. David Noel Freedman (New York: Anchor Doubleday, 1992), 243.

a suspected adulteress."[19] Roland Boer suggests that such recent, especially postmodern, biblical interpretation begins with an error: "Two [ideas] stand out: somehow Numbers 5 very quickly becomes a text concerning adultery; and interpreters have an overwhelming desire to enhance the potency of the 'waters of bitterness.'"[20] As an alternative, Boer suggests that this text details a ritual for a jealous husband, owing to the great ambiguity of the circumstances attending this legal regulation.

5:11–12a Beginning the Ritual

Verses 11–12a begin in the usual way, introducing legal material by having the Lord tell Moses to say something to the Israelites. This literary trope sets up the reader for certain expectations. Chief among these expectations is a legal scenario that covers all of the possible eventualities that may come up in a particular case. The text will dash these expectations immediately, however, as the ritual being described here is filled with a great deal of exceptions and confusions. At the end, the reader may not finally be able to make sense of the material. In other words, this is not the usual legal case: it does not discuss the different conditions that might pertain to a woman suspected of adultery, but focuses instead on the jealousy of a husband. Many English translations, such as the NIV, miss this, and follow the usual procedure to call this section, "The Test for an Unfaithful Wife."

5:12b–15 A Complicated Case

Verses 12b–15 severely complicate the nature of the case, making it clear that this law is not about a woman who has potentially committed adultery at all. Instead, it is about a husband's suspicion that his wife has committed adultery. Not only does verse 29 confirm this, but also one may note that neither man involved – the supposed lover or the husband – faces any potential penalty (see below). However, as Boer notes, comparing this with other texts regarding adultery is beside the point (e.g. Exod 20:14; Lev 20:10–21; Deut 5:17; 22:13–29). For in this text, the legal requirement applies if a man is jealous of his wife and suspects her of adultery, whether or not she has gone through with it.

---

19. Eve Levavi Feinstein, "The 'Bitter Waters' of Numbers 5:11–31," *Vetus Testamentum* 62:3 (2012): 300.
20. Ronald Boer, "The Law of the Jealous Man," in *Voyages in Uncharted Waters: Essays on the Theory and Practice of Biblical Interpretation*, ed. Wesley J. Bergen and Armin Siedlecki (Sheffield, UK: Sheffield Phoenix, 2006), 87.

In the scenario envisioned here, the question of whether the wife has defiled herself is rather secondary, since conclusive evidence of any misdeed is lacking. Such a case in a traditional society such as ancient Israel might call for a trial by ordeal, which happens here. The interpreter must remember, however, that the jealousy and suspicion of the husband has set these events in motion – not the behavior of the wife. Boer notes: "in the introduction what we get is something like a legal version of the 3 am obsessions of a jealous man, twisting in his bed, wide awake. The fourfold repetition is a dead giveaway: the act is hidden; she is undetected; there was no witness; she was not caught in the act."[21] The woman, however, finds herself in a most uncomfortable position: "if we shift focus to the woman's perspective, then the law makes little sense at all: she's trapped if she has and trapped if she hasn't. All that is solid melts into the air. Even the item that holds the whole law together – the man's jealousy – is beginning to look decidedly shaky."[22]

5:16–28 A Trial by Ordeal

Following this horribly confusing legal introduction is the description of the trial by ordeal (vv. 16–28). Traditional societies such as ancient Israel often used ordeal trials when clear evidence to prove a certain criminal act did not exist. For example, an ordeal trial might have helped in a case when a thief did not have allegedly stolen property in his or her possession. The second law of the Code of Hammurabi – a famous law code from the ancient Near East – describes such an ordeal trial. This law commands one accused of theft to jump into the river (probably the Euphrates River). If he dies, the accuser takes over the property of the now-dead accused. However, if the river, which the Babylonians considered divine, acquits the accused, then the accuser is killed, and the accused takes over the property of the now-dead accuser. Here, however, even if the woman is innocent, the husband bears no guilt and suffers no punishment.

This ritual for jealous husbands once again proves to be unique among ancient Israel's law, for as Alice Bach notes, "it is the only trial by ordeal" to be found anywhere within the Torah.[23] According to Katherine Doob Sakenfeld, "The key to understanding the procedure is the requirement that the woman

---

21. Boer, "Law of the Jealous Man," 88.
22. Ibid.
23. Alice Bach, "Good to the Last Drop: Viewing the Sotah (Numbers 5:11–31) as the Glass Half Empty and Wondering How to View It Half Full," in *Women in the Hebrew Bible: A Reader*, ed. Alice Bach (New York: Routledge, 1999), 505.

say 'Amen, Amen' (v. 22), thus accepting the potential results of the curse to be laid on her if she is guilty."[24] Interpretation of this ordeal trial typically focuses on the potency of the so-called "bitter water that brings a curse" (v. 18). It seems clear that water mixed with dirt mixed with shavings from a scroll is not going to do anything to produce a miscarriage. Furthermore, it seems that the priest must know this. For the priest writes the curses down on a scroll, then promptly washes them off into water, which he then makes the woman drink. Thus, the reader comes to the unavoidable conclusion that the ritual only serves to calm the suspicions of the husband.

The fact that the "grain of remembrance" (vv. 15, 17 AT) is also called the "grain offering for jealousy" (vv. 15, 17) creates additional confusion, which further complicates the case. In an even more confusing twist, the fact that the waters of bitterness are supposed to cause a miscarriage points to a rather odd criterion for judging whether adultery has taken place – namely, that a pregnancy has resulted. If this case were really about adultery, then it seems strange that the only acceptable proof would be the termination of the pregnancy resulting from such illicit acts. Then again, one must bear in mind that in ancient Israel, as perhaps in many ancient Near Eastern societies, adultery was more properly a property problem rather than a relationship problem. In other words, it had to do with the inheritance of property rather than a sin committed against a man. Later on in Israel's story – in the case of David, Bathsheba, and Uriah (2 Sam 11–12) – the text still does not consider Bathsheba as a victim, though David does face punishment (2 Sam 11–12).

5:29–31 Judgment in the Case

Unlike the code of Hammurabi, where the one who brings an accusation without proof is subjected to the same punishment as the accused if the accusation is determined to be false, the jealous husband in this case gets off scot-free (vv. 29–31). The epilogue finally reveals that this law is about jealousy rather than adultery. The text would certainly have been much easier to interpret if the introduction to this unique trial by ordeal had agreed with its conclusion. Then again, even the disagreement between introduction and conclusion further troubles this troubling text. It is confusing indeed. Sakenfeld's conclusion is apt: "The law invites readers to reflect upon the many ways in which diverse

---

24. Katherine Doob Sakenfeld, "Numbers," in *Women's Bible Commentary,* ed. Carol A. Newsom and Sharon H. Ringe, expanded ed. (Louisville: Westminster John Knox, 1998), 53.

cultures have sought to control women's sexual behavior, as well as upon the terror reigning among women wherever such customs prevail."[25]

The reader may find one possibility for penalty against the man who has brought this unnecessary charge just a few verses prior to the ordeal text, which read: "If a man or a woman commits any sin against another human being, acting in bad faith against the LORD, that person becomes guilty and must confess the sin. He or she must make pay full restitution plus one-fifth to the injured party" (vv. 6–7 AT). Yet the ordeal text itself gives no indication about what the man might face if he makes a false accusation. Given the patriarchal context of Numbers, this is not surprising, although 5:6–7 may be a place where the patriarchal assumptions lying behind the text unintentionally subvert themselves.

6:1–21 Nazirite Vows

Throughout religious history, certain individuals and groups have desired to perform extra religious duties as a means of attaining either salvation or a special favored status before God or the gods. For example, the Christian monastic movement through the centuries has included many people who seemed to have had a closer connection to God, which they cultivated through prayer, fasting, discipline, study, and simplicity. Within Judaism, such groups included not only the Nazirites, who are the focus of the present investigation, but also the Rechabites (see Jer 35), the Essenes (largely unknown in the NT but figuring prominently in the writings of Josephus), and, in modern times, the Hasidim (Hasidic Jews). The last of these groups owes its origin to the great master Rabbi Israel ben Eliezer (also known as Baal Shem Tov, or Lord of the Good Name), who lived from 1700–1760 AD.

Groups such as these often live in an uncertain relationship with the mainstream of the particular religious tradition from which they draw their inspiration. Thus, the Essenes in the first-century AD – who were largely responsible for collecting the group of texts now known as the Dead Sea Scrolls – were of the opinion that the Jerusalem priesthood had become hopelessly corrupt. They even went so far as to call the high priest in Jerusalem "The Wicked Priest," who in their way of looking at things was constantly at war with their leader, "The Teacher of Righteousness."

Other groups have launched protest movements against various abuses of the majority. This is the case with the Franciscan monks, who took vows of

---

25. Ibid.

extreme poverty as a foil to the elaborate, ornate, wealthy medieval church. The dominant culture typically responds to such protest movements with an attitude of suppression, either by trying to absorb the protest movement or to destroy it. The protest movement keeps pushing the dominant culture to exhibit behavior that is more in line with its vision of justice, and so tension marks the relationship, as neither is willing to back down.

The Nazirites, who come into focus in the present text, were not a group *per se,* for it seems that only individuals took this oath, and it is unclear if Nazirites ever established a communal living arrangement – a monastery, so to speak – apart from the main community of Israelites. Though the Essenes established such communities several centuries later, not all Essenes lived in monasteries like the Qumran community near the Dead Sea. Some lived within mainstream society, and some (possibly including John the Baptist) lived more like Nazirites, on the margins of society, but perhaps for that reason closer to God. Not all Nazirites separated from society, as some maintained close connection to the wider society, such as the prophet/priest/judge Samuel and Samson (see the exposition on verses 3–5 for more on Samson).

6:1–2a Introduction

This text detailing the vows of the Nazirites begins in the usual way. The Lord tells Moses to say something to the Israelites (vv. 1–2a). In the second part of verse 2, however, things become interesting. First, the vow is open to both men and women. Second, the verb comes from the same root as that which is translated "Wonderful Counselor" in Isaiah 9:6 (here it is a noun, there an adjective). The word indicates that the proposed vow, while perhaps not miraculous, is difficult, extraordinary, surpassing one's normal powers of accomplishment. The NIV's translation of this word as "special" ("If a man or a woman wants to make a special vow") does not seem quite strong enough. Even in the law describing what the Nazirites should do, the text recognizes that not everyone is up to this vow. Even for those with extraordinary capacities, it will not be easy.

Following this extraordinary verb, the text features an interesting collection of sounds. The NIV's rendering, "makes a special vow, a vow of dedication to the LORD as a Nazirite," is typical of English translations that fail to grasp the beauty of the Hebrew. The NIV has changed the word order to render the verse in intelligible English. The Hebrew word order of verse 2 follows: "A man or a woman if they [the singular stands for the plural] want to do a difficult vow, the vow of the Nazirite, to separate themselves to the LORD" (AT). The key phrase is the last five Hebrew words (to vow, the vow, Nazirite, separate, to the LORD): *lindor neder nazir lehazir leyhwh.*

The four words prior to the Lord's name separate – pun intended – into two pairs of words. Each pair comes from the same root. On the one hand, *lindor neder* literally means, "to vow a vow." This is a typical construction in Semitic languages such as Hebrew, where a noun is the object of a verb that comes from the same root. On the other hand, *nazir lehazir* means, "Nazirite, to separate." Here, the proper noun precedes the verb with which it shares the root. Therefore, the entire construction is verb-noun-noun-verb.

6:3–4 The First Condition: No Wine
Verses 3–4 spell out the first condition of the Nazirite vow: total abstention from wine or even, apparently, unfermented grapes. In addition, verse 4 indicates that the vow of a Nazirite need not be permanent. Yet during the entire period of separation, the one making the vow must not touch grapes. A later group known as the Rechabites shares this absolute prohibition of wine. Jeremiah 35 informs us that this group could not by rule build houses or plant vineyards, but must instead live in tents throughout all their days. The LORD then speaks to Jeremiah, using the Rechabites as an example of faithfulness over against the unfaithful Judahites. Because the Rechabites maintained their faithfulness as one of these fringe groups, they will be rewarded (Jer 35:1–19).

A further interesting point comes in the legal speculation about the Nazirite vow in post-biblical Jewish writings. One could become a Nazirite through one's own choice or through the decree of someone else, such as a parent, or – in the case of the most famous Nazirite in the Old Testament, the judge Samson – "through a declaration by an angel before birth."[26]

6:5 The Second Condition: No Haircuts
Verse 5 adds an additional stipulation: the Nazirites must never cut their hair. This restriction plays a role in the story of Samson (Judg 16). For when the Philistines were trying to defeat his extraordinary strength, they coaxed his Philistine wife, Delilah, into extracting his secret. Samson deceives Delilah three times before finally revealing that the Lord will take away his strength if he cuts his hair. Indeed, Samson had already broken the other Nazirite vows, but after breaking this final vow, he loses his strength. The episode ends with

---

26. Dennis T. Olson, "Nazirite," in *The Oxford Companion to the Bible,* ed. Bruce M. Metzter and Michael D. Coogan (Oxford: Oxford University Press, 1993), 552.

Samson becoming, in a manner of speaking, a suicide bomber, bringing down the Temple of Dagon (the Philistine god of grain) on himself and everyone else.

6:6 No Dead Bodies

Verse 6 adds a third stipulation for those who take the Nazirite vow: they must not have contact with a dead body. Verse 7 seems to imply that this is limited to a human body, for even if one of the Nazirite's immediate family dies, the Nazirite must not go near the body. This is a radical, counter-cultural call.

I remember the practice of the most famous heretical Christian sect in the Philippines, where members will not visit the graves of deceased loved ones, even on All Saints' Day (also referred to as All Souls' Day on November 2), when seemingly everyone in the country visits cemeteries. However, presuming that the Nazirites must be wrong because they refrain from doing what a heretical sect also refrains from doing is a fallacy, for Jesus sounded a similar radical call to leave even family behind in furthering the mission of the kingdom of God. Jesus said, "If anyone comes to me without hating his own father and mother and wife and children and brothers and sisters, indeed even his own life, such cannot be my disciple" (Luke 14:26, AT).[27]

6:7–12 The Nazirite is Dedicated to God

Finally, the Nazirite must not allow himself or herself to be defiled, for as verse 7 goes on to say, "the symbol of their dedication to God is on their head" (NIV). The Hebrew literally says, "the separation of his God is on his head," seeming to indicate that the condition of the Nazirite's head (perhaps a comment relating to the hair which must always remain uncut) is the key mark of distinction. Verses 9–12 strengthen this suspicion, stipulating that the Nazirite must shave his or her head of dedicated hair if unintentional contact with a dead body happens. This idea of inadvertent or unintentional sins needing atonement will appear again in chapter 15. It also reflects the priestly community's concern, which is expressed in the regulations of the sin offering in Leviticus 4. If this unintentional contact occurs, the Nazirite is to shave his or her head again after making atonement for the sin. Then one may renew the vow, with all of the stipulations applying anew. The days of separation begin again at zero,

---

27. Many interpreters see this as an example of Jewish hyperbole or exaggeration. In other words, in comparison to the devotion one should have for Jesus, the devotion one has for everything else looks like hate. One's devotion for Jesus must be the single most important thing in one's life. Jesus' instruction here cannot be understood literally without Jesus requiring his followers to break the Fifth Commandment ("You shall honor your father and your mother.")!

because the "previous days do not count, because they became defiled during their period of dedication" (v. 12).

6:13–21 Ending the Nazirite Vow
The final section relating to the vows of Nazirites has to do with ending the time of separation (vv. 13–21). As noted above, the vow can be permanent, as seems to be the case with Samuel, but it need not be so. In cases where the vow is not permanent, the Nazirite who has completed his or her term has to bring an offering to the priest in order to be released from the vow. This further demonstrates the radical nature of the Nazirite vow and that it is not simply a matter of individual preference. One might be tempted to think so, since a particular community of Nazirites did not develop at any time in Israel's history, at least not within the OT. Upon ending the time of separation, the Nazirite shaves his or her head, but unlike the case of unintentional defilement, the hair is put on the fire for the peace offering and burnt. This serves as a visual reminder that the limited time of service is ending and confirms that the hair – whether uncut during the vow or cut because the vow has been fulfilled – forms the most important physical symbol of the vow made to the Lord.

The final verse indicates that any additional vows that the Nazirite desires to make may be made above the vows of the Nazirite, though these are not required. The Nazirite vows are already quite strict, and the phrase, "in addition to whatever else they can afford" (6:21), suggests that it is not necessary to make any additional vow. Nazirite vows made by women are not subject to nullification by their fathers or husbands, in contrast to 30:2–8. This may indicate something further about the strictness of the Nazirite vow.

6:22–27 Priestly Blessing

This short blessing or benediction is one of the best-known texts from the book of Numbers. Were a survey taken of benedictions given in churches throughout the world, it would likely show that ministers used Numbers 6 as often as other benedictions in the Bible.

In my experience, many churches and ministers miss the importance of a benediction by simply collapsing it into a closing prayer or, even worse, leaving it out altogether. The difference between a closing prayer and a benediction, however, involves a directional change as well as an authoritative one.

A minister offers a closing prayer, as all public prayers, addressed to God *as a representative of the people*. Of course, no ordination or special setting apart is necessary for one to offer a public prayer to God on behalf of oneself and other people. Anyone can pray to God at any time, with absolute assurance of open access to God. This is the genius of the Protestant notion of the priesthood of all believers. Though priests and ministers serve a definite, indispensable function in the life of the community of faith, one may still approach God for oneself whenever one sincerely desires to do so.

On the other hand, a minister offers a benediction to the people *as a representative of God*. Ministers – whether they go by the term pastors, priests, elders, monks, nuns, or whatever – stand in a particularly significant role within the community of faith. They represent the people before God as well as God before the people. Thus, a benediction is a special task, offered by a special person who is set apart by God and by the community of faith. Whereas anyone can speak to God on behalf of himself or herself, one cautiously proposes to speak as a representative of God. The biblical prophets often expressed the desire that God would call somebody else (see Exod 3), or even that they could stop speaking in the name of the Lord (see Jer 20). They approached their task with a heavy, careful heart, lest they do something that might anger God and bring down God's punishment upon them. In fact, throughout Israel's history, the high priest, especially when serving in the most holy place of the tabernacle or Temple, was in great danger of death at the hands of God were the priest to do something improper.

In Jewish worship even today, only a Kohen (priest) may offer this blessing from Numbers 6. In fact, this restriction is only one of the many detailed rules about this blessing. Others involve how the priest should hold his or her hands, and what he or she should think while performing the blessing. Moreover, the priest must leave the sanctuary immediately if for any reason he or she does not wish to perform the blessing. These rules demonstrate how seriously Jews take this blessing, and Christians might be wise to take a cue from their predecessors in their worship of the True God in this matter. While Christians, especially Protestants with an emphasis on the priesthood of all believers, do not limit this blessing to ministers, nevertheless it should be taken seriously.

Archaeological investigation provides further evidence of the long-standing importance of this benediction from Numbers 6 for the history of Judaism. In Jerusalem in 1979, archaeologists found two silver amulets. Inside, they found tiny, rolled up copies of the priestly blessing. Researchers dated these fragments to around 600 BC, making them some of the oldest copies of biblical materials ever found. The precise use of these amulets remains unclear; however, some have suggested that they were apotropaic amulets, or things worn in order to ward off bad luck or evil influences. Nevertheless, their presence demonstrates the importance of the priestly blessing within ancient biblical culture.

Turning to the text of this section, the first two verses set the scene, so to speak, with the LORD telling Moses what he should tell Aaron and his sons to say (vv. 22–23). These verses are straightforward, presenting no critical problems. But the second to the last word of verse 23 is a little strange. The verb translated, "Say unto them," is in the Hebrew form of an infinitive absolute. Hebrew absolutes rarely occur by themselves and normally express some kind of intensified action. When they do appear by themselves, however, they precede another form of the same verb. Exodus 19:5 gives another example. Here, by contrast, the infinitive absolute seems to function simply as an active command. The intensification of the action normally associated with infinitive absolutes is therefore lost.

The Hebrew version most often used by scholars marks off the blessing itself in poetic lines in verses 24–26. Throughout, the verbs are in the jussive form, which is something like the future tense, expressing incomplete action, specifically expressing a wish. Regular future forms (often called "imperfect") usually mean, "So-and-so will do such-and-such." Here, the jussive expresses a wish that the LORD will fulfill the action requested. While the priestly blessing certainly predicts what the LORD will do, the context of a blessing dictates that one is looking for a plea for the LORD to bless and keep one, to make his face shine down upon one, and so forth. This would further be in line with the apotropaic amulets discussed above. This blessing, which expresses the wish that the LORD will do these things, thus functions as a prayer for protection for all manner of evil. Moreover, recalling the function of Aaron and the priests as representatives of God to the people, they are calling upon God to act in the way God has promised to act.

Of further interest, the singular pronouns used throughout the blessing do not come across in modern English translations, since these do not retain older distinctions between singular and plural in second-person pronouns ("you"). Moreover, the "you" here is masculine, reflecting the fact that Hebrew society, like many ancient societies, was patriarchal. This does not mean that the blessing excluded women. True enough, modern Orthodox Jewish practice requires that at least ten men be present in order for this blessing to be valid. This group of ten men, known as the *minyan*, may include the rabbi himself if necessary. Other, less rigid Jewish congregations allow both men and women into the *minyan*, which in either Orthodox or non-Orthodox cases functions as something like a quorum for worship of the LORD to take place.

The final verse turns toward the predictive sense of future or incomplete action. Thus, it picks up the commands from verse 23 above. While these verbs are not in the imperative or command form, a sense of urgency or compulsion does seem to permeate verse 27. By ordering the Lord's special representatives to bless the people, literally to put his name upon them – to mark them out as belonging to him – the Lord is promising that he will be with them throughout their journey in the wilderness and even on into the Promised Land. Thus, the priestly blessing fits in perfectly with the overall theme of the book as described in this commentary.

BLESSING AND CURSING IN TRIBAL SOCIETIES[1]

There is an old proverb which runs, "Sticks and stones may break my bones, but words will never hurt me." This is often used as a defense against verbal abuse, teasing, or bullying. I was often the victim of such bullying when I was growing up. My teachers and my parents told me to use this line in an attempt to defuse the power of the words my tormenters slung at me. Unfortunately, this proverb, unlike some that become more or less true through lived experience, is a lie. In my experience, this saying proved ineffective as a defense against bullying. Moreover, the words my enemies used did, in fact, hurt me. They wounded me, perhaps on an even deeper level than sticks and stones – or punches and kicks – would have damaged my body. I am thankful that the abuse I suffered never reached the level of physical violence. However, I realize that words can break one's spirit, even as sticks and stones may break one's bones. The priestly blessing in Numbers 6 is the opposite of this false proverb, but both speak to the power of words.

In tribal societies such as Papua New Guinea, the power to bless and curse is very important. Words can either give life and health or take them away, exchanging them for death and disease. The biblical writers realized this as well: "The tongue has the power of life and death, and those who love it will eat its fruits" (Prov 18:21); "His mouth is full of lies and threats; trouble and evil are under his tongue (Ps 10:7); "keep your tongue from evil, and your lips from telling lies" (Ps 34:13); I said, "I will watch my ways and keep my tongue from sin; I will put a muzzle on my mouth while in the presence of the wicked" (Ps 39:1); You use your mouth for evil and harness your tongue to deceit" (Ps 50:19); "May my tongue sing of your word, for all your commands are righteous" (Ps 119:172); "The tongue of the righteous is choice silver, but the heart of the wicked is of little value" (Prov 10:20); "The soothing tongue is a tree of life, but a perverse tongue crushes the spirit" (Prov 15:4); and many more besides.

Modern societies, both Western and Asian, place much more authority on written words. Contracts, for example, must be written in very specific ways. Lawyers are trained to spot the tiniest mistake in a written document that may be exploited to the advantage (or disadvantage) of their clients. Throughout the book of Numbers, words have far more significance than numbers, as has been noted throughout this commentary. Curses and blessings affect not only the person or persons to whom they are directly spoken, but also perhaps to many subsequent generations as well. This is why the murmuring of the people was such

> a problem, and why the bad report of the spies and the people's assent to it caused them to be forever banned from the Promised Land (see exposition on 13:25–14:10). Words spoken in torment of another are sometimes more powerful than sticks and stones; words spoken in support of another are sometimes more soothing than the most healing balm. Words spoken in praise of God are more important still.
>
> ---
>
> 1. Neville Bartle, my friend and colleague, shared this contextual application in a private communication. The first paragraph, detailing Western views on the power of words, is original to the author.

7:1–8:26 CONSECRATION OF THE TABERNACLE

It is not enough to build the tabernacle for the Lord's presence to remain with Israel. Instead, the people must consecrate it, or make it holy, in order for it to serve its intended purpose. This idea occurs throughout the history of religion. In other ANE religious traditions, divine cult images (idols) require consecration through proper religious ritual in order to serve as an effective representation of the particular deity in whose honor they are made. The Israelites, having from the start an aniconic (imageless) tradition, still participated in this widespread religious phenomenon by consecrating, not the image of the Lord, but the things which were to be used in the service of the Lord.

Many different things were used in the service of the tabernacle and, later, the Temple. Archaeologists have, for example, located ceremonial forks that bore the Hebrew inscription *leyhwh*, "for the Lord," clearly indicating that such a device was to be used in connection to the various sacrifices that would take place in the holy shrine. Because it was used in this way, and before it could be so used, it needed to be consecrated. The following two chapters in the book of Numbers describe various scenes of consecration and dedication of various objects belonging to the tabernacle. The long chapter 7 describes offerings that heads of the various tribes bring into the tabernacle. Next, chapter 8 is broken into three sections. The first of these (8:1–4) describes the lamps that are to be used in the shrine. The final two sections deal with the Levites, those charged with religious duties. First, the ordination of the Levites is detailed (8:5–22). After this, one finds another text regarding age limits for the Levites (8:23–26), which contrasts with the multiple other discussions of the same topic. As the commentary below will show, these differences more than likely reflect changes in Israelite society or even differences of opinion. Oral and/or written versions of these traditions existed even prior to the time when the book of Numbers began to be assembled in the seventh or sixth – or even as late as the fifth or fourth – centuries BC.

7:1–89 Offerings for the Tabernacle

The entirety of chapter 7 concerns a description of offerings brought in for the dedication of the tabernacle. As will be seen, this text connects back to the events of Exodus 40 as well as within the book of Numbers (chs. 3, 4, 5, 9, 10, 16, 17, 19, and 31). Each of the tribes will send a representative to give a lavish offering to the tabernacle. This seems to highlight the unity of Israel amongst its diversity. At the beginning, an obvious historical question looms large. Simply put, where might the materials constituting these huge offerings have been found in the desert? Surely, it strains credibility to suggest that these heavy things came with the people from Egypt, even though Exodus 12:36 does suggest the Israelites engaged in a jolly bit of looting on their collective way out the door. It seems more likely, by contrast, that these offerings reflect a kind of idealistic scenario. Perhaps they envision the time when the children of Israel would return from exile in Babylon. As noted above, this is the most likely historical context for the redaction of the material – predominantly from the Priestly tradition – which formed the book of Numbers.

The commentary that follows will note three ideas of particular significance. First, the order of offerings reflects the tribal marching order listed in chapter 2: Judah, Issachar, Zebulun, Reuben, Simeon, Gad, Ephraim, Manasseh, Benjamin, Dan, Asher, and Naphtali. Aside from the clear difference in content, the two lists differ in two ways: chapter 2 provides a summary of the groups of three tribes, whereas chapter 3 does not; chapter 2 includes the Levites in the march, whereas they are not included in the procession of offerings. Second, each of the tribal leaders brings an identical offering. Because of this, the commentary will only offer a detailed discussion of the offerings for the first section, which describes the offering from the tribe of Judah (vv. 12–17). Third, the tribal leaders are the same as those listed in chapter 2. This is worthwhile to note, if only because it suggests something of the value of a leader standing in for the people, making a sacrifice that the people themselves might have made when approaching God.

7:1–11 Introduction

The first section of the chapter (vv. 1–11) serves two functions. First, it introduces the scene by indicating that everything took place on and following the day Moses finished setting up the tabernacle and consecrating it for the service of the LORD. The offerings for the tabernacle will go on for a total of twelve days, each day given over to one of the tribes, who will send a representative. In this introductory section, however, a first offering is given, one ox for each tribe and one wagon for each pair of tribes. Thus, there are twelve oxen and six wagons. The Gershonites and the Merarites received these gifts, two-thirds going to the latter of these two groups. It is interesting that the apparently youngest of these three tribes (i.e., the one whose eponymous ancestor was youngest among the sons of Levi) receives the lion's share of the gifts, while the middle one (the Kohathites) receive nothing. As to the Kohathites, this slight is explained by the fact that they have been chosen to bear the holy things on their shoulders. Thus, those who have the job that seems the most boring, but in reality is most important, do not seem to receive wages for their service (v. 5).

The second function of this introductory section recalls Exodus 40, which also describes the finishing of the tabernacle and its consecration. Exodus 40:1–14 describes the consecration of the tabernacle. Verses 12–14 detail the setting aside of Aaron and his sons to be its chief ministers. In an interesting contrast, Numbers 7 does not mention Aaron at all. This is odd for Numbers, which, along with Leviticus, strongly emphasizes the role of Aaron as a leader of the people, even while sometimes downplaying Moses' importance. The absence of Aaron from the narrative would have made better sense in Exodus, for that book reverses the emphasis, going along with Deuteronomy to place Moses in prime position. Exodus even includes a startling story about Aaron slipping into idolatry (see Exod 32 and the episode of the golden calf)! Exodus may reflect northern Israelite traditions that were centered on Moses and opposed to the Aaronic priesthood at the Jerusalem Temple, which, at the time of composition, had been recently destroyed. These traditions migrated south, likely brought by Levites or priests fleeing the destruction of the northern kingdom, and they were ultimately incorporated into the Pentateuch as it now stands.

The final two verses in this introductory section (vv. 10–11) serve as an introduction to the list of the offerings. Verse 10 indicates that the offerings began on the very day of the tabernacle's consecration, continuing one tribe per day until all twelve had visited. The entire process took twelve days, thus reinforcing or reflecting the importance of the number twelve in biblical traditions.

7:12–17 First Offering: Tribe of Judah

The first tribe to bring its offering, on the very day of the dedication of the tabernacle, is the tribe of Judah (vv. 12–17). The tribal leader (*nasi*) who brings the offering (also noted in 2:3) is Nahshon, son of Amminadab. Here the word *nasi* does not appear in the Hebrew text, though LXX supplies it, along with the Syriac and the Targum of Jonathan. Were this present, the connection between chapters 2 and 7 would be clearer. Indeed, this word does appear in verses 18, 24, 30, 36, 42, 48, 54, 60, 66, 72, and 78, in reference to all the other tribal leaders.

Verse 13 describes the offering brought first by Judah, then duplicated by eleven other tribal leaders. Whereas the MT reads simply, "His offering was . . . ," the LXX reads, "He brought his offering . . ." The NIV follows the MT, which seems to be correct. Perhaps the LXX translators borrowed the phrase "brought his offering" from verse 12 (this phrase also appears in v. 12 of the NIV). The offering is quite extensive and heavy, probably reflecting, as suggested above, an idealized or hoped-for situation upon redemption from exile. The list of the offering reads something like an inventory, which will be quite large by the time the offerings are complete on the twelfth day. Verse 13 also notes that the shekel weight conformed to the "sanctuary shekel." This was a different unit of measurement than the ordinary shekel and was usually about double the value (see Exod 30:13; 2 Chr 24:6). The priests would typically determine the weight of the sanctuary shekel, which could, of course, lead to the kinds of abuse noted in Proverbs 11:1; 20:23; Hosea 12:7; Amos 8:5; and Micah 6:11.

Other shekels used in ancient Israel were the gold shekel (1 Chr 21:25), the silver shekel (1 Sam 9:8), the brass shekel (1 Sam 17:5), and the iron shekel (1 Sam 17:7). The text is unclear whether all of the shekels used in the computation of the offering were the sanctuary shekel, or whether the sanctuary shekel refers only to the silver items. The latter is probably more likely, however, given that the phrase "sanctuary shekel" only appears in the description for silver items in the passage (and at the other relevant points for the other eleven offerings).

All of the things brought in the offerings served for a particular offering, corresponding with those listed in Leviticus 1–7. Although the details here are somewhat different, all the major offerings are represented, except for the guilt offering, which is difficult to distinguish from the sin offering anyway. The silver bowls contain grain mixed with oil for a grain offering. The gold bowl contains incense, and though this was not a specific offering listed in Leviticus, it was common in Israelite worship.

The bull, ram, and one-year-old male lamb for the burnt offering reflect Leviticus 1. In that text, the offering may be either from the flock or from the herd, and so here the tribal leaders might be going for "extra credit," since the offering consists of one from the herd and two from the flock. The most important item, the one-year-old male lamb (presumably without blemish; see also Lev 1:3) is listed last. One male goat serves for a sin offering, though no further details occur in the text; contrast this with Leviticus 4–5, which offers an extensive list of conditions of sinfulness and the appropriate offerings for each. This text, in comparison, seems like a summary. Finally, the largest offering in terms of number of animals is the peace or fellowship offering. The final note in verse 17 gives a summary, which will, as noted, be repeated throughout: "This was the offering of Nahshon son of Amminadab."

7:18–23 Second Offering: Tribe of Issachar

The second to bring an offering (vv. 18–23) is Nethanel son of Zuar, representing the tribe of Issachar. Some variation exists in the different descriptions of the tribal offerings. The literal translation of verse 19 is, "He offered his offering." Though it sounds awkward in English, this use of two different forms of the same word is common not only in Hebrew but also in many other Semitic languages. Some manuscripts try to harmonize the phrasing here, though this seems unnecessary.

7:24–83 Ten More Tribes, Ten More Offerings

Nothing in the text seems particularly remarkable for the third through the twelfth offerings (vv. 24–83). Eliab son of Helon brings Zebulun's offering (vv. 24–29). Elizur the son of Shedeur represents the Reubenites (vv. 30–35). Fifth, Shelumiel son of Zurishaddai offers for the tribe of Issachar (vv. 36–41). Sixth, Eliasaph son of Deuel approaches with the offering of the Gadites (vv. 42–47). Seventh, Elishama son of Ammihud brings the offering for the tribe of Ephraim (vv. 48–53). Even though these texts evidence no serious problems of textual transmission or interpretation, it would be a serious mistake to pass over them entirely. For the repetition of these offerings in chapter 7 points to the value of regular, consistent worship practices (see above on 1:20–46). Gamaliel son of Pedahzur brings an offering for the tribe of Manasseh on the eighth day (vv. 54–59). Abidan son of Gideoni follows on the ninth day for the tribe of Benjamin (vv. 60–65). Ahiezer son of Ammishaddai comes on day ten for the tribe of Dan (vv. 66–71). On the eleventh day, Pagiel son of Ochran brought the standard offering for the tribe of Asher (vv. 72–77). Finally, their chief, Ahira the son of Enan, represents the Naphtalites on the twelfth day (vv. 78–83).

7:84–89 Summary of the Chapter
The last six verses of the chapter (vv. 84–89) summarize the whole. The LXX text adds a few clarifying comments here and there, perhaps to eliminate confusion on the part of its readers. For example, the LXX of verse 89 specifies that Moses heard the voice of the Lord speaking, whereas MT simply says, "the voice." Nothing commends this change from the Hebrew text, since the original audience would surely have understood that it was the voice of the Lord, seeing that the speech took place in the tent of meeting, which had just been dedicated with copious offerings from the Israelites.

8:1–4 The Lamps

God tells Moses that Aaron should make a seven-branched candlestick to install in the tabernacle. The instructions specify that the lamps should be in front of the lampstand. In modern times, the seven-branched lampstand – known as the menorah – serves as a key symbol of Judaism. This is due to the device itself but also to the significance of the number seven as representing perfection within Jewish mystical tradition.

As with other offerings made for and brought into the tabernacle (see especially ch. 7), Aaron makes this candlestick of highly valuable material, and the text is careful to note that Aaron accomplished this work precisely according to the pattern God gave Moses. As noted in the previous section, the repetitive offerings in chapter 7 imply a certain regularity of worship. Beyond this, one must not fail to notice the simple practical function of the menorah: to give light. Another somewhat famous menorah symbol is the nine-branched candlestick (called a Hanukiah or Chanukiah), which came into vogue as part of the celebration of the Jewish holiday of Hanukkah (or Chanukkah), which normally occurs in the month of December, though occasionally in the latter parts of November. This post-biblical holiday refers to the war to regain control of Yehud (the name the Persian Empire gave to Judah) from the Seleucid

Empire in the second century BC.[28] The miracle associated with Hanukkah is that the consecrated oil that remained to light the eternal light in the Temple, which was enough for only one day, lasted instead for eight days. Thus during Hanukkah, Jews light a nine-branched menorah: eight for the days represented by the miracle, with the ninth in the center serving to give light to the others during the festival. In addition, a Talmudic provision prohibits the burning of a seven-branched menorah anywhere outside the Temple. Thus, when this appears as a symbol of Judaism, the implied hope is for a restoration of the Temple in Jerusalem: a promise of God awaiting its long-desired fulfillment.

Considering the number seven, one also finds far-reaching significance. The symbol of a seven-branched candlestick appears in the NT book of Revelation, especially in chapters 2–3, where John writes letters to the seven churches of Asia Minor. In addition, the various predictions of overlapping judgments – seals, bowls, trumpets – come in groups of seven. Moreover, a week lasts seven days, and the Sabbath at the end is sanctified by God as the day on which God rested from creation. Taken together, one sees the value of seven as a divinely inspired number. One should be cautious, however, particularly when taking account of the week, so as not to be tied to a particular day in the week. More will be said about this later in the commentary about offerings for the Sabbath (see 28:9–10) and the stoning of a Sabbath-breaker (see 15:32–36).

8:5–22 Ordination of the Levites

I remember my own ordination in July 2013. Because of various twists and turns in my road, the ceremony of laying on of hands came twenty-one years after my entry into the ordination process. I recall not feeling as emotional as I thought I would upon completing this long journey. In some ways, of course, this formal step was not only the conclusion of the process leading up to it but also the beginning of the rest of my life as an ordained minister. On the other hand, my ordination was not significant in terms of my occupation as a seminary professor. While it makes sense for one who trains future ordained ministers to be ordained, it is still possible to be a biblical scholar and teacher without ecclesiastical orders. While I am not and have never been a parish minister – except for a brief stint as an associate while I was in graduate school – I embrace the roles and responsibilities of ordained ministers alongside my sisters

---

28. Incidentally, the book of Daniel may have been written at least in part to lend theological and intellectual support to this war effort.

and brothers. To remind me of these roles and responsibilities, I keep a copy of my ordination certificate hung up on the wall of my office, right next to the door. This is positioned so that not only can I see it from my desk, but also I must pass right by it every time I leave the office to go to a class, meeting, chapel service, or even when I leave to go home in the evening. Because it is the last thing I see as I leave the office, it reminds me that a particular task has been laid on me, and not for my own aggrandizement, but to remind me that I am a servant, not a leader: one of humble station, not exalted.

This text in the book of Numbers does not explore what the Levites might have been thinking as they experienced their ordination. Instead, the focus is on what God instructs Moses to do to these ordination candidates and what they are to do to themselves. The overwhelming concern of the ritual is the purity of the Levites who are being ordained. Just as the sacrifices that these men will bring must be pure and without blemish (see 19:2), so also must the men themselves be pure before the Lord.

Verses 9–10 communicate a particularly interesting idea. The whole Israelite community is to participate in the laying on of hands. In my ordination, the general superintendent (my church's term for bishop) laid his hands directly on my head, but the other ordained ministers in attendance laid their hands on the one doing the ordaining. This created an unbroken line of ministers affirming my inclusion in the orders of ministry. The effect of this was to proclaim God's selection of me as God's representative to the people.

In Numbers 8, by contrast, the people lay their hands, presumably in a similar unbroken line, on the Levites. Perhaps this is due simply to the practical matter that there were no other ministers who could perform this function. Alternatively, this could signify the opposite of what my own ordination service did: it marked off the Levites as the people's representative to God. Indeed, the Levites always stood in this double position (God's representatives to the people and the people's representatives to God), and perhaps all of God's minister-servants stand in this kind of double position. Ultimately, this question must be left open, as no OT text goes on to describe how subsequent generations of Levites were to be set apart for their service.

One particular way in which the Levites stand as the people's representatives before God is in taking the place of the firstborn of all Israelite households. Whereas the firstborn animals are given over to God as an offering (v. 17), the Levites – because they have been set apart by God – substitute for the firstborn of Israelite human males. This is a roundabout way of preventing the abominable practice of child sacrifice. Some of the Canaanites whom the

Israelites displaced may have practiced this, though clear evidence does not exist. Thus, their representation of God before the people and of the people before God not only serves a religious function but also prevents a horrifying practice within Israel.

8:23–26 Age Limits for the Levites

For the fourth different time, this text discusses age limits for the Levites. In chapter 3, the numbering of the Levites included those who were one month old and above. In 4:21–28 and again in 4:34–35, the Levites were counted from the age of thirty to fifty. Here they are counted from the ages of twenty-five to fifty. In the introduction above, I suggest that the differences are not worth worrying about. For at least the last two hundred years, biblical scholarship has considered such discrepancies as the melding of different traditions into the final form of the book of Numbers. A similar conclusion seems inescapable here.

In support of this conclusion, there are not any significant textual notes in this passage. In fact, the only note in the BHS apparatus comes in verse 26. For the LXX, instead of reading "his brothers," reads "his brother." The full reading of verses 25–26a thus comes to be, "After the age of fifty, he shall return from the service core and not do anything more, ministering to his brother in the Tent of Meeting by keeping guard, but he shall not do other things" (AT). The LXX translators apparently perceived an error in the MT, since this is the only time the MT uses a plural ("his brothers") in the entire passage. I prefer the MT reading, because the ministry of the fifty-plus Levites here envisioned was, in fact, for the benefit of all the "brothers," which is to say, all the people. The NIV, for its part, makes all of the singular references in the passage plural; this seems also unnecessary, except for the note – present in the Hebrew – that this instruction "applies to the Levites" (v. 24).

9:1–14 PASSOVER CELEBRATION

In many ways, the Christian ritual of the Lord's Supper – or Communion, or the Eucharist, which are different names for the same thing – is patterned after the Jewish Passover. These two events are perhaps the highest points in all of God's redemptive work for humanity. As such, it is unfortunate that Communion is often neglected by evangelicals. More liturgical traditions, by contrast, usually put a great deal of thought and preparation into the celebration of Communion, giving it the high place it deserves. Even as I say that, however, I recognize that sometimes the solemnity overpowers the celebration. In other words, if Communion is only treated as a memorial of Jesus' death, it can be quite bland and even boring. If, on the other hand, it is treated also as an anticipation of the Resurrection and the life of the world to come, it can come off looking more like a party than a funeral. Maybe Communion could, in fact, be celebrated joyfully, in the same way that Filipino fiestas are celebrated: both as recalling key moments in the town's, region's, or nation's history, but also as cementing the values of family which are so central to Filipino and other Asian societies.

In the Old Testament, the Passover was first instituted as part of the events surrounding the Exodus. In Exodus 12, the blood of a one-year-old lamb (taken from the sheep or the goats) was to be spread on the doorposts and lintels of the Israelites' houses. During the Tenth Plague, the angel of death would "pass over" the Israelite houses and not kill the firstborn son inside. The ritual of the Passover, second in importance in the Jewish calendar to Yom Kippur (the Day of Atonement; see below on 29:7–11), recalled both the deliverance that God allowed for the Israelites from this plague along with the oppression that made this deliverance necessary.

While further instructions for the Passover appear in Numbers 28:6–15, chapter 9 text recounts a particular celebration of the festival. This Passover was celebrated, "in accordance with all its rules and regulations" (v. 3), on the fourteenth day of the first month. The "first month" refers back to Exodus 12, in which Moses proclaims the month in which the Passover takes place to be the first month of the year. Sometime later, the celebration of the new year transferred to the season of autumn, usually September or October of the solar year. Many Jews now recognize the secular new year on January 1 along with Rosh Hashanah in the fall. Rosh Hashanah – Jewish New Year – now precedes the Day of Atonement by ten days. These ten days are called the High Holy Days and are a time for solemn reflection on the goodness of God. Both options – taking the month of Passover (March–April) as the first month or the month of Rosh Hashanah as the first month – seem to accomplish the same thing in different ways: both emphasize the foundation of Israel by and through the grace of God. No other beginning was possible.

In the middle of this text (v. 6), a problem arises. Some people are rendered unclean because of their contact with a dead body (see below on Num 19:11). They come to Moses to find out what they should do. Moses goes to God and receives a most startling answer: celebrate the Passover, clean or unclean! The only stipulation is that these people are to wait until the second month, on the fourteenth day. This seems to be in contrast with the stipulations of Numbers 19, that someone who touches a dead body is unclean for only seven days. However, the beginning of the festival was connected – along with everything in the calendar – with the appearance of the new moon, and seems to be where the resolution lies. So long as the people in question "follow all the regulations" (v. 12) this is an example of the proverb: "Better late than never."

Those unable to celebrate the Passover at the proper time will not miss the ritual, and this provision speaks to the need to provide opportunities to people who miss important rituals, such as Holy Communion. While Christians do not necessarily use the categories of clean and unclean, sometimes people are unable to attend Communion services. Sometimes they are in the hospital; sometimes they are unable to leave their houses at all. Regardless of the reason, however, the principle is still valid. Those who cannot attend, no matter the reason, must have the opportunity to share in the Body and Blood of Jesus Christ, which is connected to the Passover in significant ways. Not only does Holy Week occur close to the time of Passover, but Jesus called himself the Passover Lamb!

9:15–23 THE CLOUD COVERING THE TABERNACLE

The presence of God descends upon the tabernacle. The traditional understanding of how God appears is as "a pillar of cloud" in the daytime and as a "pillar of fire" in the nighttime. This description comes from Exodus 13:21 and this collection of verses from Numbers 9. In verse 15, both the Hebrew original and a variety of ETT describe the cloud as looking like fire. The NIV says, "From evening until morning the cloud above the tabernacle looked like fire."

The distinction between cloud, fire, and cloud that looks like fire is important as it betrays a significant stylistic feature, if not a significant difference in the description of the event. In any case, this is part of the identity-forming story of the Israelites, and one should expect some variation, particularly if one does not stand in the face of history of scholarship and insist on an untenable theory of Mosaic authorship. In any event, as long as the cloud, the fire, or the cloud that looked like fire stays over the sanctuary, the Israelites do not move. When this manifestation that demonstrates God's presence with the people leaves, the people leave (see the commentary on 10:11). The latter verses of this text summarize how the people respond to the movement of the cloud: sometimes the cloud moves in the morning after it settles down (v. 21), sometimes it settles for a few days (v. 20), sometimes it settles for as long as a year

(v. 22). The next major movement for the cloud will be on the twentieth day of the second month of the second year, which marks the Israelites' departure from the all-important location of Mount Sinai, and thus the transition to the next major stage of their journey with God in the desert, moving from the land of slavery to the land of promise.

Preachers and teachers sharing this text with faith communities can find ready connection with the idea of God's timing. Often, we do not know when to go to another place – literally or figuratively – and when to stay where we are. However, those who belong to God can take comfort in God's ongoing presence. We who are on a journey with God may find inspiration in the story of God's journey with the Israelites in the desert as recounted in the book of Numbers. Regardless of the circumstances we are facing, God is with us. Throughout Scripture, when God reminds us that he is with us, he also reminds us that he will never leave us (see Gen 24:27; Deut 4:31; 1 Kgs 6:31; Neh 9:31; Ps 16:10; John 14:18; Acts 2:27).[29]

10:1–10 THE TWO TRUMPETS

In the opening section of chapter 10, God commands Moses to make two trumpets to accompany the physical sign of the cloud (or cloud that looks like fire). God gives several different instructions about how these horns should be blown. If both sound at once, all of the people are to assemble; if only one sounds, only the leaders are to gather. Furthermore, these trumpets make different sounds, which have different meanings. When the "signal for setting out" (10:7) sounds, first the tribes to the east are to set out, then at the second blast the tribes on the south are to set out. These six tribes (see ch. 2 above) are the only ones named in this passage, though the implication is that all of the tribes, including the Levites at the center with their responsibilities regarding the ark, would be included.

The word translated "trumpet" here is a favorite of the Priestly writer, also appearing in some other OT texts, mainly of a late historical date. The better-known word *shofar*, which has come into English, does not occur here, but does appear in Joshua 6:4 before the battle of Jericho. The trumpets in use here were probably straight, slender metal tubes, which distinguishes them

---

29. There are, indeed, some instances where God's departure from Israel is given as a punishment for sin (e.g. 2 Chr 24:18), but this abandonment is always only temporary, ending as soon as the judged people turn from their ways and desire to be near God again (see Jer 7:5–7, which predicts this, along with Isa 54:7, which makes it even more explicit).

further from the shofar, which even into modern times has retained its curvy shape. The different material and shape of the two kinds of horn certainly contributed to different sounds, and the different sounds to different uses. In any event, Aaron – and his sons throughout history – should blow these trumpets, especially at festival times over the sacrifices that are offered to God. Their use in sanctuary ritual sets them apart as primarily a sacred instrument, although the shofar was also often used in rituals like this. The Israelites are also called to use these trumpets before going into battle, thus assuring that God will remember them and give them victory over their enemies.

NUMBERS 10:11–21:3
FROM MOUNT SINAI TO MOUNT HOR

OVERVIEW

As indicated in the introduction, the Israelites have been camped at Mount Sinai since Exodus 19. In terms of number of chapters, this is the place where they spend the most time. This speaks to the importance of Sinai and the making of the covenant there, a fact that will have preeminent importance in Israel's thought and history even up to the present time. Before and during the life of Jesus, the Jews were divided on the question of precisely what was given on Sinai, and hence what remained binding on their practice in both ethical and religious domains. The group that came to be known as the Pharisees emphasized the oral law – or interpretations of the written law given by God to Moses on Mount Sinai. Other groups, most notably the Sadducees, thought only the written law was binding.

Though no similar distinction between the written law and the oral law exists in Christianity, an analogy might be drawn between early Protestant debates with Roman Catholics concerning whether Scripture alone was sufficient for salvation and practice (the Protestant view) or whether the interpretation of Scripture must be mediated through church tradition (the Catholic view). Moreover, various Protestant groups remain divided over matters of biblical interpretation, particularly regarding issues such as standards of dress, the role of women in public ministry, and doctrines of the end times. Though vigorous debate is a noble pursuit, it is unfortunate when matters of interpretation cause dissension and division among Christians. Though each group (not necessarily each individual) needs to have the freedom to interpret Scripture within its historical context(s), disagreements should not get in the way of Christ's mission to go into the world – or to go on our own journey with God – and make disciples of the nations. Something is clearly amiss when doctrines solidify the power of the dominant group, for Jesus said those who follow him should not reach for power over one another (Matt 20:25; Mark 10:42; Luke 22:25).

The Israelites now leave Sinai behind geographically and historically, but theologically, Sinai will always be a key part of their identity. In much the same way that the Cross, the Empty Tomb, and the Ascension are inseparable parts of the Christian history of salvation, the Exodus and the giving of the

Torah are inseparable in the Jewish tradition. God brought the people out of Egypt and to Sinai to demonstrate that he was the Lord and was worthy to be praised (Exod 20:2). Though Jeremiah predicts (see Jer 16:14–15; 23:7–8) that the return from exile will exceed the Exodus in the people's imagination, this never comes about. Even today, though Jews have experienced severe persecution – the worst being the Nazi Holocaust – they have retained in their theology the importance of the Exodus, this first act of God's deliverance.

This section of Numbers traces the Israelites' journey from Mount Sinai to Mount Hor. At Mount Hor, Aaron and Miriam die, leaving Moses to guide the Israelites on their journey with God. In the same chapter that records the deaths of his siblings, Moses also loses the right to enter the Promised Land. Moses remains the lone leader of the people until Deuteronomy 31, which names Joshua as his successor. The following section is bookended by two departures: the Israelites' departure from an important historical place at the beginning and the departure of two important historical persons at the end.

10:11–36 DEPARTURE

Exodus 19:1, as noted elsewhere, records that the Israelites reached Mount Sinai on the first day of the third month after leaving Egypt behind forever.[1] The Numbers text reports a similarly specific date: "the twentieth day of the second month of the second year." The confluence of the number two is interesting in this date notation. In addition, given all that took place at Sinai, it is fascinating to note that the Israelites spent just a few days shy of two years there. Following the lunar calendar per the Hebrews, each month would be twenty-nine or thirty days long, so the twentieth day of a month would be a

---

1. A remnant did go back to Egypt during the exilic period, and a rather important Jewish community was also established in Elephantine near Aswan in the middle of the Nile River (even including a temple!), but we are dealing with the difference between history and ideology here. In any event, it is true that the Israelites were never again slaves in Egypt. On the one hand, the prophet Jeremiah strongly discourages the remnant from going to Egypt (see Jer 42:7–12 for God's order not to go, as well as 44:26–30 for the judgment upon them). On the other hand, the Elephantine temple does not merit mention in the OT, even though it was founded during the sixth century BC. The Hebrew word *sinim* appears in Isaiah 19:12 as part of an oracle of deliverance. A slightly different form, *sevenah* or *sunah*, occurs as part of a judgment against Egypt in Ezekiel 29:10 and 30:6. In all three cases, the NIV translates this word as "Aswan." Some have associated this Hebrew word with China, because of the similarity of the root with "Sino," the Latinized form of the Qin dynasty. Yet this association is mistaken, an example of the etymological fallacy. My students in China, among others, use this association as evidence that the OT writers knew about China, but this cannot be so. Though the failure to mention China does not render the Bible false, suggesting that the Bible *does* mention China in order to "prove" its veracity is also bound to fail.

little more than a week before the end of the month, which in this case would have completed the second year.

In accordance with the instructions established in chapter 9 – but, interestingly, not including the trumpet blasts from earlier in chapter 10 – the cloud lifts up from the tabernacle, and the people set out on their way, moving from Sinai to the Wilderness of Paran. The Wilderness of Paran is a large, rather ill-defined area in the middle of the Negev desert. This lack of definition along with the uncertain identification of Mount Sinai results in ambiguity about how far they went on this first journey. Verse 33 says that they "traveled for three days," but this is a typical expression for a non-specifically short distance. The overall journey will ultimately take some forty years – a similarly typical expression for a non-specifically long time – but it begins, in the words of the old Buddhist saying, "with a single step."

The majority of this text (vv. 14–28) is given over to a description of the marching order, which matches the order in chapter 2 (including the names of the leaders) with one exception. The Levites are broken up into two groups: one leaves before the camp of Reuben, and the other leaves afterwards. In chapter 2, the Levites are listed all together after the camp of Reuben. The Gershonite and the Merarite clans of the Levites, who have responsibility for the tabernacle, go after the camp of Judah. After the camp of Reuben come the Kohathite clan of the Levites, who carry the holy objects. The text notes that the tabernacle was to be set up before they got there, which suggests that the division of the Levites gives the first two Levite clans enough time to set up the tabernacle before the third clan arrives. However, it is curious that the Kohathites do not take out the holy objects before the tent is broken down. Apparently, they stand around holding the holy objects until it is their turn to leave. Alternatively, they would have had to wait around after getting to the new place before setting up the holy objects.

The final verses (vv. 29–36) of the chapter detail the conversation between Moses and Reuel, his father-in-law. Moses' father-in-law is given the name Jethro throughout the book of Exodus, a consequence of the different sources behind the Pentateuch. It is unclear whether Hobab, Reuel's son, accompanies Moses and the Israelites, for even though the text does not specify his presence, it does not mention that he takes his leave. The last two verses report a song of Moses, which is reminiscent of many of the Psalms, though not exact (e.g. Ps 7:6). The glory of the Lord goes before Israel throughout its entire journey, even though it takes longer than it should. Surely this, too, is an example of grace.

Numbers

11:1–9 THE PEOPLE COMPLAIN ABOUT FOOD

The following four sections deal with the people's complaint about not having enough food and God's provision of food for the journey through the desert. Yet God's provision comes at a significant price, for fire from heaven comes and consumes "some of the outskirts of the camp" (v. 1). Though some of God's punishments are rather worse,[2] this one reminds the people that they should fear the One who called them out into the desert. Apparently, this is something of a "warning shot," and so no people are harmed. The people cry out to Moses, who prays to God, who takes away the punishment. Thus the place is named Taberah, which comes from *ba'ar*, one of the many Hebrew words that can be translated as "burn."

Verse 4 suggests that the "rabble" who appear alongside the people are the original complainers in this particular episode. Whereas the people complain of their general hardships in verse 1, calling down the burning anger of the Lord, the "rabble" make the more specific complaint about food. The word translated "rabble" is unique to Numbers 11:4, referring to a mixed lot of peoples who had joined themselves to the Hebrews during their journey. Some of these may have been the 'Apiru, whose name comes from an Akkadian root and refers to a group of mixed-ethnicity that lived on the fringes of society in the Fertile Crescent during the second millennium BC. Interestingly, given the provision of quail to satisfy the people's demand for food, the hieroglyphic sign for these people in Egyptian sources includes a plural suffix made out of a quail chick.

The Hebrew writer gives these people the funny-sounding name *'asafsuf*. Though it is quite likely that the Hebrew writers – at least at the time the final form of Numbers was assembled during the time of the Babylonian Exile – were familiar with the term *'Apiru*, they may have chosen not to use it because of the similarity in the Hebrew and Aramaic languages to their own ethnic designation. If this suggestion is true, then one may infer an attempt from the Jews to distinguish themselves from the "rabble," which they might have seen as inferior to themselves. In a modern context, the careful reader should neither miss nor condone the negative overtones of this "othering."

The content of the rabble's complaint is that manna does not stand up well in comparison to the rich food enjoyed in Egypt. This is a remarkable statement for two reasons. First, this is the first mention of manna in the book of Numbers, which implicitly leads the reader back to the parallel account of manna and quail in Exodus 16. Second, if the "rabble" were also slaves with

---

2. Consider, for example, the rebellion of the Kohathites in Num 16–17.

the Israelites, they are claiming here that living in slavery is better than not having a variety of things to eat. This sentiment presents a great deal of difficulty, for it requires the interpreter to enter into the mind, as it were, of those who would hold and give voice to such an idea. On the one hand, stepping out into the desert to follow a dream of liberation and freedom entails a great deal of risk. On the other hand, it is hard to believe that staying in an abusive situation would be preferable to life in the desert. However we interpret this text, it stays at the descriptive level, going on in verses 7–9 to describe how the manna came down. The sequence seems odd: the people, especially the "rabble," complain about the manna, comparing it to the rich food they enjoyed while living as slaves in Egypt; then the text describes how the manna looks, what the people do with it, and how it is produced. The detail that the manna "tasted like something made with olive oil" (v. 8) is especially colorful, giving a later audience a sensory description of what their ancestors ate while journeying with God in the desert.

11:10–15 MOSES' LAMENT

Hearing the "rabble" and the Israelites' complaint causes Moses to lament to God. This lament comes after God becomes angry again, though there seems to be no threat that God will set the edges of the camp on fire again. Moses cries out to God, wanting to know why God has set such a tremendous burden on him. Laments are common in the OT, especially in the book of Psalms, where they form a plurality of the poems (60–65 of the 150, depending on how one classifies some of the psalms). Laments sometimes accuse God of not protecting the lamenter from suffering (Ps 22) or not fulfilling his part of the bargain (Ps 44). The content of this lament is that God has not protected Moses. Moses does not go as far as Job in his laments, who accuses God of wrongdoing (though Job 1:22 suggests that Job did not blame God). Instead, Moses' complaint echoes the prayer of Jonah, who asks God to end his life, because he is so angry about the salvation of the Ninevites (see Jonah 4:3, 9). The fact that the Bible preserves such laments is wonderful, because they give modern believers space to cry and recognize that things do not always go well for believers – and especially pastors! Tragically, sometimes believers abandon their faith or pastors abandon the ministry – or in extreme cases end their lives – because things do not go as they think they should. Yet Moses, Job, Jonah, and the Psalmists complain to God, and this reveals how God can accept our grieving, hear our accusations, and continue to love us.

11:16–30 GOD'S RESPONSE

God demonstrates love for Moses by easing his burden. God instructs Moses to appoint seventy leaders "who are known to you as leaders and officials among the people" (v. 16). It seems clear from the text that Moses does not appoint the leaders himself, but simply recognizes their standing among the people and recommends them to God.

This text gives a rather different impression from a similar story elsewhere in the Pentateuch. In Exodus 18, Moses' father-in-law, Jethro, the priest of Midian – whose flocks Moses was tending on the day he was called to be Israel's greatest prophet – comes and urges Moses to "select capable men from all the people" (Exod 18:21). This vision of the sharing of leadership is more top-down, for the people do not seem to have a say in the appointment of the leaders. Moreover, Jethro doesn't bring God into the process until the end of the instruction (Exod 19:23).

Yet here, God wants Moses to recommend people for leadership positions, and God says that he will take some of the spirit that has rested on Moses and give it to the seventy elders. This interesting twist seems to confirm what uninformed leaders might think about delegating authority: they will lose power. Although God takes away some of the spirit given to Moses, God gives the spirit to the seventy, empowering them to do what God is calling them to do. Theologically, the reduction in the spirit given to Moses does not in any way limit or reduces God's empowerment of Moses to do the work God wants *him* to do. Indeed, even though in the OT, the general view of the empowerment of God's spirit is that it is for a limited time in order to accomplish a specific task, God gives all of God's spirit all the time. Infinity reduced by half, or even divided among seventy-one people (Moses and the newly anointed leaders), is still infinity.

After the charge to Moses to recommend seventy leaders to share the power and the burden, God returns to the question of meat, which started the episode, and issues a challenge to the "rabble" complainers. This challenge takes the form of "You want meat? I'll give you so much meat you get sick of it!" Too much of a good thing is too much – even the provision of God.

Moses laments again in verses 21–22, wondering where he will get so much meat to make the people eat a month's worth of food in one day. This statement reminds the reader of the dismay Jesus' disciples express before the feeding of the five thousand. An especially relevant parallel comes in Mark's version of the story, when the disciples complain: "[Feeding all the people] would take more than half a year's wages" (Mark 6:37)! Here, Moses calculates the amount needed in terms of material: entire flocks and herds and all the fish in the sea (v. 22). God responds with a challenge: does Moses believe in God's provision, or not?

The final seven verses of the passage (24–30) return to the appointing of the seventy leaders and how God gives his spirit to them. After the Lord comes down in the cloud, the seventy elders prophesy – which probably means that they have an ecstatic experience of some kind – yet the text is clear that they "did not do so again" (v. 25). This text reminds us that we ought to be careful about associating a particular spiritual gift or physical behavior – an utterance, vision, or healing – with the manifestation of God's spirit, where this one thing is the only evidence of being filled with God's Spirit. One can also err in the other direction, suggesting that such physical manifestations do not evidence the filling of the Spirit. Deciding this question will require careful discernment from the community.

There is a further intertextual trace in verses 26–28, when Eldad and Medad are caught prophesying (making ecstatic utterances), apparently without authorization. When Joshua expresses shock about this incident, Moses replies: "I wish that all the LORD's people were prophets and that the LORD would put his spirit on them" (v. 29). In this moment, Moses recognizes, as noted above, that a "reduction" of the spiritual power given to him is not really a reduction at all. This posture contrasts with some leaders in Asian contexts who refuse to give up power.[3] Of course, Eldad and Medad were not – so it seems – part of the original seventy on whom the Spirit was deposited. Nevertheless, Moses sees no reason to rebuke them, for he recognizes that God may, in fact, be generous with his spirit and give it to whomever God wills (see 1 Cor 12:1–11).

Two aspects of the event – Joshua's shocked response and Moses' wise answer – are reminiscent of a different biblical text: Mark 9, which recounts an episode where the disciples tell Jesus that they have stopped someone from casting out demons in Jesus' name. Apparently, like Eldad and Medad, he did so without authorization, and so the disciples are proud for shutting this seeming impostor down. However, in words that echo Moses' speech in Numbers 11, Jesus shuts down the disciples, saying, "no one who does a miracle in my name can in the next moment say anything bad about me, for whoever is not against us is for us" (Mark 9:39–40).

---

3. As an outsider, I do not wish to comment on political situations in Asia, but I believe it is proper to note the contrast between Moses and leaders such as Ferdinand Marcos or Xi Jingping.

The post-exilic prophet Joel, who stands as a kind of bridge between the end of the prophetic movement and the beginning of the apocalyptic movement announces a similar promise of God (see Joel 2:28).[4] Commenting on this text, Norman Podhoretz explains: "With a sudden twist, God answers and says that all will be well . . . He will pour out His spirit upon everyone, young and old, all of whom will become prophets."[5]

11:31–35 PROVISION OF QUAIL

Once again, the people receive provision from God, even in the face of their complaining. Though a skeptic might say that this was simply a natural occurrence, the Bible testifies that God made the wind shift and blow a tremendous amount of quail amongst the Israelites. The taste of quail is similar to chicken, though the birds tend to be quite small. Quail eggs are a popular ingredient in salads and other similar dishes in the Philippines. The text says that no one who went out to gather quail gathered less than ten homers. One homer is equivalent to about 220 liters, which hints at the size of the miracle. While this may be an exaggerated number, the point is that both here and in the parallel story from Exodus 16, God provides an overabundance of food to meet the Israelites' needs.

A comparison with the Exodus account reveals some important differences. First, both Exodus 16 and Numbers 11 connect the provision of quail with the provision of manna; yet in Exodus, the quail come first, whereas in Numbers, the manna comes first. Second, the earlier verses of Numbers 11 (see above) do not give specific details about the first arrival of the manna. Third, this chapter does not include the instruction about not gathering manna on the Sabbath. Rather, this chapter seems to assume that the manna has already been coming for quite some time, since the people are already tired of it. Fourth, one finds no suggestion that one could gather too much (as in Exod 16:20 regarding the manna). Finally, Exodus 16 does not mention the plague noted in Numbers 11:33–34. Instead, Exodus 16:12 simply says that the provision of meat will prove God's identity to the Israelites. This punishment perhaps indicates the priestly ideas behind Numbers, where righteousness is all about giving proper respect to God.

---

4. However, "First Zechariah" (Zech 1–8) and "Second Zechariah" (Zech 9–14; or Second [9–11] and Third [12–14]) might be better candidates as this bridge.
5. Norman Podhoretz, *The Prophets: Who They Were, What They Are* (New York: Free Press, 2002), 298.

12:1–16 DISPUTE IN HAZEROTH

This episode relates a dispute between the sibling leaders of the Israelites – Moses, Aaron, and Miriam – and it illustrates some key issues relating to the overall interpretation of Numbers. First, this story elevates Moses over Aaron, which is generally uncharacteristic of Numbers, since it supports the perspective of the Aaronic priesthood. The Jewish scholar James Diamond comments that Numbers "continues the material and the point of view of Leviticus, which is totally a 'priestly' book, that the *Kohanim* [priests] were the chief agents by which the Israelite God was accessed and the sacrificial rites the means of this access. But at various points in the middle of Numbers we get a few narratives that present a very different perspective."[6] Here, Moses triumphs over Aaron as well as Miriam. Yet in a curious twist, even though both Aaron and Miriam make the accusation, only Miriam experiences the consequences in the form of a physical malady.

This text may reflect debates within a later, established religious hierarchy, and these debates may "have been retrojected onto the wilderness traditions . . . [T]he precise nature and origin of the conflict remains a matter of some scholarly debate."[7] One possible origin could be a conflict between northern and southern priests, which took place after the fall of the northern Kingdom. (See the commentary on chapter 7 for more on this idea.) In any event, one would expect the supremacy of Moses to be affirmed in Deuteronomy, where the roles of Miriam and Aaron are diminished, but it is surprising in the priestly document of Numbers. In the purported setting of Deuteronomy, Moses recounts everything that has happened to the Israelites since crossing the Red Sea, a retelling that includes instructions about what they should do when they get there – without Moses, since he is forbidden to enter the land. Incidentally, this interweaving of the Pentateuchal sources surfaces again in Numbers 27, when God tells Moses why he cannot go to the Promised Land. Yet Deuteronomy 1 has a very different take, and so the fact that Numbers 12 takes up Moses' against Aaron and Miriam presents interesting interpretive possibilities.

The dispute is touched off (v. 1) by the apparent marriage of Moses to a Cushite woman. Cush is the Hebrew term for Ethiopia, and the LXX translates the term accordingly. Genesis 10:6 and 1 Chronicles 1:8 both list Cush as among the sons of Ham, who are generally located in Africa, according to

---

6. Diamond, *Stringing the Pearls*, 66.
7. Athalya Brenner, *A Feminist Companion to the Latter Prophets* (Sheffield: Sheffield Academic, 1995), 190.

the three general divisions of the world under which these genealogies operate. Cush occurs alongside Mizraim (Egypt), Put (or Phut; Libya), and Canaan; thus, all of these men and the peoples of which they are the eponymous ancestors were all located in "the region bordering the Mediterranean Sea on the southeast."[8] Elsewhere in the OT, Cushites are described as distinct from the Israelites by virtue of their dark skin (see Jer 13:23).

Several oddities about this story become immediately apparent. First, it is unclear why this marriage set off a dispute among the Israelites' top leaders. In Western interpretation, particularly among fundamentalists, "this text has figured significantly in religious debates over interracial marriage."[9] Using this text to arrive at such a conclusion demonstrates the way people sometimes try to use the Bible for their own purposes. Yet Moses is being affirmed in this passage rather than criticized. Even though the affirmation has nothing to do with his "interracial" marriage, using this text to argue against such unions is unsuited for the purpose.

Second, it is also uncertain if a Cushite woman would have been available to marry Moses in the desert anyway. Certainly other ethnic groups joined the Israelites during or just after their departure from Egypt (see above on the "othering" in 11:4), and some others may have joined them in the desert as they attempted to create a new, apparently egalitarian, society in rebellion against the oppressive powers in Egypt and Canaan.[10] At any rate, Cushites were well known in ancient Israel, though there is no injunction against marrying them, such as the one concerning Moabites (see the commentary on ch. 25 below).

Third, and perhaps most importantly, the sudden vanishing of this woman from the text seems odd, for in verse 2, the critique that Aaron and Miriam level against Moses has nothing to do with the ethnic origin of the prophet's wife. Though Sakenfeld notes that "the Cushite wife must not be overlooked,"[11] the text immediately loses interest in her. It is possible that earlier versions of this story — whether oral or written — dealt with the issue of the interracial marriage in a more substantive way, but the final form of Numbers seems uninterested in the topic. Perhaps a lengthy dispute about the validity of Moses' marriage was replaced by a significant dispute about leadership, specifically

---

8. Mitchel Modine, *1–2 Chronicles: A Commentary in the Wesleyan Tradition* (Kansas City: Beacon Hill, 2014), 48.
9. Sakenfeld, *Women's Bible Commentary*, 52.
10. Jorge Pixley, *Biblical Israel: A People's History* (Minneapolis: Fortress, 1992), 20–22. See also Norman K. Gottwald, *The Hebrew Bible: A Socio-Literary Introduction* (Philadelphia: Fortress), 285–287.
11. Sakenfeld, *Women's Bible Commentary*, 52.

whether the word of the LORD was confined to one person or a group of people. Such a debate would have found relevance in the post-exilic period, when the traditional ways of doing things were quite naturally called into question.

CAN GOD SPEAK THROUGH THE BUDDHA?

The dispute about leadership in Numbers 12:1–3 raises the question of how God speaks to people. God often speaks to us through intermediaries. Sometimes these intermediaries are people, such as Moses, whom the book of Deuteronomy calls the greatest of all God's prophets. Sometimes these intermediaries are friends, family members, or pastors. But sometimes these intermediaries take the form of something we would not expect God to use to speak to us. Later on in the book of Numbers, we will see God speak to the prophet Balaam – who is not an Israelite, but still receives a message from Israel's God – through the intermediary of a donkey. As we will see, there is no particular reason why the donkey could not worship God.

My friend Neville Bartle spent many years as a missionary to Papua New Guinea. Once he met a Korean woman named Kim, who was pursuing her Master of Divinity degree at a seminary in the United States, and she told Dr. Bartle that "It was the writings of Buddha that led me to Christ." Seeing his surprise, she explained what she meant.

Kim had grown up in a Buddhist family in Korea and had been very devoted to the Eight-Fold Path and the precepts of Buddha. She wanted to be the best person that she could be. However, as she grew, continuing to read and meditate on the Buddhist scriptures, she found that the hunger in her heart was not satisfied. She wanted to know the truth. She noticed that the Buddha always identified himself as a teacher. He said that he pointed to the truth but he never claimed to be the truth.

If the Buddha was not the truth, but merely pointed to the truth, she reasoned, then someone else must be the truth, and so she began to look at other religions. Later on, a friend gave her a Bible. It was the first time she had owned a Christian scripture. She began to read and meditate on the Bible the way she had previously done with the Buddhist scripture. One day she read these words of Jesus: "I am the way and the truth and the life. No one comes to the Father except through me" (John 14:6). Seeing these words, she realized she had found the answer to her quest. So today, whenever someone asks her about her faith, she says that the writings of the Buddha led her to Jesus, who not only pointed to the truth, but who was the truth.

As verses 2–3 report, the dispute between the leaders is clearly not about Moses' Cushite wife, which suggests that before the final form of the text was reached, a resolution of this initial charge was replaced by the question of whether God only spoke through Moses. Verse 3 indicates that no one has ever been as humble as Moses, which suggests an alteration of the text, since elsewhere Moses is not depicted as humble (see, for example 20:10–12). The NIV turns this into a parenthetical comment, which certainly seems appropriate.

The squabbling between the siblings causes the Lord to call them all into the office, as it were, to scold them for bickering (v. 4). The Lord then says that Moses is a particular kind of prophet: one to whom God spoke "face to face, clearly and not in riddles" (v. 8). This reminds the reader of a similar statement in the Gospels, in which Jesus tells the disciples that the secrets of the Kingdom of God have been given to them, but not to the people at large, and so Jesus speaks to the disciples plainly, but to the people in parables (Mark 4:10–12; see also Matt 13:10–13; Luke 8:9–10).

The Lord angrily departs from Aaron and Miriam because they were not afraid to speak against Moses, as they should have been. Once the cloud lifts up from the tent of meeting, Miriam is covered with leprosy. The NIV footnote maintains that the Hebrew term for "leprous" or "leprosy" referred to several diseases affecting the skin. Whatever the specific ailment, Aaron perceives that his sister has a "defiling skin disease" (12:10), which scares him to apologize, asking Moses not to hold this sin against them. Aaron's statement piques interest for two reasons: first, it seems to indicate that Moses has the power to afflict or heal, to punish or to relent from punishment. This affirms what God says about Moses' stature in the previous verses. Second, only Miriam experiences punishment, though the text makes it clear that both Aaron and Miriam have spoken against Moses. (For example, the verb "you were not afraid" in verse 8 is in the plural form.) Miriam's punishment recalls the law of jealous husbands, in which the woman bears guilt if the ordeal proves her guilty; yet the man does not bear guilt if his suspicions are groundless (see commentary on Num 5).

In an even more bizarre twist, God says in verse 14 that Miriam would have been unclean for seven days if her father had spat in her face. No other OT text refers to what seems to have been a familiar practice. Spitting in one's face does bring great shame to the victim, but this seems an odd justification for God's behavior, since Miriam has not been spit upon. Rather, she has received unequal treatment from God, since both she and Aaron spoke against Moses' authority. Yet the text leaves this apparent inequity without comment, except to say that the people stay around in Hazeroth until Miriam's shame has passed, and then they begin their journey and settle "in the Desert of Paran," which is apparently another part of this large area (see the commentary above on 10:12).

13:1–24 SENDING THE SPIES

This text disagrees with Deuteronomy 1 regarding whose idea it is to send spies into the land.[12] Here, the narrator reports that the spies are sent at God's direction. In contrast, Moses – or the literary character of Moses – suggests in Deuteronomy 1 that the people have this idea. Moreover, according to Deuteronomy 1, God is not present in the discussion at all! While one could discuss whether this represents a lack of faith on the part of the people or, alternatively, that God ratifies the plan of the people, perhaps a better solution would be to recognize the difference in literary character between Numbers and Deuteronomy. This gives further weight to the consensus theory of biblical scholarship, which suggests that the books of the Pentateuch were composed several centuries after the facts they report, drawing on multiple and varied accounts. Both Numbers 13 and Deuteronomy 1 agree about the people's reluctance to go in and attempt to take Canaan because of the report of the ten so-called "bad" spies, as well as Moses' role in turning away God's wrath, which is kindled because of this reluctance.

Verse 3 and Deuteronomy 1:23 agree that Moses selects the representatives of the people who are to act as spies. The spies come, one from each tribe, and the text reports that "All of them were leaders of the Israelites." They are not the same leaders mentioned in chapters 2–3, who appear again in chapter 7, bringing their copious offerings for the tabernacle. Moreover, the tribes in verse 4 are listed in a different order than the two previous lists: Reuben, Simeon, Judah, Issachar, Ephraim, Benjamin, Zebulun, Manasseh, Dan, Asher, Naphtali, and Gad. In chapters 2 and 7, the order is as follows: Judah, Issachar, Zebulun, Reuben, Simeon, Gad, Ephraim, Manasseh, Benjamin, Dan, Asher, and Naphtali. While this change probably does not have an ultimate significance, it may reflect the later ascendancy to prominence of the tribe of Judah, from whom the great Davidic monarchy will come. A similar reversal may be found in Genesis 49, where Reuben is disqualified for having slept with Bilhah, his father Jacob's concubine. The genealogies of 1 Chronicles reflect

---

12. Similarly, there is textual disagreement between Num and Deut regarding the sin that prevents Moses from entering the Promised Land (see the commentary below on 20:2, 13).

this change as well, listing the sons of Judah before those of Reuben, who are relegated there to the third position (1 Chr 5:1–10).

Verses 4–16, which comprise the majority of this text, give the details of the names. Most striking, this is the first appearance of Joshua, son of Nun, whom Moses will appoint (according to ch. 27) as his successor to bring the Israelites into the Promised Land. This man is first identified as Hoshea (v. 8); his name is later changed by Moses to Joshua (v. 16). The prominent medieval exegete Rashbam – an acronym for Rabbi Samuel (or Shamuel) ben Meir (d. 1174) – suggests that a name change such as this was a common feature of nominating a second in command. If this is true, then it is something of a foreshadowing, since no one else in this list – even Caleb, who will give a good report along with Hoshea/Joshua – is similarly renamed. The renaming of significant persons (not just second-in-command) is a well-known feature in the Bible, with examples such as Abram/Abraham, Sarai/Sarah, Jacob/Israel, Simon/Peter, and Saul/Paul. The latter two examples, both from the NT, are admittedly tenuous. On the one hand, Simon was already known as Cephas (Cephas is the Aramaic equivalent of Peter – one might consider this as similar to the American nickname "Rocky"), according to Matthew 16:18, which links the naming with Peter's confession of Jesus as the Messiah. In John 1:42, however, Jesus seems to give this name to Simon, linking it to the calling of Peter. On the other hand, Acts maintains simply that Saul was also called Paul (Acts 13:9), without indicating that God changed his name ("Paul" was more easily recognizable to the Gentile converts among whom Paul mainly labored).

The final verses detail Moses' instructions to the spies (vv. 17–20) and follow their movements in carrying out these instructions (vv. 21–24). The spies are to look for the nature of the land, the nature of the people, and the nature of the cities. All three of these ideas figure in the report given by the spies in the next passage of this commentary (13:25–14:10). Even though the majority report is negative, the spies keep Moses' instructions. In other words, it is not a matter of, "If only you had done what Moses told you to, you wouldn't have given such a sinful report."

13:25–14:10 THE SPIES REPORT BACK

The spies' collective sin is not their failure to carry out Moses' instructions, but rather the reaction that their words generate in the minds of the people. The text reports that the spies return after forty days. As the commentary to the Israelites' departure from Sinai (10:11–36) notes, the Hebrew expression "forty days" often simply means an unspecified long period of time. One could easily imagine the spies returning in groups of two or three, which leads to two possibilities: either the reports are received together once all twelve spies have returned (which v. 27 seems to suggest), or else the text summarizes the reports after the spies return. I favor the former possibility, since the spies would not journey all together upon entering the land, though they probably walk together until they approach the border, as verse 21 suggests. One can imagine a bit of trepidation as the days wear on, with Moses and the people waiting for each spy or group of spies to return. Once all twelve spies return safely, there is likely much rejoicing for God's protection.

Whether the reports come from individual spies or small groups, Moses and the people wait to hear them all at once. The report begins positively, with the spies showing off the large clusters of grapes they found. Then they confirm that the land flows with milk and honey, which mirrors the metaphorical description of the Promised Land as far back as the call of Moses (see Exod 3:8, 17; 13:5; 33:3; Lev 20:4; and several later texts).

Alas, the report quickly takes a bad turn as the spies describe the strong and fortified cities and the large people, thereby convincing the majority of the spies – along with the people – that the land cannot be taken. The description of the Israelites' size relative to the Nephilim is the stuff of legend. (The Nephilim are mentioned only one other time, in the odd mythological fragment of Genesis 6:1–5.) The spies also suggest that the Nephilim, whom the narrator identifies as the ancestors of "the Anakim" (AT), believe the Israelites to be like grasshoppers in relations to them. This interesting insight into the perceptions of the enemy produces fear among the people.

In defense of the ten spies, if they were merely suggesting that a direct assault would be futile, then their argument would have merit. For only indirect assaults, or stratagems, can turn apparent disadvantages into advantages. Writer Malcolm Gladwell makes this argument by turning his attention to the story of David and Goliath. Gladwell writes: "the act of facing overwhelming odds produces greatness and beauty. [However,] we consistently get these kinds of conflicts wrong. We misread them. We misinterpret them. Giants are not what we think they are. The same qualities that appear to give them strength are often the sources of great weakness."[13] Yet Numbers 13 does not delve into the potential motivations behind the report of the ten "bad" spies. The response

---

13. Malcom Gladwell, *David and Goliath: Underdogs, Misfits, and the Art of Battling Giants*, Kindle Edition (New York: Little, Brown, & Co., 2013), 6.

to this report is either complete courage or complete fear. Caleb's attempts to argue against the majority report prove to be as futile as the attack seems to the majority. This binary opposite runs as follows: either one faithfully accepts what God has given or charges forth without delay or one does not.[14] Whatever the reason for reticence, the reticence seems to be the sin.

The spies' bad report and the people's reaction lead, yet again, into a lament of the people and an attack against Moses. In Numbers 14:4, the people even suggest electing a new leader, who will take them back to Egypt. Such a move has been hinted at before, particularly when the "rabble" in the early verses of chapter 11 complain about missing the rich food they had in Egypt, but this is the farthest such speculating comes thus far in the book of Numbers. The people desire to abandon their journey with God in the desert and return to slavery. From the perspective of the narrator, this desire seems strange, since in Exodus 3 God tells Moses that the people have been crying out for a deliverer for a considerable amount of time. Apparently, the people were not prepared for the difficulties of life in the wilderness. Liberation, once enacted – whether miraculously, as with the Exodus, or not – requires patient work before it can be fully achieved. Thus many movements for liberation in the modern world (for example, the civil rights Movement in the USA, or the People Power Revolution in the Philippines) tend to founder once the shine from initial victories wears off. Oftentimes, the temptation is to give up in the face of seemingly insurmountable challenges, and the Israelites prove here that they are no exception.

The negative feelings grow even worse. Joshua, who is now referred to exclusively by his new name, and Caleb, who brings a positive report in chapter 13, try to intercede with the people on behalf of the leaders. In this moment, Joshua and Caleb put themselves at great risk, for the people consider stoning them. It is unclear precisely whom the people want to stone, for verse 10 simply says, "the whole assembly talked about stoning them," and the immediate antecedent is Joshua and Caleb.

Yet there are four possible targets for the proposed stoning. First, the direct targets of the stoning could be Moses and Aaron, since they have brought the people into this dire situation by giving them the wild idea of freedom. Second, Joshua and Caleb could be indirect targets, because they are blocking the path of the stones that the people want to use to kill Moses and Aaron.

---

14. This is a favorite point of attack from postmodern critics, since life experience is almost never cast in such stark binary terms.

Third, Joshua and Caleb could be direct targets, because they are trying to dissuade the community from believing the negative report of the other ten spies, and they are encouraging the community to go into a suicide mission. Finally, the direct targets of the stoning could be Moses, Aaron, Joshua, and Caleb all together, because they are collectively at fault for the futile situation in which the people presently find themselves.

Although the second of these possibilities seems attractive, in the way it ascribes compelling virtue to Joshua and Caleb, such a reading misappropriates the OT text by finding a cartoonish example to emulate. Thus, the last possibility seems most likely: all four should be stoned for encouraging the people to believe that they can and should be free. As readers, we know more than the characters at this point. We know that the people will find success, even though only Joshua and Caleb of the Exodus generation will make it to the Promised Land. We also know that Moses, Aaron, Joshua, and Caleb will not die at this point, though they could not have known this at the time.

God's appearance in verse 10 is a kind of *deus ex machina*, which is a phrase from Greek drama in which the gods appear at the end of the story to magically fix all of the problems created by the human characters. But God does not fix things by appearing in this text – at least not yet. First, God has a discussion with Moses, and Moses intercedes on behalf of the people just as Joshua and Caleb intercede to save Moses and Aaron from the angry mob.

Sometimes leaders in faith communities find themselves facing resistance and rejection, even when they have made every effort to remain faithful to God. In these stressful times, leaders need advocates who are willing to stand between themselves and their opponents – taking on the arrows or bullets. Though opposition within a church may not come to physical violence as it does in this text, an intermediary helps the leader avoid despair and also helps people avoid irrevocable damage.

14:11–45 MOSES TURNS BACK GOD'S WRATH

The commentary above demonstrates how Joshua and Caleb stand as intercessors with the people on behalf of Moses and Aaron, attempting to protect their leaders from a certain death in an emotionally driven mutiny. In this next section, Moses intercedes not only for Joshua and Caleb, but for all the people, even those who want him dead. The tension in this scene is high: stones may already be in the hands of the people. Yet the narrative takes another detour as God continues to journey with his people in the wilderness.

God's peculiar statement in verses 11–12, along with Moses' response in verses 13–19, lends a fair amount of comedy to this tense situation. God essentially says to Moses, "Duck so I can kill these people and start over with you!" Curiously, Moses does not appeal to God's mercy – which has already been demonstrated abundantly in the people's journey in the wilderness – but to God's reputation. Moses argues that the Egyptians will hear how God powerfully defeated them, only to bring the Israelites into the wilderness and then kill them when nobody else was around.

In verse 14, Moses says that the Egyptians will spread the word of God's failure to the inhabitants of "this land" (i.e. the land in which the conversation takes place). If God brings his people out to kill them, no one will fear God in the future. If other nations do not fear the God of the Israelites – especially if the only Israelite left is Moses – then the hope of taking the Promised Land will die.[15] Thus Moses proposes that God put his mercy on display, yet again, and convey a consistent character.

Moses convinces God by appealing to the divine nature, but God makes a counter offer: no one from the Exodus generation will make it into the Promised Land. God says that the Israelites have tested him "ten times" (v. 22), which is surely not intended to be an exact number, as suggested by the medieval Spanish Jewish scholar Ibn Ezra (d. 1167). In this case, it's unnecessary to count the number of times since the Exodus that the people have tested God's patience. Furthermore, this phrase is similar to the "forty days" referenced above in describing the time it took the Israelite spies to look over the Promised Land and then return to the camp in the Wilderness of Paran.

The exceptions to this counter offer appear in two separate places in the remainder of the passage: Caleb is mentioned alone in verse 24, and Caleb and Joshua are mentioned jointly in verse 30. This doublet may owe its explanation to the standard theory of multiple sources. But an alternative theory is that verses 26–35 might have been added to the text at some undefined point in order to reconcile an apparent discrepancy between verses 6 and 24. Moreover, God has been speaking to Moses alone from verse 11–25; whereas verse 26 opens with the statement, "The LORD said to Moses and Aaron." This inclusion corrects another apparent discrepancy in the text: the disappearance of Aaron from the narrative after verse 5, when the two brothers fall face down before the people, as if ready to accept their fate.

---

15. Moses' concern here seems to be valid, since in Joshua 2:9–11, Rahab helps the Israelite spies in Jericho because of the stories she and her people have heard about how God has helped the Israelites and destroyed their enemies.

Although Moses and Aaron do not die by stoning, they are among the Exodus generation, who will die before crossing over into Canaan. This irony, when the reader knows more than the characters, has been seen before. Yet interestingly, the narrator – who also knows that Moses and Aaron will not enter Canaan – merely hints at this truth in the dual report that Caleb and Joshua will be the only ones from their generation to see the Promised Land.

Miriam – who has not been present during this entire episode – will die at the beginning of chapter 20, with Aaron to follow at the end. In the middle of this chapter, Moses commits the sin for which God judges him unworthy to enter the Promised Land.[16] Yet it is not Moses' sin at Meribah that keeps him out of the Promised Land, but the fact that he must suffer the fate of the entire Exodus generation. Recognizing this gives some strength to Moses' declaration in Deuteronomy that his inability to enter Canaan is because of the people's rebellion against God (see Deut 1:37).

It is legitimate to ask whether Moses' punishment was fair, especially given the apparent dispute between Numbers and Deuteronomy about Moses' sin. It is insufficient to say that this decision is up to God. While this is true, many evangelicals are no longer comfortable emphasizing the wrath and judgment aspects of God's character. While these are biblical ideas, they are dwarfed in both the OT and NT by God's love, grace, and redemptive activity.

Elaborating on the judgment pronounced upon the Israelites, God says in verse 34 that the wilderness wandering will last for forty years, a number that matches the number of days that the spies took to investigate the Promised Land. Again, this figure means simply, "a long time," though the clear difference is that the spies took days, while the wilderness wandering will now take years – enough time for those who were of the Exodus generation to die.

Two points stand out here. First, Deuteronomy 1:2 notes that it should have taken only eleven days to go from Egypt to Canaan by the shortest and simplest route. Instead, in "the fortieth year, on the first day of the eleventh month," Moses speaks to the people on the plains of Moab (Deut 1:3). Second, and more importantly for theological reflection on the book of Numbers, a key change takes place here: at this point, the journey with God in the wilderness – which is how this commentary refers to the story as a whole – becomes the wilderness wandering – which is how traditional interpretation describes the forty years in the wilderness. The Exodus generation – those who saw with

---

16. The commentary for chapter 20 notes that the specific sin seems too insignificant to warrant such a harsh judgment.

their own eyes what God did to the Egyptians (Exod 19:4) – will give way to a new generation, who did not see these things, and who therefore have to rely on God alone when it comes time to enter the Promised Land. Joshua has the assurance that God will be with him just as God was with Moses (see especially Josh 1:1–9), but the people of the next generation will have to trust that God will act even though they have no direct experience of God acting. As Jesus says to the Apostle Thomas, those who have not seen and yet have come to believe anyway are perhaps more blessed than those who believe because they have seen (John 20:29).

15:1–21 INSTRUCTIONS FOR OFFERINGS

The heights of comedy and drama in the previous text now give way to a comparatively bland instruction concerning proper offerings. God's command here stipulates that offerings of various animals, given for various reasons, should include wine or olive oil "as an aroma pleasing to the LORD." This phrase occurs six times in chapter 15 (vv. 3, 7, 10, 13, 14, and 24), the first five of which fall under consideration in this section.

The idea of a sacrifice being a pleasing aroma to God also shows up in Genesis 8:21, when Noah and his family offer a sacrifice after emerging from the ark. This intertextual connection saves this text from being yet another "boring" legal text in the Torah. For when Noah offers his sacrifice in Genesis 8, God has just spared him and his family from the great flood: they are the only ones, according to that narrative, to have survived. Noah does not intercede on behalf of the people and animals on the earth in the way that Moses intercedes for the people in the narrative above. However, he does offer a sacrifice, and the aroma fills God's nostrils, anthropomorphic language that contributes to the literary artistry of the text. Then God's normal character of graciousness and mercy returns. Here in Numbers 14, Moses talks God down from a plan to wipe out the people because it is not in keeping with God's normal character of graciousness and mercy. Once again, God responds by instructing Moses how to add offerings with pleasing aromas to any sacrifice that the people bring.

A further connection between Genesis 8 and this text comes in verse 16, which stipulates that the same regulations apply to both Israelites and non-Israelites. Both groups, when bringing sacrifices to God, should bring pleasing offerings as well. The same idea occurs in Exodus 12:49, the institution of the Passover, where God says that foreigners who are willing to eat the Passover meal must submit to circumcision (pertaining to males; Exod 12:48), but otherwise the whole world is potentially included. Similarly, in the case of Noah's sacrifice, the entire world is included: for just as the Israelites in Numbers 14 come through a purging when they experience the turning back of God's wrath, so the entire world in Genesis 8 comes through a purging when they experience God's wrath in the great flood.

15:22–29 ATONEMENT FOR UNINTENTIONAL SINS

The instructions for offerings continue in this next section, with successive texts dealing first with unintentional sins and then with intentional sins. John Wesley famously makes a distinction between "sins properly so called," which are "willful transgressions against known laws of God." These are deliberate, rebellious acts which run against the will of God for one's life: violations of the law of love, failure to do acts of charity, failure to attend on the means of grace, and so on. By contrast, "sins improperly so called" are the attitudes and dispositions that remain behind in believers even after God cleanses them of deliberate transgressions. Thus, for example, one who has a problem with her temper might not "sin," strictly speaking when, after becoming a Christian, she still lashes out in anger occasionally. Both kinds of sin, it is important to note, require the atoning work of Jesus, and this work brings forgiveness for both, but sins "improperly so called" do not carry the same level of guilt as sins "properly so called."

The section immediately following, which deals with punishment for intentional sins, sounds similar to Psalm 19:12–13, which includes prayers for atonement for both kinds of sin. In addition, one may recall here the Nazirite vow. Numbers 6 stipulates that Nazirites should never touch a dead body, even if it is a family member (vv. 6–8). This is equivalent to intentional sin or defilement of the Nazirite vow. The next three verses include a provision for what should be done in case someone dies unexpectedly, near enough to the Nazirite to cause defilement (vv. 9–12). In such a case, the Nazirite needs to shave the head, shave it again after eight days, and bring an offering for the sin. Then, only after atonement has been made, the Nazirite vow starts over with day zero.

The key point here is that sin affects the community as a whole.[17] The community, upon learning of an unintentional sin by one of its members,

---

17. This is a different theology of sin than many evangelicals are used to, since sin is often treated as an individual problem that requires personal repentance. Only rarely is some kind of

brings a sacrifice and seeks atonement from God. As noted in the section above on general instructions for sacrifice, both Israelites and foreigners are included within the regulations offered here. The grace of God covers everyone, in theory everyone in the whole world. In this way, this text loops back to the general instructions to sacrifice, and again to Moses making intercession for the people and convincing God to be gracious, and yet again to Noah making a new start for all of creation, not only for his family, but also for all of the animals and birds that God created. This is a good word indeed: the unlimited grace of God for the entire world.

15:30–31 PUNISHMENT FOR INTENTIONAL SINS

The offerings cover not only unintentional sins, but also intentional sins. As noted by John Wesley above, these are "willful transgressions against a known law of God." Theologically, a text such as this is shocking in that it seems to exclude the possibility of turning away from one's sins and back to God. Yet, of course, such a turning is always possible: it is a truism that even the worst sinners may repent and turn back to God, and God will redeem them. This theme appears quite often in the Bible. In one example, 2 Chronicles 33 reports the wickedness of King Manasseh and – in a radical departure from 2 Kings 21 – his later repentance. Furthermore, the repentance of King Manasseh inspires a writer in the deuterocanonical literature to write a prayer that the king might have said at that moment.

However, voluntarily turning away from God or wanting nothing more to do with God are different matters entirely. Any process for dealing with sin, even of increasing severity, that the Israelites might have practiced in the desert is neither directly stated nor implied here. Any sin, according to this text, is blasphemy against the Lord and must be dealt with in the severest manner possible. It is important to note that this severe text must be balanced by other texts detailing a more graceful response to sin, such as Psalm 103:12, which reminds us that "as far as the east is from the west, so far has [God] removed our transgressions from us." God is ever reaching and ever willing to

---

restitution offered toward the person offended. Here, however, any sin by any member of the community puts guilt upon all. This idea lies at the heart of the theology of the Pharisees in the NT, who are so often the opponents of Jesus. If all sin could be purged from the community, they believed, the Messiah would come. Though this idea led to some abuses, for which Jesus rightly criticizes the Pharisees, it may be that modern evangelicalism has gone too far in making sin and repentance merely matters of the individual's relationship to God.

forgive – though the message of the Bible seems to be that God's love is not coercive: God will not force anyone to come to God.

Taking this and the previous text together, one sees that both unintentional sins – which John Wesley calls "mistakes" or sins improperly so called – and intentional sins are in need of divine favor, which is brought about through sincere repentance. Psalm 19:12–13 makes a similar distinction between "hidden" or unintentional faults and "willful sins." This text again makes it clear that no sin, even a deliberate one, is outside the realm of divine forgiveness. God fails to forgive no sin except the one for which the sinner does not seek forgiveness.

15:32–36 THE STONING OF A SABBATH BREAKER

One such intentional sin, and the community's response to it, forms the focus of this next section. In the commentary on the lamps in the tabernacle above (see 8:1–4), the principle of a one-day-a-week rest is identified as more important than the specific day chosen.[18] Thus, in modern times, one could observe Sabbath on Saturday, as is traditional. In other languages, such as Spanish and Tagalog, the very word for Saturday, *Sabado*, comes from "Sabbath." The Sabbath is not the same as the Lord's Day, Sunday, the traditional day for Christian worship, which was selected because of its connection to Jesus' resurrection on the first day of the week. However, especially for church leadership – pastors, discipleship directors, etc. – Sunday is the furthest thing from a day of rest. This stands as further reason why the day of Sabbath and the day of worship should not necessarily be the same, since the minister is also part of the community and must keep Sabbath. The earliest Christians observed both the Jewish Sabbath and the Christian Lord's Day. Both Sabbath rest and worship could occur on any day of the week. In fact, in many circumstances, due to a shortage of clergy, a shortage of facilities, or work schedules of members, communities require creative worship scheduling. For both Sabbath – one's personal time of rest and being with God – and worship – the communal act of the body giving praise to God – can be moved according to the circumstances of one's life, though neither should be set aside. While Saturday and Sunday might be the ideal times, one should not consider one's practice deficient if Sabbath and worship come on different days.

In this text, the focus is on one who has broken the Sabbath. A man is caught gathering wood on the Sabbath. Most interesting, perhaps, is the note

---

18. See commentary on Numbers 28:9–10 for more on the importance of keeping Sabbath.

in verse 34 that the people do not quite know what should be done with him. Emile Durkheim comments that "many of the stories in the Pentateuch teach us that there were criminal acts whose criminality was undisputed, but where the punishment was determined only by the judge who applied it. Society was well aware that it was faced with a crime, but the penal sanction that was attached to it was not yet defined."[19] Although certain problems exist with Durkheim's theories – specifically, that he often makes larger claims than his evidence warrants – nonetheless he has captured the question of this text well. The people know that what the stick man has done is an offense against God, but they do not know what to do about it. Just before this comment, Durkheim establishes that "lower societies" often first define laws with regard to religious offenses; in other words, law begins with religion, not the other way around. Durkheim writes, "Thus in lower societies the most numerous offences are those that are injurious to the public interest: offences against religion, customs, authority, etc. We have only to see . . . the abundant growth of repressive legislation concerning the various forms of sacrilege . . . these crimes are the most severely punished."[20]

Leviticus 24 tells a similar story involving one who blasphemes God by making improper use of the holy name of God (Lev 24:10–16). Moses and the people wait for God's judgment and then carry it out immediately. The same thing happens here: the Israelites keep the offender "in custody, because it was not clear what should be done to him" (v. 34). Finally, God's judgment comes: the whole assembly should stone him outside the camp. This is a shocking text, but one must recall that the times are different. This is one of the many biblical texts that, in all honestly, later practice has correctly set aside. Other such laws are the food laws in Leviticus 11 and Deuteronomy 14. Jesus specifically set aside these laws for Christians in the NT. Though no NT text specifically sets aside the idea that Sabbath breakers must be stoned, nevertheless modern practice would understandably frown on such a barbaric practice. This does not mean that believers may wantonly ignore Sabbath. However, the penalty remains on the spiritual level, experienced by the worshipper who fails in this responsibility, rather than physical, resulting in the worshipper's death.

---

19. Durkheim, *Division of Labor in Society*, 51.
20. Ibid., 50.

> **SABBATH OBSERVANCE**
>
> Growing up in a Christian home, I rarely missed Sunday services. In fact, our parents took us to church almost every time the doors were open, even when our church was several miles from our home. I never considered that one could worship God in a church service on a day other than Sunday (or Wednesday, for midweek services). Later on, I met some people from a church which insisted that Saturday, not Sunday, was the appropriate day for worship. Even later still, "contemporary" or "seeker-sensitive" worship services intentionally moved worship away from the traditional day of Sunday. Even later still, I became aware of Roman Catholics and others who worshipped on any day, or even multiple days of the week, even if they continued to preserve Sunday as the principal day.
>
> Insistence on Saturday worship as following the ancient practice of the Jewish Sabbath runs into a few logical problems. On the one hand, it seems to miss the clear evidence in the NT (mostly in the Book of Acts) that the earliest Christians worshipped in the synagogue on the Sabbath and together on Sunday, or the Lord's Day. On the other hand, given the argument that God never rescinded the seven-day pattern, insistence on Saturday worship assumes that God began the work of creation on Sunday. This further assumes a literal six-day creation, an idea which even many evangelicals question. At the end of the day, if one feels convinced that Saturday worship is appropriate, one should follow that conviction. In no case, however, should one impose one's view on this question – or one's view of appropriate styles of worship, or anything else – on others. This is an error, not only against the Bible's call for unity, but also against human decency.

15:37–41 FRINGES ON THE GARMENTS

Here the LORD commands Moses that the people should make fringes on their garments in order to remind them of the LORD's commandments. This sounds a theme that Deuteronomy will heavily emphasize concerning the desire to remember and the dangers of forgetting what God has done (e.g. Deut 8:1–10 on remembering and 8:11–20 on not forgetting). Deuteronomy also emphasizes, in certain places, the idea of having a tangible reminder as a guide. A reminder such as this must be a physical object, something which can be seen with the eyes or, more often, touched with the hands. An example of this comes in the phylacteries – small boxes containing bits of paper with four biblical texts written on them (Exod 13:1–10; Exod 13:11–16; Deut 6:4–9, 11:13–21) – which the Israelites are commanded to bind on their hands, between their eyes, on the doorposts of their houses, and the gates to their land (Deut 6:8–9; 11:18; Exod 13:9, 16).

In contrast to Deuteronomy, which includes the things that go with someone – bound between the eyes and on the hands – as well as stationary things – on the doorpost and the gates – the instruction in Numbers only involves something which goes with the person. In Deuteronomy, the physical objects reinforce the teaching in Deuteronomy 6:7 that the Israelites should talk about God's commandments whether they are going or staying, sitting or standing, lying down or getting up. In Numbers, the fringes for the garments will always go with the person. Indeed, some Jews, especially the Orthodox, maintain Deuteronomy 6:8–9 and Numbers 15:37–41 to the letter. The fringes these believers wear on their clothing are usually tied into 613 knots, one for each of the commandments of God preserved in the Torah, which were revealed, according to tradition, on Mount Sinai to Moses.

In these laws, remembering is not meant to be simply a mental exercise. Instead, the physical object participates in the act of remembering, both as a summons and as a guide. As a summons, the object reminds the believer to remember the LORD whenever she sees it. As a guide, the object helps the believer in her act of remembering. By placing her hands on the knots in the fringed garments, she remembers the commands of the LORD. By tying the commandments of the LORD on her hands or hanging them by her door, she remembers that the LORD's commands control every area of her life.

The connections noted above between the present text and the Shema in Deuteronomy 6:4–10 find further support by James S. Diamond. Diamond notes that the priestly source of the Pentateuch is concerned primarily with sight as it relates to familiarity with the commands of God. Referring to this text as "the third paragraph" of the Shema, he writes: "If the first two paragraphs of the Shema [Deut 6:4–10 and 11:13–21] foreground hearing, the third paragraph, which details the commandment to 'see;' the tzitzit [fringes] [Num 15:13–17], balances things off by holding up seeing as the pathway to awareness."[21] A further intertextual connection comes in the question posed to various prophets, "What do you see?" (e.g. Jer 1:11, 13; 24:3; Amos 7:8; 8:2; Zech 4:2; 5:2). The prophets answer this question, and then God (or,

---

21. Diamond, *Stringing the Pearls*, 43.

in Zechariah's case, an angel) gives a symbolic interpretation to whatever the prophet has seen.

Finally, the reader may wonder why this law specifically commands the Israelites to include one blue thread on each of the tassels. Post-biblical Jewish interpretation paid particular attention to this fact. Ben Zion Bookser, for example, notes: "Resembling the sky, the abode of the deity, and of the ocean [*sic*], from which all life commenced, the color blue was seen as a special locus of the divine. [That] the Bible prescribed a blue colored thread . . . added to the mystical idealization of this color."[22]

Later on, Bookser quotes a section of *Sefer HaBahir*, one of the earliest documents in the Jewish mystical movement known as Kabbalah. The unknown author of this text also speculates on the importance of blue and white together:

> Why do we have a thread of blue . . . and why do we have thirty-two threads [of the white, eight threads in each of the four corners of the garment]? This is comparable to the cast of a king who had a beautiful garden in which there were thirty-two paths. He appointed a watchman . . . What did this watchman do? He appointed guardians over them.
>
> And why was the thread of blue added? Said the watchman: Perhaps these watchmen might say: the garden is ours. He gave them a sign and said: See this is a sign of the king that the garden is his, and that he established these paths, and they are not mine; and here is his seal.[23]

One may still see this blending of white and blue amongst Jews today. In synagogue worship, Jews regularly wear prayer shawls about their shoulders, covering their heads with them while they pray. Jesus may be alluding to this practice when, in his instructions on prayer, he tells his disciples to go into their "rooms" and shut the "door" (see Matt 6:6). Jesus attaches this to a prohibition against showy displays of piety. However, a prayer shawl could also serve to close oneself off from the world and its distractions in order to focus entirely upon communion with God. Furthermore, the modern state of Israel – regardless of how one may evaluate its policies in light of biblical values – maintains this association between white and blue. The Israeli national flag contains a blue Star of David in between two broad strips of blue, all three of these symbols resting on a field of pure white.

---

22. Ben Zion Bookser, *The Jewish Mystical Tradition* (New York: Pilgrim Press, 1981), 51.
23. Ibid., 86.

Numbers

16:1–17:28 THE REBELLION OF KORAH AND ITS AFTERMATH

The rebellion of Korah represents one of the most serious challenges to Moses' leadership recorded in the book of Numbers. Considering how many join up, this rebellion seems much more significant than a mere collection of malcontents. Even though readers familiar with Numbers and the entire Pentateuch know well enough not to fear any possibility that Moses will be toppled, those witnessing the contest are surely much more in doubt. This is the case with many similar debates recorded throughout the Bible. One thinks, for example, of the debate between Jeremiah and Hananiah in Jeremiah 28. The crowd has to choose between two very different prophecies based on limited information, and they do not know who is right. If Hananiah's prophecy had been correct, we would not be reading the book of Jeremiah today. Similarly, if the rebellion of Korah and his associates had been successful, we would not consider Numbers among the "books of Moses." Instead, Moses would have gone down as simply another leader who started out with good promise but failed to deliver in the end.

The back and forth nature of the dialogue in these chapters makes them some of the most artful in the entire Hebrew Bible. As noted before, the readers have considerably more knowledge than the participants in the narrative. In other words, the readers know from the book of Numbers, the Torah, and the entirety of Jewish tradition that Aaron and the Aaronide priesthood – which are the real focus of attack here – live on as cherished institutions for centuries, perhaps only finally broken down by the destruction of the Jerusalem Temple in 587 BC. Seeing that this is the case, one must exercise caution by not castigating the rebels for failing to see what they should have known all along. Indeed, it is plausible that the story could have gone entirely differently: the Korahites could have won their case. Thus, one should place quotes around the words "rebels" and "leaders," since, even though Moses and Aaron are the "leaders" at the time of the rebellion, the "rebels" may well have believed their cause to be right, expecting vindication from God.

The literary artistry in the passage cannot fail to amaze. Two particular features of the text contribute to this artistry. First, both the "rebels" and the "leaders" accuse each other of "going too far," or asserting more than is their fair share in the community. Second, the "rebels" make wonderfully ironic use of a well-loved phrase, "a land flowing with milk and honey," applying it in an unexpected way to level a strident critique against Moses and Aaron.

In the church today, conflict is sadly often a part of our life together. Sometimes pastors and other leaders are called to mediate conflicts, and sometimes they are brought into conflicts – either by receiving an attack or by initiating an attack against someone else. In an ideal world, all the members of a faith community would always get along with each other, would never be jealous of each other, and would grow in faith together. Since we do not live in an ideal world, learning how to deal with the inevitable conflicts is an important part of the preparation to lead or simply to be members of a community of faith. Seminaries would do well not only to include courses in conflict management and resolution in the formal curriculum, but also to offer conflict resolution seminars and workshops for laypersons.

Moreover, sometimes conflict needs to take place in order to correct an unhealthy situation or to foster greater connectedness among the members and between the members and the leadership. Leaders should not exercise their power over the members in an overly authoritative way (Mark 10:42–45; Luke 22:25–30). Members should also not raise conflict over trivial matters – the color of the paint on the walls, for example – but should carefully examine whether the conflict they are raising is vital to the mission of the church in the world. Above all, everyone involved in a conflict should maintain humility, gentleness, and grace – for it surely grieves the Father, wounds the Son, and quenches the Holy Spirit when brothers and sisters are divided (contrast Ps 133:1).

16:1–3 Initial Challenge

The initial challenge against Moses and Aaron is over qualifications for leadership. Unlike a later challenge in 21:4–9 (see below), the people do not directly challenge God (see also Exod 17:7). Instead, they dispute whether Moses and Aaron deserve the leadership. The claim is that Moses and Aaron do not have a monopoly on holiness, for they say, "The whole community is holy, every one of them, and the Lord is with them" (v. 3). The commentary for chapter 3, in the context of the genealogy of the Gershonites, refers to the key Protestant doctrine of the priesthood of all believers. Here, as there, one must be careful not to extend this important theological idea to deny the importance of God's call to ministry. While all have access to God for themselves, and all are called into ministry of various kinds, only a few are called into the ministry of leading God's people. Scenarios that call one's leadership into question are no doubt common. The typical element in such charges centers on the worthiness of the individual for the position of leadership. Indeed, Moses himself expresses doubt about whether he is worthy to lead the people out of Egypt (see Exod 3). In Moses' call experience, God assures him that God will go with him. Even though Moses knows this, he does not go to the LORD in prayer in the next passage, but instead responds with a rather angry defense.

16:4–11 Moses' Defense

Moses, instead of going to God directly to prayer, as he has before – even if the prayer was largely a complaint (see 11:10–15) – proposes a kind of ordeal to see who "belongs to him [God] and who is holy" (v. 5). This text foreshadows something that will happen in chapter 17, namely the miraculous budding of Aaron's staff as a sign of God choosing him and his sons to lead the Levites and to claim the title of High Priest with hereditary succession. The present text does not indicate exactly how God will indicate God's choice. Moses simply orders the Korahites to take censers and, the next morning, to put coals in them before God. Though the text does not explicitly say so, it is likely that the sign of God's choice will take place by making the coals glowing hot, even though no one has put any fire coals in them. Alas, the reader remains disappointed at the end of the text, for no description of what should happen to these censers and the coals within them appears in the text, nor is there any description of what happens to the censers after the ordeal. Such a description would have solved the question of what the ordeal involved. One must conclude that the authors/compilers/editors of the text had no particular interest in the nature or resolution of the ordeal, so either they didn't create it in the first place or left it out of the final form of Numbers.[24]

Moses probably has grown tired of rebellion after rebellion, but his failure to go to God at the first instance is striking, perhaps sowing the seeds of his ultimate rebellion against God when he strikes the rock at Meribah to bring water out when God tells him to speak to the rock (20:2–13). In addition, this text captures the reader's interest because it primarily concerns the defense of Aaron, not Moses.

Yet, as noted previously, this is only one in a series of challenges throughout the book of Numbers to the leadership of Moses – which, according to the larger narrative, has been established by God (see Exod 3). In chapter 12, Aaron and Miriam oppose Moses' leadership, leading God to strike only Miriam (not Aaron) with leprosy. God then answers Moses' prayer for healing. In chapter

---

24. This is an admittedly circular argument.

15, after the spies return, the people gather to stone Moses and Aaron, but Joshua and Caleb intervene to save their lives. In this section, Moses stands as a defender for Aaron, whose authority to be priest is called into question by the rebellion of the Levites. In fact, Moses tells them: "You Levites have gone too far" (v. 7). Of course, this charge matches what the "rebels" say about Moses and Aaron (v. 3), and so the reduplication of the phrase serves to link the two parts of this episode together.

Moses' essential complaint against the Levites centers on his contention that they "have gone too far" because they are trying to wrest the priesthood away from Aaron, even though they have already been set apart for special duty by God. Moses thus casts the argument in strictly theological terms: "It is against the LORD that you and all your followers have banded together. Who is Aaron that you should grumble against him?" (v. 11). This statement is striking in light of Moses' complaint to God in chapter 11 that the people – and, for that matter, God – have been complaining against him! Later in Israel's story, the prophet/priest/judge Samuel will make a similar complaint to God, namely that in asking for a king, the people are rebelling against him personally. But God assures Samuel that the people are rejecting God, not Samuel. Moses here says that by attacking Aaron, they are attacking God.

Modern ministers and other students of the Bible must tread with great caution here, for a text such as this invites tremendous abuse. In many contemporary contexts, a minister or leader places herself or himself on decidedly unsteady ground when she or he claims that a criticism of the minister is a criticism of God. Just as Aaron and Miriam dispute with Moses about whether prophetic authority rests solely with their younger brother, so also the Korahites dispute whether priestly authority rests entirely with Aaron. It is possible that this text originated out of just such a dispute later on in Israel's history, perhaps even after the kingdoms were divided and Northern Israelites were asking the same question as the Samaritan woman in John 4 – whether Jerusalem really is the only legitimate place to worship God. In other words, one must not forget the context of this passage, and it must not become a proof-text for an overbearing stranglehold on authority on the part of ministers and leaders. For if God does in fact speak through the ones God chooses to be leaders, God also can say important things through those whom God does not choose to be leaders, and ignoring or silencing these voices brings great peril to the community as a whole.

16:12–15 Dathan and Abiram Refuse Moses

As the story of the Korahites' rebellion continues, things get worse for Moses and especially Aaron before they get better. Dathan and Abiram, the sons of Eliab, whom verse 1 report as being "insolent," refuse Moses' command to appear before God. In a bit of rhetorical flourish, they mockingly refer to Moses' vivid description of the land – a description that originally came from God – by saying that Moses has brought them *from* "a land flowing with milk and honey to kill [them] in the wilderness" (v. 13). This statement echoes the contention of the "rabble" in chapter 11, who complain that Moses has led the people out of Egypt with its rich food – and slavery – to starve them to death on the meager food supply they find in the wilderness. Moreover, Moses has failed to deliver on his promise to take them to a land flowing with milk and honey. On top of all this, Moses wants to "lord it over [them]" (v. 13)! Without using the precise phrase, the "rebels" here are accusing Moses of having gone too far (see vv. 3, 7). As stated above, the artfulness of the text is undeniable.

16:16–22 Setting the Case before God

Moses responds to the attempted "rebellion" by renewing his call for the Korahites to bring the censers full of coals before the Lord on the next morning. This time, he adds Aaron to the mix. As above, the Korahites are to fill censers with burning coals and incense and bring them to the tent of meeting. Unlike Dathan and Abiram, who in the previous section refuse to appear, the Korathites do as instructed, perhaps because they have just as much interest in the resolution of the debate as Moses and Aaron. Verse 17 confirms that 250 Levites are involved in the protest against Aaron's exclusive hold on the Israelite priesthood. Adding Korah himself to this group lends a total of 251, though it is unclear if Dathan or Abiram, or both, change their minds and decide to join the group. Although the next section will include Dathan and Abiram, they do not seem to be present when the ordeal itself takes place. Once again, the text does not make clear the precise nature of this ordeal.[25]

As the text continues, even though nothing happens to the censers, God apparently makes a choice between Aaron on one side and Korah and his 250 accomplices on the other side because God tells Moses and Aaron to get out of the way so that God can kill all of the "rebels" at once. This reminds the careful reader of what God tells Moses after the ten spies return with bad

---

25. It is uncertain if this case truly *is* an ordeal, since God is not involved in the process. See commentary on 17:1–13 for more on this.

reports (see above on 14:11–45). There, Moses talks God down from God's intention to wipe out all of the Israelites and start over with Moses by asking God to think how such an action would look to the Egyptians, of all people. Here, Moses and Aaron try to talk God down again, but they adopt a somewhat more typical line in their argument by suggesting that killing everyone for the sin of just one person is unjust.

This line of argument reminds the reader of the bargain that Abraham makes with God regarding the inhabitants of Sodom in Genesis 18:23–33. Abraham, starting with the assumption that most of the inhabitants of Sodom are wicked, wonders whether it is just to "sweep the righteous away with the wicked" (Gen 18:23). He asks first if God will still destroy the city if fifty righteous people are in it; God says God will not. Then Abraham asks about forty-five righteous people, then forty, then thirty, then twenty, then ten. God agrees each time that if the given number of righteous people lives in Sodom, God will not destroy it. The bidding does not go any lower, and this text thus doubtlessly forms one of the scriptural and legal justifications for a long-standing principle in Judaism: that ten Jews – usually it is ten men, though in some Conservative and Reform congregations women may count – are required for public prayers to take place. This quorum is called a *minyan*.

In the present text, Moses and Aaron approach this from the opposite side, asking if one person's sin justifies killing everyone. This is surely because the overwhelming majority is righteous, not guilty of sin. The text leaves this question tantalizingly unanswered, whereas God responds favorably to Moses' entreaty in chapter 14. However, God's choice is made clear in the next section.

16:23–50 The Rebels Are Isolated; God Punishes

The verse numbers in the NIV depart from the Hebrew text after verse 35 of the present chapter. The Hebrew text that is numbered 17:1–15 is numbered 16:36–50 in the NIV. Miller and Hayes suggest that this entire chapter is one of a complex of stories that refer to conflicts between various priestly houses.[26] This is in line with what the commentary suggests above, that those who are in "rebellion" here might have a point. Assuming these texts reflect historical reality – whether or not it is exactly as described here – the reader must remember that at the time of the dispute, the people involved did not have the same information or level of knowledge as the readers; these questions needed additional adjudication. This adjudication comes in the next chapter, with the

---

26. Miller and Hayes, *History of Ancient Israel*, 106.

miraculous budding of Aaron's staff, but first the "rebellion" itself must find resolution. The violence of this text disturbs the reader. Even in light of what is said above about challenges to authority needing to be for purification and not for simple rebellion, God judges those who have come against Aaron.

In verse 20, God tells Moses and Aaron to get out of the way so God can kill everybody. In verse 24, God tells everybody to get away from the tents of Korah, Dathan, and Abiram. All of the rebels die, which negatively answers the question Moses and Aaron pray in verse 22. Without doubt, these tribes are judged to be rebels, so from now on the quotes will be removed.

A seeming discrepancy calls for investigation. In Moses and Aaron's prayer (v. 22), as noted, they ask God why all the people should die for one man's sin, echoing Moses' earlier strategy of intercession (14:13–19), in which he talks God out of killing all the people and starting over with one righteous man, as with Noah (see Gen 6:8). In the present passage, Moses tells everyone to get away from the tents of Korah, Dathan, and Abiram: "Do not touch anything belonging to them, or you will be swept away because of all their sins" (vv. 24, 26). Earlier all of the guilt was laid on Korah, but here Dathan and Abiram are included. This is probably due to Dathan and Abiram's refusal to follow Moses' orders to create an ordeal trial back in 16:12–15, but it remains curious, since on the surface it seems that the refusal to join the ordeal ceremony is not as serious as instigating the rebellion.

In the next section (vv. 28–35), Moses finally seems to get the ordeal trial that he has been wanting. He offers two possibilities: the people involved in the rebellion will live out their days and die a natural death, or else the earth will swallow them up and they will die immediately. Deuteronomy 18:15–22 offers a famous test for prophets: the confirmation of their prophecies will judge them. Though that later text has its own problems, and though it is irregularly applied (especially in Jer 27), the principle remains. God will confirm the word of the prophet if the prophet has spoken a true word. In this passage, God does in fact confirm Moses' words, to disastrous effect: "the earth opened its mouth and swallowed them up, and their households, and all those associated with Korah, together with their possessions" (v. 32). It seems, once again, that Korah is the focus of the punishment, leaving to one side Dathan and Abiram. But these latter two are surely caught up with the 250 who are consumed by God's fire in verse 35.

Two more episodes round out the text. First, the censers brought by the 250 are hammered into bronze coverings for the altar in the tabernacle (vv. 36–40). An equivalent to setting the rebels' severed heads on a spike, this "was to remind the Israelites that no one except a descendant of Aaron should come to burn incense before the LORD, or he would become like Korah and his followers" (v. 40). Second, the people complain to Moses about having killed God's people (vv. 41–50). God once again orders Moses and Aaron to step aside so that he might kill everyone at a go, and Moses and Aaron intercede once again (vv. 45–46). The text seems to lack details here, for Moses suddenly orders Aaron to take burning coals and run through the camp to stem some plague that has broken out among the people. A total of more than fifteen thousand people – more than 250 in connection with Korah and 14,700 in the plague – go down to the land of the dead in this episode. The violence God exhibits here makes many readers uncomfortable and has led many throughout history to declare the OT unfit for the Christian canon. The interpreter must honestly face this discomfort. If the church has rejected, correctly, the option to leave the OT out of the canon, then disingenuousness with a text like this – as in trying to explain it away or pretend it is not there – will ultimately harm credibility, if not outright destroy it. One can find solace in the fact, however, that "we need not endorse the savagery of our holy book to recognize the beauty in its ideas."[27]

17:1–13 Aaron's Staff

As noted above, the verse numbers in the NIV are different from the Hebrew. These verses are numbered 17:16–28 in the Hebrew. The commentary on 16:4–11 describes Moses' proposal of an ordeal to decide between the claims of Aaron and Korah, the latter of which is ultimately determined to be in rebellion. Here, another kind of ordeal trial takes place, this time at God's insistence. Because God involves himself in the ordeal process, the reader has more assurance that this text involves an actual ordeal, in contrast to the former text, which is more speculative. Strangely enough, however (and again as a foreshadowing of how the test will turn out), Aaron's name goes on the staff from the tribe of Levi, whereas the names of the leaders from each of the other tribes go on the respective tribes' staffs. One supposes that, because chapters 2 and 7 – in which the marching order of the tribes and the offerings brought for the dedication of the tabernacle appear – identify no leader for the Levites, this heads off at the pass any potential charge of "rigging the game" in favor of Aaron and his descendants. (Of course, the Levites are not included

---

27. Steve Almond, "Chanukah Your Hearts Out!" in *How to Spell Chanukah*, ed. Emily Franklin, (Chapel Hill: Algonquin Books, 2007), 40–41.

in the list of offerings for the dedication, since their charge is to receive and catalogue all the offerings brought in.)

Verse 5 reveals why God has set up this ordeal trial. The reason is not, as one would suppose from the context, to establish the hereditary Aaronic priesthood. Instead, the reason for the ordeal is so that God will not have to listen to the Israelites' complaining anymore (v. 5). If this complex of texts reflects debates from much later in Israel's history, then the present text represents the "answer" of the Aaronides to the challenges brought against them.

After Moses takes all the staffs from the tribal leaders and places them in the tabernacle, God reveals his choice of Aaron the next morning by causing Aaron's staff – representing the Levites – not only to sprout, which was the original criterion of the test (v. 5), but also to produce flowers and almonds. In this way, God demonstrates an abundance of grace in selecting the Levites. In addition, this is but one of many times in which God uses a miraculous sign to indicate the choice of a person. Aaron's staff turns into a snake before Pharaoh and devours the snakes similarly produced by the Egyptian priest-magicians (Exod 7). Negatively, Moses' staff later becomes the instrument of his own undoing, when he strikes a rock and makes water come from it, rather than speaking to it, per God's commandment (Num 20).

Taking this and the previous chapter together, they represent a grand debate for the nature of the Israelite priesthood. If this is the case, however, they seem to be in reverse order. For in the rebellion of Korah and his associates, the debate is among factions of Levites. By contrast, in chapter 17, the debate is amongst the tribes. If the history of the events unfolded as these chapters describe them, one can easily imagine both tests going another way: God could just as easily have chosen the Korahites over the Aaronides if God had desired that. Similarly, God could have taken the priesthood from the Levites and given it to, say, the Tribe of Zebulun.

These pretend scenarios are rather unlikely, however, since the prevailing scholarly opinion is that these chapters reflect later issues in Israel's history. Thus at some point in the nation's history, Israelites questioned the legitimacy of both the Levites to serve in the tabernacle (or the Temple) and the descendants of Aaron to maintain their hereditary control of the priesthood. For that matter, such questions could very well have arisen multiple times. Some of these other challenges might be reflected in texts such as Numbers 12 (see above), though that raises a question about Moses' legitimacy from Aaron and Miriam and therefore is a little different from what is found here. The golden calf episode in Exodus 32 might also have served to call Aaronic legitimacy into question. Some have suggested that Northern Israelites might have written this text to question whether the Aaronide priesthood remained valid.

Notwithstanding the importance of these questions, the story as we have it informs us that God chooses Aaron and the Levites to perform the various ministries of the tabernacle and, later, the Temple. The amazing way in which God confirms this causes great consternation and fear among the people. After Moses places Aaron's staff in the tabernacle – it will eventually go into the Ark of the Covenant itself – the people are fearful lest they die for coming near the tabernacle. The fearful questions in verses 12–13 are left without resolution, except for the hint in the following chapter (especially 18:1–5) that Aaron and his sons have the responsibility – on pain of their own death for failure – to make sure that the holiness of the sanctuary is maintained. Thus, ministers today should not elevate themselves above the community simply because God chose them to be ministers; rather, God's selection is both awesome (in the sense of awe-inspiring) and terrible (in the sense of fear-inspiring).

18:1–32 THE LORD'S CHARGE TO AARON

Having established the legitimacy of Aaron's priesthood with the sign of the staff, God tells Aaron what he is to do. In this chapter, one finds the only two references to God's speech to Aaron alone in the book of Numbers (see vv. 1, 20). In fact, God speaks to Aaron directly without Moses only one other time in the Torah at Exodus 4:27. That text is the call of Aaron to meet Moses, following the call of Moses and the revelation of God's name in Exodus 3. Moreover, Aaron is included in God's addresses to Moses only six times (Exod 7:8; 9:8; 12:1, 43; Num 20:12, 23). By contrast, God speaks to Moses alone seventy-six times. One wonders about the implications of these facts, especially given the respective roles of Moses (prophet) and Aaron (priest) in relation to God. Surely, the interpreter should not infer from this that prophets are more important than priests in every case, or that God does not desire to speak to priests. Perhaps the safest conclusion is that this is little more than a curious feature of the story, although that seems unsatisfying as well.

18:1–5 Obligations

God wastes no time in putting a serious obligation on Aaron, his sons, and the Levites. They are to bear the blame for any offenses committed against the sanctuary. Modern interpreters must be wary of making too much of a text like this. One could commit this error by teaching that all behavior in church must be serious and solemn to a high degree, effectively banning all fun and frivolity. This would be unfortunate, for it would cast a dour pall over Christianity and make enjoyment a sin. Such thinking might extend itself to teaching that Christians must be serious all the time, even outside of the sanctuary. A much better reading of a text like this would be to acknowledge that one's treatment of the sanctuary is important, so that not everything is permissible (see Col 3:23), but the enforcement of this recognition should not become heavy-handed or quasi-Pharisaical.

Another valid principle in the text is the recognition of different levels of religious personnel. Most churches – Catholic, Orthodox, and Protestant – distinguish among the roles and responsibilities of laypersons and different kinds of ministers. Thus, some orders of ministry have different areas of responsibility (different obligations, rights, and privileges) than others, which are different again from laypersons. It is important to maintain such distinctions, not for the purpose of arrogance on the part of ministers or self-deprecation or envy on the part of laypersons, but in order to insure proper order and discipline in the worship service. Indeed, religious personnel, especially ordained ministers, have a far greater burden than privilege. "Professional Christians," or those whose calling and occupation are connected with the operation of a local church, have an obligation to maintain proper order so that the witness of the church is not impaired within the community. Again, this is not meant to deny access to others, but to answer the call of God, which is always subsequent to the grace of God by which ministers are installed in the first place. "The will of God will never lead you, where the grace of God cannot keep you," an old Christian saying promises. With that great promise comes great responsibility – and though this can certainly be taken too far, it must never be taken lightly. In the next section, God adds the Levites to his roster of permanent servants, to serve alongside the priests, though in a different role.

18:6–7 The Attachment of the Levites

This text makes a bold statement: the Levites, far from being a privileged class of people who can demand respect from others, are a gift from God to the people. A perspective like this could change not only how the laity view members of the professional clergy but also, more importantly, how professional clergy view themselves. In American English, the phrase "God's gift to . . ." usually connotes a significant degree of arrogance on the part of whoever is being described. Usually the form takes on a negative tone, delivered by a detractor in the attempt to humble the person or lead others to believe that the person has stepped over some perceived boundary. Thus, people often say, "So-and-so thinks he's God's gift to women," or, "So-and-so thinks she's God's gift to the world."

One could surely read this as coming from the Levites themselves to bolster up the Levites' place in the community, which reflects the usage noted above. However, in a more positive reading, being described as God's gift to Israel gives the Levites a particular level of responsibility that is accompanied by a call for humility. They are a special class, but this does not mean that individual members of that class are special. Instead, the Levites, both individually and collectively, lead from a position of servitude. This is especially true since the Levites depend on the offerings of the people rather than having a tribal allotment of land for their upkeep and maintenance (e.g. Num 26:57–62). This more positive reading is supported by the fact that the Lord's command is addressed to the Levites themselves rather than the community at large.

Pastors, priests, and other ministers err greatly when they regard themselves above other members of society. Though the priestly profession commands a certain level of respect, arrogance on the part of ministers does great harm to the witness of the church throughout the world. When religious leaders believe that they are beyond reproach, that their decisions and actions cannot be questioned because God has chosen them, they have committed a sin. For as Jesus warned the disciples: "You know that those who are regarded as rulers of the Gentiles lord it over them, and their high officials exercise authority over them. Not so with you. Instead, whoever wants to become great among you must be your servant, and whoever wants to be first must be your slave, just as the Son of Man did not come to be served, but to serve, and to give his life as a ransom for many" (Mark 10:42–45; see also Matt 20:25–27).

18:8–20 Assignment of the Gifts to Aaron

This text recognizes the necessity of some kind of recompense for not having any land assignment given to Aaron and his descendants (see, e.g. 26:57–62 and 35:1–8, the latter of which marks Levitical cities within the areas belonging to the other tribes). God offers them a special allowance: the rest of the Levites are included in this arrangement, when God grants the Israelites' tithes for their support (see just below). Everything that is not burned is to be given to the priests. Although through this text God expresses a rather large allowance of grace to God's ministers, the potential for abuse is clear even on a superficial reading.

In fact, later priests did abuse this principle. Most notable among the abusers were Hophni and Phineas, the sons of Eli. Through an unnamed prophet, God pronounces judgment on the house of Eli (1 Sam 2:27–36). Making reference back to this particular text in Numbers, God indicts Hophni and Phineas – and, by extension, Eli – for "fattening [themselves] on the choice parts of every offering made by my people Israel" (1 Sam 2:29). I once had a book of Bible trivia that indicated, citing an earlier verse in this chapter (1 Sam 2:14), that priests were allowed to do this! This reinforces the importance of reading biblical texts in their context. The Bible will be grossly misinterpreted and misapplied if the reader ignores this injunction for reading God's word.

If God had not given this gift to Aaron and his descendants, inviting them to enjoy a portion of every sacrifice, then Hophni and Phineas may not have fallen to the depths of hypocrisy. Yet the excesses of Eli's sons (among others in the priesthood) could have sprung out of entirely different origins. In other words, one may speculate about what might have happened if God had not directly instituted the practice of priests being "paid" out of a portion of the sacrifices the people offer. Such a tradition may have developed through the natural course of time, since neither the Levites in general nor the descendants of Aaron in particular were given any land in order to support themselves. Even if this practice had emerged without divine authorization, whoever made that decision would not have been culpable for future excesses.

From verse 15 on, the text focuses on the priests responsibilities. Chief among these is the redemption of the firstborn. In at least two different places in the book of Exodus (chs. 13 and 34), God commands that the first offspring of every womb – whether animals or humans – belongs to him. Nevertheless, the firstborn child of every household is to be redeemed through an appropriate sacrifice. In two earlier chapters in Numbers (chs. 3 and 8), the Levites are set aside as those dedicated to God in place of the firstborn sons of the other tribes. This gives the position of the Levites considerable ideological and theological weight, adding an additional aspect of their overall duty to stand as the people's representatives before God.

Here, also, God says that unclean animals – those unfit for human consumption and for sacrifice to God (or, one might say, unfit for either human or divine consumption) – must be redeemed (v. 15). Cows, sheep, and goats may not be redeemed, for these are holy (v. 17). At no other point in the Torah are cows singled out as holy to God. Perhaps one may draw a connection to the ritual of the heifer in Deuteronomy 21, where the blood of the heifer absolves the guilt of the people for a murder whose perpetrator is unknown. The reason why sheep and goats, the other two animals not eligible for redemption, are excluded from this rule is rather more straightforward. The Passover lamb could be prepared from either of these two flocks (12:5), which were really considered one (the separation of the sheep and the goats in Matt 25 notwithstanding).

The final verse of this passage drives the point home in a spectacular way. Just as the priests are to be God's special possession out of all the tribes, God is to be the priests' special possession. This does not mean, of course, that only the priests have access to God. Certainly, abuses from such an attitude abound in both the Bible and contemporary experience. Nevertheless, the positive aspect of this statement should not be lost and can serve as a promise to contemporary ministers without doing violence to the text. Ministers often are not well paid; true servants (for this is what "minister" means) do not seek wealth for themselves, but instead look to God for their ultimate reward. This ultimate reward comes with a heavy responsibility and a fearsome punishment is in store for those who, like Hophni and Phineas, continue to abuse their privileges and exploit the people in their care with impunity and without repentance. Related to this, ministers must avoid the awful teachings of the prosperity gospel movement. The journey with God in the Desert – actual in the Israelites' case, figurative in the case of modern ministers – has its own rewards: but these rewards are not financial.

18:21–32 Assignment of the Tithes to the Levites

As noted above, God supports the Levites here by setting aside the Israelites' tithes, just as he makes provision for Aaron and his descendants in 18:8–20. The tithe is probably not an Israelite innovation in the history of religion, a fact that would situate the support of Israelite religious personnel within an already established practice. The insistence on bringing in tithes found in Malachi 3:10 probably does not belong in discussion of this text. Not only is the situation which Malachi addresses in his post-exilic context quite different than that faced by the Israelites on their journey with God in the desert, but the argument Malachi makes sounds more desperate. Most texts having to do with the tithe in the OT are either legal texts, such as Leviticus 27, Deuteronomy 12, 14, and 26, or narrative descriptions, such as 2 Chronicles 31 and Nehemiah 10. All of those texts assume as a matter of course that the Levites take their support from the tithe. The Malachi text, however, encourages the Israelites, even in their difficult situation, to maintain their obedience to God, for God will not restrain the blessing. The Malachi text is not a threat, but a challenge: give when you think you cannot, and just wait and see what God will do for you!

Verse 26 of the Numbers text continues God's commands regarding the tithe. The Levites, having received the tithe, are to present a tithe of the tithe back to God. The Levites' tithe goes to the priests (v. 28), and it must represent the best that the Levites have to offer (vv. 29–30). There is a threat attached to this, but one must notice that the threat comes upon the Levites, not on the people as a whole.

None of the texts mentioned above lay a threat upon non-compliance, but rather promise abundant blessing for faithfulness. Lest one mistakenly think that this throws open the door to works righteousness, and in particular, the prosperity gospel version of the same, nowhere in the OT texts on tithe – and indeed in texts regarding offerings in the entire Bible – may one find the suggestion that giving extra offerings earns one "extra credit" with God. In other words, the Israelites have an obligation to support the priests and Levites because they lack the land and other resources to support themselves. If they had these resources, maintaining them would take up their time and attention rather than allowing them to be dedicated to the work of the sanctuary. Moreover, the Levites themselves are required to tithe the tithe, supporting by means of this the priests, who themselves do not have land and resources to support themselves. Each group of people, then, supports with their tithes those who are closer to the center of the sanctuary than they themselves: the people support the Levites, and the Levites support the priests. Though the text does not mention this, surely the priests would tithe the tithe of the tithe, presumably giving it to the high priest, who then would tithe the tithe of the tithe of the tithe, presumably adding it in with other offerings and dedicating the whole to God.

19:1–10 THE RITUAL OF THE RED HEIFER

In 18:17 above, God tells the Israelites that they cannot redeem the firstborn of cows, sheep, and goats, but they can redeem the firstborn of other animals, and they have to redeem the firstborn of humans. This is the only time a biblical law specifically mentions a red heifer. Deuteronomy 21 also mentions an occasion on which the inhabitants of a particular town are to slaughter a heifer in sacrifice. The law requires this sacrifice in the case of the discovery of a dead body in the countryside, with the additional circumstance of the identity of the murderer remaining unknown. In that case, the elders of the nearest town – one wonders what the measurement process would have looked like – must sacrifice a heifer in order to absolve themselves of the guilt. Both of these sacrifices require that the heifer in question has never been worked and never worn a yoke. This chapter adds that the heifer must be without defect, as is the case for every sacrifice.

As noted, one may find no other mention in the OT specifically of a red heifer. One suspects that either Israel – or the other societies of which Israel had knowledge – consider the birth of a red heifer a significant omen, especially since the text gives no other reason for this sacrifice. That Eleazar, Aaron's son, takes the blood of such a heifer and sprinkles it "seven times toward the front of the tent of meeting" (v. 4) lends support to this theory. After the slaughter, the priest then watches the burning of the heifer outside the camp. When one notices that all of this takes place outside the camp, and further that it renders the priest unclean – so that he must wash himself and remain "unclean till evening" (v. 8) – one feels that this reflects some ancient superstitious ritual. Moreover, the person who gathers up the ashes of the heifer – placing them in a receptacle for possible later use – also becomes unclean, which further suggests a special kind of significance for this ritual.

The fact that the Bible reflects such superstitious or animistic behavior should not overly worry the reader. On the one hand, the Israelites grew up in a particular cultural environment, and though the roots of monotheism embedded their collective psyche quite early, it certainly did not drop fully formed – out of heaven, so to speak – but improved through a gradual, steady process. On the other hand, seeing such animistic or animistic-like rituals in the Bible may help in the contextualization of the Bible in Asia-Pacific, since many societies in Asia-Pacific carry animistic elements in their history, and in some cases even maintain animistic practices in the modern era. The Israelites, then, seem not much different from modern societies, and modern societies seem not much different than the Israelites.

THE RED HEIFER AND ESCHATOLOGY

Many readers of the Bible, especially evangelicals tending toward the more fundamentalist side of the ledger, find themselves quite interested in prophecies about the end times. For example, I remember being concerned about the end of days happening when the European nation of Germany reunited in 1990. My unschooled logic ran in the following way. First, the group of economically powerful nations known as the "G-7" includes the seven richest countries in the world: Canada, France, Germany, Great Britain, Italy, Japan, and the United States. Revelation 13 – which ends with the famous number of the beast, 666 – speaks of a beast with seven heads, one of which "seemed to have had a fatal wound, but the fatal wound had been healed" (Rev 13:3).[1] Germany's dissolution into two countries (East and West Germany) following the Second World War was, in my estimation, such a mortal wound; this wound was healed in 1990. Therefore, I concluded that the G-7 was the "beast coming out of the sea" prophesied in Revelation 13:1. It was only after I gained some biblical and theological knowledge that I learned how mistaken my interpretation was.

A similarly odd logic pertains to the symbolism of the red heifer in this passage. Many believe that the end of days will be brought about when the Temple is restored in Jerusalem. When the Temple is restored, the sacrificial system will resume, and the Messiah will return. This logic is quite odd, especially for evangelicals who claim to "take the Bible literally" (lack of space prevents exploration of this claim). The principal reason why this is so has to do with the fact that the Jerusalem Temple has nothing to do with Christianity. One must recall Jesus' words to the Samaritan woman: "a time is coming when you will worship the Father neither on this mountain nor in Jerusalem . . . Yet a time is coming and has now come when the true worshipers will worship the Father in Spirit and in truth, for they are the kind of worshipers the Father seeks" (John 4:21, 23).

In the second place, in following the standard procedure of "taking the Bible literally," this text has little to no eschatological significance. The red heifer in Numbers 19 is to be sacrificed in order to purify anyone who has come into contact with a corpse. Within the original context of Numbers 19, this is the end of the story. One must remember that while the written compilation of Numbers probably came centuries later, during the monarchical period, the internal setting is prior to the conquest of the land. Thus the internal setting is before the existence of the Temple; the external setting is prior to the destruction of the Temple; in fact, the destruction of the Temple is still some 500 years into the future; no one has come along to predict it as God's threatened punishment for sin.[2]

Third, one may inquire precisely what is meant by a "red heifer" in order to keep away from odd eschatological interpretations. Because this text has in fact been interpreted eschatologically, this exploration seems necessary. Rabbi Yehuda Sherpin discusses the red heifer text in an online article.[3] Cows with reddish-looking skin were not particularly rare in ancient Israel. However, the Bible severely limits the types of animals that can be used in this purification ritual. First, an acceptable heifer is a cow that has never had calves, is not pregnant, and has never even mated with a bull. Second, the red heifer must be in its third year of life; in other words, it is more than two years old, but less than three years old. Third, it must not have any defects: the same stipulation applied to all other animals used in sacrifices. Fourth, it must never have done any work or even been prepared for work by having a yoke placed on it.

Rabbi Sherpin cites a passage from the great medieval Jewish philosopher Maimonides, who indicates that nine red heifers have been found and offered between the time Moses gave this law and the destruction of the Second Temple by the Romans in 70 AD. The arrival of a tenth red heifer would signal the beginning of the end of days, since the Temple would soon after be rebuilt. This does not indicate a specific time, however, since only a small amount of the ashes of each heifer would be used whenever it was necessary to perform this ritual. Sherpin concludes that this teaching is about yearning for the end of days. It is important to note that the Jewish theology of redemption is quite different than the Christian theology of redemption: for Jews, the Messiah has not yet come; Christians believe that Jesus is the Messiah sent from God. This is the final, and perhaps the most important, reason to reject interpretations of a passage such as this, which tend too far in the direction of end-times theology.

---

1. The translation should read "mortal" wound, since receiving a "fatal" wound means dying immediately; such a wound cannot be healed. A "mortal" wound is a wound leading to death, but not immediately.
2. Solomon's prayer of dedication for the Temple (1 Kgs 8:23–53) came later, and even verse 46 of that chapter does not suggest that the Temple had been destroyed.
3. Yehuda Sherpin, "For Real, How Rare Is a Red Heifer?" *Questions & Answers* 16 (March 2017), accessed April 25, 2017, http://www.chabad.org/library/article_cdo/aid/3613245/jewish/For-Real-How-Rare-Is-a-Red-Heifer.htm#-footnote1a3613245. The remainder of this section summarizes and paraphrases Rabbi Sherpin's article.

19:11–22 DEALING WITH CORPSES

This text notes that coming into contact with a human corpse renders a person unclean for seven days. This stipulation applies for all Israelites, but it perhaps holds special significance for those whom the community has set apart in some way for the service of God. In other words, priests and Levites should take particular caution lest they touch a dead body. Leviticus 21:1–3 makes these stipulations explicit: a priest must not touch a dead body, making himself unclean, except for a near relation. A priest rendered unclean in this way would not qualify to serve in the temple of the LORD, because he would defile it by attempting to carry out his duties while being ceremonially unclean.

Things are a bit more serious in this regard for those who have taken the Nazirite vow (see 6:1–21). Nazirites face the most stringent of penalties for touching a dead body. First, unlike the priests, they cannot even attend the funeral rites of a near relative. Moreover, their time of service essentially starts over if the death of someone nearby causes unavoidable contact. Regulations such as these regarding holy persons' contact with dead bodies perhaps illumine some of the background behind Jesus' Parable of the Good Samaritan in Luke 10:25–37. The priest and the Levite who pass by on the other side – implicitly regarded as not showing neighborly hospitality to the man whom the thieves had beaten up – may have been avoiding potential contact with a dead body. The Samaritan, by contrast – who in the Jews' minds does not need to worry about defilement – approaches the man and cares for him because he might still be alive.

However, this text does not distinguish between priests, Levites, and "laypersons." All who encounter a dead body must purify themselves by washing twice: on the third and the seventh days after the contact which made them unclean. If they do not cleanse themselves, they run the risk of defiling the tabernacle, and the Levites above all must preserve the ceremonial cleanness of the tabernacle, as this is the physical manifestation of God's presence among the people. Everyone who goes into a tent in which someone has died, every open container inside such a tent, or anyone who touches a dead body, bone, or grave out in the open becomes unclean and must therefore be cleansed.

Verses 12 and 20 doubly emphasize that cleansing must take place in order to secure the holiness of the tabernacle. Verse 18 suggests that someone who is clean must take a branch of hyssop and sprinkle the tent, the furnishings, and everyone who goes into the tent. It is important to note that only a clean person can clean other persons and things. This illustrates a well-known principle in ancient Israel: something unclean renders something clean unclean, rather than something clean rendering something unclean clean (see v. 22). Laws like this may be difficult to understand; however, many Christians take great care to keep vessels used for Holy Communion from profane or non-holy purposes. Sometimes, even church buildings are set apart through some kind of ritual, made ready for the service of God. In the case of a temporary building that has been set apart as a church, a ritual to return the building to secular purposes may be in order once the church community moves on to another temporary home or a more permanent one.

20:1 MIRIAM DIES

Ironically, and with a twinge of sadness, the arrangers of Numbers follow up the instructions on dealing with corpses with a short note concerning the death of Miriam, Moses' sister. As it turns out, both Miriam and Aaron will die in chapter 20, leaving Moses alone in the preeminent position of leadership. This situation will remain until Moses designates Joshua as his successor in Deuteronomy 31. Aaron's death later in the chapter merits significantly more attention, though one should not interpret this to mean that Miriam's death is less tragic. The fact that Miriam's death receives mention at all testifies to the importance of Moses' big sister. On the one hand, many Israelites have already died at this point in their journey with God in the desert. Most of these other deaths receive no mention at all. On the other hand, Miriam's death doubtlessly has personal significance for Moses. Though he himself might not have had clear memories of what happened to him as he floated in a basket on the Nile River (see Exod 2:1–10), Miriam's involvement was critical to the success of the venture. The text does not say that the people mourned Miriam, though they surely did, not least for the fact that the leaders of the Exodus have now begun to die, setting up the transition to the leaders of the conquest, primarily Joshua son of Nun.

20:2–13 THE PEOPLE COMPLAIN ABOUT WATER AND MOSES SINS

This story has a parallel in Exodus 17, which is usually explained in Western scholarship by the two different sources that make up the Pentateuch. Exodus 17:7 reports that Moses named the place where this incident – or a similar one – took place "Massah and Meribah." The first of these names means, "testing," while the second means, "contention" or "strife." A different form of the same root occurs throughout the classical prophets, wherein the prophet summons the people to hear God's complaint or lawsuit against them for various violations of the covenant (see, for example, Hos 4).

In later texts, these two names become almost synonymous for unfaithfulness and rebellion toward God. In a final speech to the people (Deut 33:8), Moses refers to this event (see also Deut 6:6; 9:22). The religious poetry in the book of Psalms will also make use of the names Massah and Meribah (see 95:8, in the context of a poem often used as a call to worship). Here, in verse 13, the narrator gives the name of the place as Meribah, without the accompanying name Massah. Meribah also occurs without Massah in Psalm 81:7, which says that God tested the people at Meribah, rather than the people testing God. Also, in Psalm 106:32, the poet reports that the people "angered the LORD at the waters of Meribah," and trouble came to Moses because of them. The prophet Ezekiel, however, overturns the negative connotations of Meribah by including Meribah Kadesh as part of the boundary of the new Jerusalem vision at the end of the book (see Ezek 47:19; 48:28).

A further interesting point comes in verse 12. Here and in verse 23 (below), God addresses Moses and Aaron at the same time. Interestingly, both of these instances involve God's judgment against Moses and Aaron: they have not been faithful nor shown the proper respect to God by doing what God has told them to do. (God also speaks to both in 14:26 and 16:20, but in those places they are not being punished.) Although Moses' sin does not appear as a direct challenge to God here (as it does in Exod 17), God will judge Aaron first and Moses in chapter 27. Thus, this text foreshadows things to come. The commentary to chapter 14 above notes Moses' contention that the people's sinfulness causes him to be barred from the Promised Land (Deut 1:37), which may have some justification. Near the end of Deuteronomy, Moses quotes God, turning the discussion about his inability to enter the Promised Land into something closer to the truth (see Deut 32:51). However, leaders, like all people, are responsible for their own actions and are called to a higher standard, because their failures may lead other people to fail. Though God's judgment seems harsh (see 27:14), Moses cannot get out of his own guilt by shifting the blame to the people.

20:14–21 THE EDOMITES DENY SAFE PASSAGE

The fourth oracle of the prophet Balaam (see below on 24:15–24) targets Moab and Edom for judgment. The long-standing enmity between the three nations of Israel, Edom, and Moab shows up in various texts throughout antiquity. A few examples will suffice for illustration. First, 1 Kings 11 describes an attack by an Edomite named Hadad, who was of the royal line – though it is not clear from the text that he is king. Second, the poet of Psalm 60:8 (see also Ps 108:9) casually dismisses Moab, Edom, and Philistia as worthless enemies. Third, Jeremiah includes Edom in his Oracles Against the Nations (see Jer 49:7–22). Fourth, both Amos (1:11–12) and Obadiah (entire) among the Minor Prophets have something to say against Edom.

From the Israelite side, this enmity rested on two distinct but related issues. First, in terms of their origins, the Israelites maintained the same close relationship with the Edomites as they did with the Arabs. Indeed, perhaps the connection with the Edomites was even closer, since Jacob (the ancestor of the Israelites) and Esau (the ancestor of the Edomites) were twin brothers. The second issue happens here in the book of Numbers: the Edomites deny safe passage to the Israelites, threatening to make war against them if the Israelites cross into the Edomites' territory.

Though it is perhaps natural or expected to read this text in favor of Israel, since the Israelites are the "heroes" of the story, one should not so quickly think the Edomites are out of line. Many times throughout history, invading forces have claimed that they will not harm a nation that grant its forces safe passage, but invariably something happens to make the nation granting safe passage regret its offer. Israel itself (more specifically, Judah) faces a similar issue (see 2 Kgs 23:29–30; 2 Chr 35:20–25) when the armies of the Egyptian Pharaoh Necho II desire to march through Judahite territory to join battle with the Assyrians against the armies of Babylon (the latter commanded by the general and soon-to-be-famous king Nebuchadnezzar II).

Despite two reassurances that neither the Israelites nor their livestock will even drink a drop of water without due compensation, the Edomites steadfastly refuse to allow the Israelites to pass. This refusal contributes to the general enmity that existed between these two nations throughout their existence. The extreme example of this comes from the prophet Obadiah, who devotes, as noted above, his entire short book to a diatribe against Edom. The specific events recounted in Obadiah reflect the destruction of Judah by the armies of Babylon – thus the end of its existence as an independent nation – while the event here has to do with the beginning of Israel's existence; nevertheless, the enmity remains. The final verse of this text (v. 21), comments simply that the Israelites took the long way around. One wonders why they did not join in battle against the Edomites, but this possibility remains a speculation, since it is not discussed in the text.

20:22–29 AARON DIES AT MOUNT HOR

As noted above, Miriam dies at the beginning of this chapter (v. 1) and Aaron dies at the end (v. 28). Though Moses will not die until the end of the book of Deuteronomy, he commits a sin in this chapter that causes the Lord to disqualify him from entry into the Promised Land (v. 12). In verse 23, God addresses Moses and Aaron together. In verse 24, God says that Aaron will die here because of what both he and Moses did to disrespect the Lord.

In this passage, Aaron does not enjoy an opportunity to defend himself, as Moses does in Deuteronomy 1. Indeed, Aaron has not spoken at all in the text since his plea for mercy in 12:11, after he and Miriam oppose Moses' exclusive claim to leadership. The commentary there notes that only Miriam suffers the punishment of leprosy, a judgment that mirrors the jealous husband in chapter 5, who escapes punishment even if his suspicions turn out false. In the commentary above on Miriam's death, we note that one should not make too much of this difference, for in both instances, one may note evidence of editorial shaping of the accounts.

It remains interesting that only Aaron receives judgment in verse 24, even though God says the judgment comes upon him because both Aaron and Moses disobey God in the incident with the rock. God thus defers the judgment against Moses until later (see 27:14). One wonders if the editors have intentionally deleted a reference to Moses' judgment here, in keeping with the suggestion above that this text and chapter 12 both betray evidence of editorial manipulation.

In any event, God tells Moses to take Aaron and his son, Eleazar, up on Mount Hor. Symbolically, and at God's direction, Moses transfers the high priesthood from Aaron to Eleazar. This transfer takes place quite differently from the ordination of the Levites in chapter 8 and the special designation of Aaron and his sons in chapters 17–18. Here, the people do not have a significant role to play. Instead, they only hear about what happens. Interestingly, the text does not say how the people react to the news of the high priesthood being transferred to Eleazar. It only says that they mourn for Aaron for thirty days. They would not have his presence with him in the battle to follow, nor for the remainder of their journey with God in the wilderness. At the time Numbers reached its final form, Jewish theology did not include the notion of an afterlife, except as they understood how one's life would continue through one's progeny. Thus the story ends on a note of hopefulness as Aaron's high priestly duties transfer to his dutiful son Eleazar.

Numbers 10:11–21:3

21:1–3 THE BATTLE OF HORMAH

The final episode before the Israelites depart from the vicinity of Mount Hor on the last leg of the journey with God in the wilderness involves yet another battle. The Canaanite King of Arad comes against the Israelites. Arad is significant in Syro-Palestinian archaeology for being the site where archaeologists discovered an Israelite temple dating from the time of the divided monarchy. On the border between the southern kingdom of Judah and the Negev, it served – much like Jerusalem near the border with the northern kingdom of Israel – as a kind of marker for the deity to whom this land belonged, several centuries after this battle in the book of Numbers at any rate. The Arad temple even showed signs of having been carefully and respectfully closed down, perhaps after Judah finally centralized worship in the Jerusalem Temple as part of the reform movement conducted by King Josiah.

The text lacks a specific description of the battle itself. The story is limited to the Israelites' bargain with God: if God will give the Canaanites into their hands, they will destroy "their cities" (v. 2). The BHS critical apparatus indicates that "King of Arad" might be added here unnecessarily as a parallel to Judges 1:16. If the phrase is not original to the text, then this foreshadows the vows that the Israelites take before many of the battles throughout the book of Joshua. Alternatively, if the city reference is genuine or original, then this vow would be specific to this particular battle. The plural "their cities" would seem to argue for the former possibility.

Another curious phrase in this passage is: "if you will deliver this people into our hands we will destroy their cities" (v. 2). The NIV translates this as a plural, but the Hebrew is singular: "if you will deliver this people into my hand, I will destroy their cities." The NIV translators have here taken a bit of license based on smooth English. "Israel" often appears as a collective noun, attached to plural verbs. However, the Hebrew here uses singular verbs. When translating Hebrew, one must accurately render the idiom of the source language in as equivalent an idiom as possible in the target language. It seems that little difference exists between the singular and plural here, so the change is warranted.

God grants Israel's request and they keep their vow. They kill all the people and destroy their cities – the reader should remember Steve Almond's quote above ("we need not endorse the savagery of our holy book to recognize the beauty in its ideas").[28] The text ends by noting the origin of the place's name:

---

28. Almond, "Chanukah Your Hearts Out!", 40–41.

Hormah (v. 3). This term is etymologically related to the term "I/we will destroy" seen in verse 2, thus tying the text together with a neat literary flourish. This, as noted, will be the last thing the Israelites do near Mount Hor. After this, they leave Mount Hor behind and travel toward the final waypoint of their journey with God in the desert, the plains of Moab, which will later form the literary setting for Moses' final speeches in the book of Deuteronomy. On this leg of the journey, all three of the leaders of the Exodus – Moses, Aaron, and Miriam – have been disqualified from entering the Promised Land: the latter two by their deaths, the former by treating God contemptuously by striking the rock. The next segment will see the appointment of Joshua as the one who will take the community into the Promised Land.

NUMBERS 21:4–36:13
FROM MOUNT HOR TO
THE PLAINS OF MOAB

The third and final major section of the book of Numbers – or "Journey with God in the Desert" – moves the community from the waypoint of Mount Hor to the Plains of Moab, which form the literary setting of the book of Deuteronomy. Moses, as noted above (see 20:1–13), will not be allowed to accompany the Israelites into the Promised Land and will give way to a second generation of leadership. At this point in the journey, the two older siblings, Aaron and Miriam, have already died. In fact, the death of Aaron provided the impetus for the Israelites' departure from Mount Hor. Although Moses will not die until the end of the book of Deuteronomy (see Deut 34), the story has already foreshadowed his death before the Promised Land journey begins (see above on Num 20:1–13).

This final journey of the Israelites includes several significant events, which later biblical texts in the OT and NT recall. This portion includes what may be the best-known story from Numbers: King Balak of Moab and Balaam the prophet. Balak tries and fails to pronounce a curse on the Israelites through the agency of Balaam the prophet. As the commentary will show, this story makes a significant theological statement, for even though Balaam is not a prophet of the Lord, the Lord uses him to bless the Lord's people. This section also includes the second census of the people. As has been noted, these censuses form the basis for the traditional title of the book of Numbers. Finally, among other scattered laws and regulations, there is an interesting case about what to do when an Israelite man has no sons to whom he can give his inheritance. The case of Zelophehad's daughters, which is recounted here in two stages (27:1–11 and 36:1–12), reflects the ability of Israel's legal traditions to evolve in order to meet new eventualities.

21:4–9 THE PLAGUE OF SNAKES

When the Edomites deny the Israelites permission to traverse their territory (see 20:14–21 above), the Israelites have to double back on the road they have already traversed in order to go around Edom. The NIV's translation of verse 4, "along the route to the Red Sea," finds little support in the Hebrew. First, the Hebrew phrase that occurs here and twenty-two other times in the OT more accurately means "Sea of Reeds," a term referring to a marshy area that has dried up since the construction of the Suez Canal. Second, the preposition "to" does not occur in this text. In fact, the text does not indicate – through prepositions or otherwise – the direction of travel. This suggests the normal relationship between two nouns – called a construct chain – which yields the translation, "the way of the Sea of Reeds." This is the translation assumed in this commentary, which follows KJV, NJPS, and NASB, while the NIV follows ESV, NLT, and NRSV.

However, the text does not indicate how far along the road back toward Egypt the Israelites have to go. It surely could not have been far, since the way of the Sea of Reeds did not follow the seacoast the whole way any more than the so-called Way of the Sea (see Isa 9:1) followed the Mediterranean (Great) Sea for its entire length. These names refer to trade routes that spread throughout the Levant in ancient times. In any event, the Israelites have to go a bit out of their way in order to satisfy the Edomites that they will not cause any damage to the land of Edom.

This detour leads the Israelites, once again, to complain. However far the distance, the people grow "impatient," according to the NIV (v. 4). Moreover, although water comes from the rock for them in the previous chapter (see 20:2–13) – a scenario that results in Aaron and Moses disqualifying themselves from entry into the Promised Land – the people act as if they have not tasted fresh water for a long time, as if they are on the verge of dying. Although one may easily understand the complaints, one may also understand the growing frustration of Moses, who now finds himself the lone leader of the people.

This text does not report that Moses complains to God in his turn. Instead, the text says that the people directly "spoke against God and against Moses" (v. 5). The great historical review in Psalm 78 uses this phrase as well, attaching it to the water brought from the rock in Exodus 17 and above in Numbers 20. Psalm 78 may refer to either event, since they probably make up two different versions of the same story.

In response to the people's complaints, God sends poisonous snakes through the camp. These snakes bite many people, causing them to die in great agony. One wonders why God kills so many. Yet the people quickly repent of their sin and ask for a remedy from the snakebites. God orders Moses to make a bronze snake and place it on a pole, so that anyone who suffers snakebite may look at it and receive healing. One also wonders why God does not simply heal the affected Israelites.

This story has some intertextual traces, one later in the OT and one in the NT. During King Hezekiah's religious reform, the king orders the removal from the Temple precincts the bronze serpent that Moses makes here, which by that time has taken on the name "Nehushtan," which means bronze (see 2 Kgs 18:4). In the NT, Jesus refers to this passage during his conversation with Nicodemus, saying that "just as Moses lifted up the snake in the wilderness, even so must the Son of Man be lifted up" – an allusion to Jesus' crucifixion – so that everyone may have life by believing in him (John 3:14). The hymn "Look and Live" expresses the same sentiment: "'Tis recorded in His Word, Hallelujah! / It is only that you look at live."[1]

21:10–20 JOURNEY FROM OBOTH TO MOUNT PISGAH

This passage condenses several stages of the Israelites' journey into one. Seven out of eleven verses trace the Israelites' movement from one place to another, and verse 19 mentions two movements. The entire journey recounted in these verses totals just a few miles, and the text does not indicate how long the journey takes. When the people end up on Mount Pisgah, they find themselves inside the territory of Moab. Moabite territory will serve as the literary setting for Moses' final speeches in the book of Deuteronomy.

Perhaps the most significant line comes in verse 20: "where the top of Mount Pisgah overlooks the wasteland." The Israelites, having just come through a plague of deadly snakes, find themselves in a wasteland, walking about from place to place, biding time until something happens. Though this passage in Numbers does not carry much interest, a couple of interesting things happen.

This experience of waiting when not much interesting seems to be happening connects with the concept of "Ordinary Time" which applies to two seasons in the Christian liturgical calendar. The first season of "Ordinary Time" is held between the Epiphany (January 6) and the beginning of Lent, a season of fasting in preparation for Holy Week and Easter. The second season of "Ordinary Time" refers to the weeks between Pentecost – the holy day commemorating the birth of the church and the descent of the Holy Spirit (see Acts 2) – and the beginning of Advent, which marks the "new year" in the Church calendar. Since Pentecost is always fifty days from Easter, and since the date of Easter changes owing to the movements of the moon, both seasons of

---

1. William A. Ogden, "Look and Live," in *Sing to the Lord*, reprint (Kansas City: Lillenas, 1993), no. 372.

"Ordinary Time" vary in length from year to year. For example, in 2016, the first season of Ordinary Time between January 6 and Ash Wednesday was quite short, whereas the second season of Ordinary Time between Pentecost and Advent was quite long. During Ordinary Time, nothing particular is planned in terms of holy days. However, this does not mean that God's Spirit does not move and excite God's people during these seasons.

Similarly, there are several interesting moments within this "ordinary" stretch of verses in Numbers. First, verse 14 cites a lost document called *The Book of the Wars of the Lord*. This text stands alongside many others, such as *The Book of Jashar* (Josh 10:13), *The Chronicles of the Kings of Israel* (or Judah; see, among others, 1 Kgs 14:19, 29), *The Book of the Visions of Iddo the Seer* (2 Chr 9:29). The medieval work *The Book of Jasher* (at 90:48) suggests that *The Book of the Wars of the Lord* was a collaborative effort by Moses, Joshua, and the children of Israel. Whatever the nature of this work, its presence in Numbers gives credence to the dominant theory of Western scholarship on the Pentateuch, which is that these five books came together after having drawn upon multiple ancient sources. (Admittedly, such evidence is not particularly strong, since this is the only mention of *The Book of the Wars of the Lord* in the entire OT.)

The second interesting moment within this "Ordinary Time" text is when God tells Moses to gather the people so that God can give them water (vv. 16–18). As a side note, this text lacks the often-heard complaint of the people about the lack of water. The Israelites break into a spontaneous song in celebration of the "well that the princes dug, that the nobles of the people sank – the nobles with scepters and staffs" (vv. 17–18). This short song probably reflects some kind of ancient well-digging song. The sheer delight of a successful quest to find water speaks for itself in this passage. The song also reminds me of a little chorus often sung during my childhood: "Spring up O well, within my soul. / Spring up O well, and make me whole. / Spring up O well, and give to me / That life abundantly."

Intertextually, one remembers the discussion that Jesus has with the Samaritan woman at the well in John 4. He tells her that if she drinks from the well she will be thirsty again, but the water he offers will grant eternal life. Interestingly, this story occurs just after Jesus' encounter with Nicodemus, where Jesus refers to the bronze snake being lifted up in the wilderness as a symbol of the way he will be lifted up. Furthermore, the song in praise of the well here occurs just after the story to which Jesus refers in his speech with Nicodemus.

21:21–32 BATTLE AGAINST KING SIHON OF THE AMORITES

In a story that echoes the interaction between the Israelites and the Edomites in 20:14–21, the Israelites send messengers to King Sihon of the Amorites asking for safe passage. Indeed, the similarity between the two texts has led many to assume that these stories act as doublets of each other. In literary terms, a doublet refers to either of a set of similar narratives, where the two different versions may or may not reflect distinct historical events.[2] If they do not, then these narratives probably function to explain deep-seated historical enmity between Israel and these other people groups.

The translators of LXX apparently believed that these stories functioned as doublets of one another, since they seem to have "corrected" what they perceived as an "error" in the text of verse 21. Where the Hebrew text reads, "Israel sent messengers," the Greek reads, "Moses sent messengers." Thus the LXX harmonizes the two texts in a simple, straightforward way. Moreover, the singular verb of verse 22 ("Let me pass through your country") might lend some further justification to the LXX's correction of verse 21. However, on further inspection, this justification is questionable, for the doublet text in 20:17 uses the plural ("Let us pass through"), even though it begins with the singular noun "Moses" (20:14). Through the rest of the two texts, there are a few minor vocabulary differences, yet for the most part the two stories appear identical.

Sihon, like the Edomites, denies the Israelites safe passage through his land. The Israelites say they will stick to the King's Highway, a major trade route through the area that ran from Damascus in the distant north to the Gulf of Aqaba in the South – passing through both Amorite and Edomite territory in the process. Nevertheless, Sihon will not allow them to go through. Like the Edomites, he musters for war. Rather than going around the Amorite territory, however, the Israelites fight against the forces of King Sihon and defeat them, killing the king in the process. The text notes that the Israelites did not take over the land of the Ammonites "because their border was fortified" (v. 24). One wonders if this phrase may serve as a tacit admission of defeat. The fortified borders do not necessarily indicate that Israel will have no chance of success, and so it seems likely either that they refuse to engage once they see the fortifications; or that they engage the Ammonites and are defeated.

---

2. There are also narrative triplets, as when the Israelite patriarchs attempt to pass off their wives as their sisters (see Gen 12:10–20; 20:1–16; 21:22–34; 26:1–33).

Verse 24 reports that the Israelites take over all the territory of Sihon from "the Arnon to the Jabbok." Yet when Sihon previously fights against the Moabites, the text says he takes the land from them "as far as the Arnon" (v. 26). These two geographical notes seem to have reverse orientations. On the one hand, the Jabbok River, which is identified with the modern name Zarqa, flows ultimately toward the ancient city of Shechem, the location of Jacob's famous all-night wrestling match with an angel (Gen 32:23–32). The Arnon River, by contrast, flows into the Dead Sea in the vicinity of Jericho. In modern times, this represents nearly a hundred kilometers. Assuming the correctness of these dimensions, King Sihon covers a vast amount of territory, which is then taken over by the Israelites and will eventually be given over to the tribes of Gad and Reuben, who – along with half of the tribe of Manasseh – will live on the eastern side of the Jordan River (see Num 32).

The final verses of this text (vv. 27–30, with an historical notice in vv. 31–32) constitute a victory song of the Israelites, celebrating their defeat of Sihon. The fact that the writers/compilers of the book of Numbers cite this ancient war song – which first applied to the victory of the Amorites over Moab (vv. 28–29) – reveals two things. First, it solidifies the historical notice given in the verses immediately preceding it – namely that Israel conquers territory previously conquered by Moab. Second, it proves yet again that the writers of Numbers used and reused ancient material, even coming from other cultures to suit their own purposes. Verses 27 and 30 seem to form "bookends" for Israel, turning this victory song of the Ammonites into their own victory song. In verse 27, "the poets" call for the restoration of Heshbon, the principal city of the Ammonites. These poets are probably traveling minstrel singers, who tell and retell the great stories of the past. In other words, these poets, in a manner of speaking, were the first to "write" the book of Numbers. Put another way, the first bits of material that eventually made their way into Numbers found their origin among these poets.

21:33–35 BATTLE AGAINST KING OG OF BASHAN

The fourth major battle in chapters 20 through 21 – or, in the case of the Edomites, a near battle (20:14–21) – merits only summary treatment in the final form of Numbers. In contrast with the Edomite and the Ammonite narratives, the text does not include any discussion between the Israelites and the Bashanites. Instead, the story recounts a message from God to Moses, promising that Og and his army shall fall to Moses and the Israelites. Though the battle at Hormah (see 21:1–3) includes a prayer to God for deliverance, followed by the narrator's assurance that God will grant the Israelites' request, those elements do not occur here. This speaks to the ability of ancient storytellers to vary their material within established limits, rather than any substantial differences in the history behind these stories.

The two kings whom the Israelites defeat in this chapter – Sihon of the Ammonites and Og of the Bashanites – enter into Israelite legend at various points throughout the OT. They appear together four more times in the Pentateuch (Num 32:33; Deut 1:4; 29:7; 31:4), twice in Joshua (2:10; 9:10), once in 1 Kings (4:19), once in Nehemiah (9:22), and twice in the Psalms (135:11; 136:19–20). One wonders why these two kings – out of all the rulers whose defeat, capture, or death the text claims for the Israelites and their army – should merit such boasting. It could be that these two kings control areas which, in due time, will form part of the territory of Israel. As noted above, the tribes of Reuben and Gad, along with half of the tribe of Manasseh, settle on the eastern side of the Jordan River. Though these battles are not the first in the narrative, they are important in preparing the way for the Israelites to inhabit the Promised Land. Thus, Sihon and Og pass into legend, though not in the way either of them may have wanted. Israel keeps the memory of these two kings alive because their victories over these territories testify to the greatness of God – both in promising them the land and also in delivering on that promise.

22:1–24:25 BALAK AND BALAAM

This block of material forms the seventh *parashah* (weekly Torah portion) from the book of Numbers, which is used in Jewish synagogue worship throughout the world. Theologically, this story demonstrates that the God of Israel can use a non-Israelite to accomplish God's purposes. In modern contexts, one might even say that a non-believer can be used for God's purposes. In making statements like this, however, one must exercise a fair amount of caution in order to avoid confusing one's own words with the words of God. This idea appears again later in the book of Jeremiah, which proclaims that King Nebuchadnezzar of Babylon is God's instrument to punish Judah. Here, the implications for Israel are far more positive.

Balaam figures prominently in an inscription discovered at Tel Deir 'Alla in the Jordan River valley, which dates to around 700 BC. This Aramaic text, which some call the "Book of Balaam," associates Balaam, the son of Beor, with three different deities: Ishtar, Shgr, and Shadday. The text also makes reference to the word "Elohim," a plural noun meaning "gods," but often used in the singular in the OT to refer to the Israelite God (see for example, Gen 1:1–2:4a). The fact that Balaam shows up in literature throughout the ANE connected with various deities indicates something of his importance as a known figure in history. The Israelites' version of the Book of Balaam attaches him to their purposes – and God's purposes – quite nicely.

The commentary on the Numbers' version of the Book of Balaam will proceed as follows: an introduction, an investigation of eight episodes that detail the hiring of Balaam, and Balaam's prophecy, which comes in four oracles – the first three of which include a response from King Balak, who hires him to curse the Israelites. This story perhaps carries the most humor of any in the book of Numbers. Recognizing this may help avoid the unprovable question about whether these events actually took place. One might benefit more by enjoying the story for what it is: a creative and humorous testimony about God using a non-Israelite to speak blessing over Israel. The book of Jonah tells a similar story with a twist, for God uses an Israelite prophet to speak judgment (and, after repentance, forgiveness and mercy) for those who do not belong to the "Chosen People."

BALAAM THE SHAMAN[1]

Though Balaam himself is never called a prophet in the book of Numbers, his words are called "the prophecy of Balaam" in Numbers 24:3, 15. His role is described in the Bible and also in extra-biblical evidence (see below) as a diviner, one who discerns the will of the gods and communicates that to the people. Since Balaam is not attached to a particular deity, someone can hire his services to speak the will of any of the divine figures. One must keep in mind when reading the Balaam material that it comes from a polytheistic context, much like the traditional background of a number of Asian societies – and even modern places in India with its nearly three hundred million deities!

Many Asians believe quite strongly in the reality of the spirit world. Specialists known as shamans can contact the spirits and discover secrets or other important information to pass on to their clients. Numbers 24:1 suggests that Balaam is a diviner in a roundabout way by saying, "he did not resort to divination as at other times," implying that he often, perhaps usually, used the techniques of diviners to figure out what the gods were saying.

Christianity, in contrast to animism, is divided over the question of belief in the spirit world. Many Westerners deny the spirit world, choosing instead to adopt more "rational" or "scientific" explanations for what they see and experience. As a result, they are often unable to explain when something happens that cannot be explained through these means. By contrast, Asian Christians, whose cultural background includes belief in the spirit world, often have insights into strange phenomena that Westerners lack. If the temptation for Westerners is to be too rational, the temptation for Asians is to ascribe everything to the spirit world. In other words, if Asian Christians are not careful, they may erase the distinctions between Christianity and paganism and fall into syncretism.

God can and does speak through non-Christian religions, however. This is a point on which Christians must insist. In the book of Numbers, God uses someone who does not worship him to speak a blessing for God's people. This does not mean that all religious traditions lead to God. However, Christianity has from its very beginning taught that God will go to great lengths to reach people who are searching for God's truth.

---

1. The following is a summary of a contextual application written by Neville Bartle, which he shared with me through private communication.

22:1–4a Introduction
By this time, according to the narrative, the Israelites are gaining a reputation as effective warriors. Specifically, the Israelites' defeat of the Amorites is creating great concern among King Balak and his people. These verses remind the reader of the word given to the Israelite spies by Rahab in Joshua 2:9: "I know that the LORD has given you this land and that a great fear of you has fallen on us." This fear motivates King Balak to seek help from higher powers, as it were. The Moabite king is not the only one who is disturbed by the Israelites, for verse 4 reports of a conference between the Moabites and the Midianites. These two groups will join to secure the services of a prophet to call for divine aid against the invading "horde" (v. 4). The fact that the enemies refer to Israel as a "horde" signifies two things. First, it seems likely that this is a genuine report. Even if this conversation never took place as such, it is likely that other people groups might have thought something like this about the Israelites.

Second, the term "horde" (NIV) is a derogatory term for a large group of people. The Hebrew word *qahal* has many meanings, though it is typically translated as "group" or, in a religious context, even "congregation." However, the Israelites are described here as a horde: a swarming, advancing army threatening to take control of people's lands regardless of any resistance. The NIV translation is ingenious, for it suggests that all is not sweetness and light for the Israelites as they journey with God in the desert. This text may push us to think about the implications of statements such as, "God told me to do this and such," for more often than not, the actions and decisions we make will affect other people in ways that we can only sometimes grasp or imagine.

22:4b–8 Hiring of Balaam Son of Beor
The conference between the Moabites and the Midianites – people the Israelites have not engaged before – results in the decision to hire Balaam from a distant country. The text does not report any discussion about which prophets the coalition could employ, for a rather sizeable collection probably existed. Though most prophets in the ANE associate themselves with a particular deity, the external evidence regarding Balaam associates him with three deities, only one of which (Shadday) appears in the Bible in the compound for El Shaddai ("God Almighty"). It is possible that the Midianites defer to the judgment of Balak, the Moabite king, without any discussion. Regardless, the responsibility to hire Balaam falls to Balak.

After sending a messenger, a delegation of Moabites and Midianites journey with the required sum to secure Balaam's services. Pethor, the place listed as Balaam's hometown, is of uncertain location. Perhaps it lay some ten to fifteen miles to the southwest of Carchemish, which would have put it under the control of the Neo-Assyrian Empire, at least at the time when the Pentateuch began to coalesce into its final form. An Assyrian context makes sense for Balaam, especially given his association with the deity Ishtar. The NIV reflects the subservience of Pethor to Assyria by making a distinction between Balaam's city and "his native land" (v. 5). If Pethor did not fall under Assyrian control, this distinction would prove unhelpful, since the city would control a certain amount of land around it (a political arrangement known as a city-state), especially if Pethor was of considerable size. Biblical examples abound of such arrangements (see, for just one example, 1 Chr 6:55). However, Pethor certainly does not rank as one of the most important cities of the ANE. Its uncertain location – not even generating a significant amount of debate – bears witness to its relative unimportance. Modern scholarship, perhaps on the strength of the inscription mentioned above, has identified Pethor with Deir 'Alla in the territory of modern Jordan.[3]

Despite the relative unimportance of Pethor, Balaam, its most famous resident, enjoyed – according to Numbers as well as the inscription – considerable importance. The fact that he serves as a prophet for hire certainly contributes to his reputation. Apparently, Balaam has a reputation for doing what his employers hire him to do. Perhaps this means that Balak and his associates cannot trust other prophets to deliver on what they want. More likely, however, Balaam's reputation is too strong to resist. Little did Balak and company know, however, that this reputation would work against them, for Balaam only says whatever any particular deity tells him to say.

22:8–12 God Speaks to Balaam

As it turns out, Israel's God preempts Balak's attempts to hire Balaam. When God asks Balaam who has come to see him, the interpreter must not get tripped up on God's apparent lack of knowledge, over against the theological idea that God knows everything possible to know. An attack against God's omniscience based on a text like this seems rather like grasping at straws and does not merit a serious response. In the logic of the narrative, it is more important that the Israelites' God gets involved at the very beginning of the story. In other words, from the very beginning, the quest of the Israelites' enemies

---

3. See, for example, William H. Shea, "The Inscribed Tablets from Tell Deir 'Alla (Part II)," *Andrews University Seminary Studies* 27, no. 2 (1989): 97–119.

is doomed to failure, because God is more powerful than the gods for whom Balaam usually speaks.

God informs Balaam that the Israelites – not mentioned by name in the text – are "blessed." The notions of blessing and cursing occur together in verse 12, highlighting something important about this text. God could have closed Balaam's mouth, rendering him mute either permanently or at least temporarily until Balak and his associates give up in frustration. The idea of God closing someone's mouth for a temporary period occurs in the early chapters of Luke, where Zechariah, the father of John the Baptist, becomes mute until he names the child John in writing per the angel's instructions (Luke 1:13, 19), even though the name John does not occur in their family line (1:59–64).

This dialogue between God and Balaam sets up a pattern that will occur throughout this passage. Balak will hire Balaam to say one thing, but he will invariably say another. Balak will express disappointment, and Balaam will say that he must say what God orders him to say. This pattern contributes to the humor of the story, perhaps even more so than the talking donkey, which appears below (vv. 21–30). In this immediate context, Balaam tries to dissuade the elders of Moab and Midian from hiring him. Had they been paying attention to Balaam's words, they would have saved themselves considerable frustration and, ultimately, an embarrassing defeat.

22:13–14 Balaam's Response to the Moabites

Balaam tries to get out of the job Balak offers him, a detail that could indicate to Balak that his proposed cursing of the Israelites is going to fail. Though Balak is obviously not aware of what God says to Balaam, Balak is clearly not paying attention to Balaam's response. This mirrors Jeremiah's description of the Israelites when he says that God sends the prophets early and often to warn God's people, but they refuse to listen (see Jer 7:25).

At first, Balaam tries to refuse the request of the emissaries sent by King Balak, perhaps stating his position more strongly than he ought. In verse 12 above, God merely says, "Do not go with them." But in verse 13, Balaam says, "the LORD has refused to let me go with you." When the emissaries return to King Balak, they soften the language again, reporting: "Balaam refused to come with us" (v. 14). Interestingly, only the Moabite officials bring this report back to Balak; the Midianites have suddenly disappeared (see v. 7). As previously noted, Balak may realize at this point that Balaam is delivering God's judgment in favor of the Israelites and against him. Yet no discussion of the deity takes place. In other words, Balak does not try to hire Balaam as a prophet of Ishtar, Shadday, the LORD, or anyone else. Thus the LORD, God of the Israelites, inserts himself into a conversation to which he has not been invited. Balak does not know this, and so he continues on, making his blunders even worse.

22:15–20 Second Attempt to Hire Balaam

Balak not only continues in his folly but also "doubles down" by imploring Balaam to come and curse the Israelites by sending even more people of even greater status. The text does not indicate how far the emissaries have to travel back and forth between Balak and Balaam, or how long these journeys take. If one assumes, quite sensibly, that the emissaries are coming from the royal court in Dibon, then the journey would take at least several days. These considerations all add to the sarcastic humor of the text. The compilers and original storytellers, along with their audiences, were likely overcome with laughter at the foolishness of King Balak in this text.

Yet the reader must keep in mind that she knows more about this situation than Balak – in particular that God is already involved. As a prophet, Balaam is a representative of the divine. As indicated above, most prophets serve a particular god or goddess, but some prophets like Balaam hire themselves out to a number of deities. Obviously, Balak does not hire Balaam to give the LORD's word, to pronounce the LORD's curse upon Israel. Though Balak certainly knows who the LORD is (contrast Exod 5:2), he probably wants Balaam to pronounce his curse upon Israel in the name of some deity who will allow such a curse.

He doesn't even seem to want his own principal deity, Chemosh, to curse Israel. Two reasons speak against such a strategy. First, he has an abundance of prophets living at his court who could pronounce Chemosh's curse upon Israel. However, as noted above, he does not employ his own prophets, perhaps because he fears they will prove untrustworthy. Second, Balak may not want to put his own god at risk. In verse 3, the narrator notes, "Moab was terrified because there were so many people" amongst the Israelites. Moreover, all of Moab – along with the Midianites, who have apparently already gone home – are afraid of the power of the Israelites' God, which is also the case with the residents of Jericho later in the biblical narrative (see Josh 2:11).

Desperate to hire Balaam because he is afraid of the Israelites, Balak rashly offers Balaam anything he wants. Balaam, however, shows he has a bit of wisdom: even if all the gold and silver from Balak's palace is transferred to him, he cannot do anything outside of what "the LORD my God" commands him (v. 18). The reader should not be confused by this. Unlike Rahab (Josh 2), who becomes a worshipper of the LORD, Balaam does not experience conversion here. Instead, he says this because he is following the first deity who speaks to him. In this case, the God of Israel speaks to him, and so he informs Balak's representatives that he can only do what the LORD tells him to do. This second time, the LORD allows him to go, but affirms again that Balaam must do and say only what the LORD tells him. The overarching point of the Book of Balaam in Numbers is that the God of Israel may do whatever he wants – which includes using those who do not acknowledge his existence.

22:21–30 Balaam Beats His Ass and It Talks Back

Although God tells Balaam to go with the Moabite officials, the text reports that God was "very angry when he went" (v. 22). A standard Western interpretation around this apparent contradiction suggests that at least two different versions of this story have come together. The seams remain visible, and this contributes to the difficulty of reading this text. The majority of the evidence lies on God's resistance to what Balaam tries to do, especially in the story that follows.

Before this, however, there is a most interesting development in the text. Unlike any other text in the Bible, an angel of the LORD appears to Balaam's donkey. Though the NIV consistently translates the pronouns relating to the donkey as "it," the Hebrew text uses feminine pronouns. At first glance, this seems an irrelevant detail: why should it matter if the donkey is a jenny-ass as opposed to a jack-ass? Yet, on closer examination, the presence of a *female* animal detaining Balaam says something against the dominance of men and men's interests in the narrative. Balaam has heretofore appeared as a competent man, in tune with the desires of divinity, and able to commune with the God of the Israelites – who, by the time Numbers comes to its final form, has already achieved widespread recognition.

Balaam's jenny-ass refuses to move once she sees the angel. An animal sensing danger will often react instinctively to preserve itself. Yet some animals that are trained to help persons with disabilities – for example, blindness – may learn to refuse commands whose fulfillment will bring pain to their owners/handlers. Admittedly, the story here does not describe what the donkey does in these terms. Nevertheless, the animal proves to be more knowledgeable than this knowledgeable human prophet.

Balaam beats the ass three times in an attempt to get her to move, but she consistently refuses. Recent scholarship in the humanities pays close attention to animals in literature. In reflecting on this text, Jay McDaniel and J. Aaron Simmons write: "Words finally worked, though the intricate dance of understanding was already taking place between the angel and the ass."[4] Far from being a background figure in the story, the donkey plays a central role. Indeed, one might say that the donkey becomes God's prophet in order to communicate God's message to Balaam, who really is a prophet (see Amos 7:14).

22:31–35 The Angel Speaks to Balaam

Having gotten Balaam's attention through the talking donkey, the angel addresses the prophet directly, first expressing concern for the donkey's safety. The leading edge of contemporary biblical scholarship, as noted above, pays close attention to the role of animals, and many other fields are concerned with the way human behavior affects animals and other parts of the natural environment. Christians should not ignore these important questions. The angel begins its critique of Balaam by scolding him for hurting an animal that has done nothing wrong. Though humans cannot really tell what animals think, animals, who are also part of God's creation, certainly have the ability to worship God. One sees this in the donkey's words to her master: she has been faithful to Balaam all her life, and only now – when confronted by the angel – does she disobey him.

In verse 20, God tells Balaam to go with the Moabites, but to say only what God commands him to say. When God's anger kindles against Balaam again, God sends the angel to impede his path. Yet when Balaam confesses his sin and says he will turn around if God asks, God once again gives him the same instruction as in verse 20: "Go with the men, but speak only what I tell you" (v. 35). Thus, on one level, the incident with the donkey seems irrelevant, since in the end God tells Balaam the same thing as before. However, on another level, we can infer to a certain extent some implications about the message being communicated to an animal and the fact that God's angel shows concern not only for humans, but also for animals.

---

4. Jay McDaniel and J. Aaron Simmons, "So Many Faces: God, Humans, and Animals," in *Divinanimality: Animal Theory, Creaturely Theology*, ed. Stephen D. Moore (New York: Fordham University Press, 2014), 217.

CAN GOD SPEAK THROUGH A PIG?

The following story comes from Neville Bartle, who served as the district superintendent for the Church of the Nazarene in New Zealand. He spent many years as a missionary in Papua New Guinea. Early on in his ministry, he learned a strange lesson: that God could speak through a pig.

Pastor Gandi, a local pastor, came to him and said, "Something very strange has happened in the local village and the people are really worried." He explained that the parents of a lovely young Christian woman named Martha, who was very active in the local church, were both in hospital with pig bites.

"The pig that bit them was not some wild pig, but their pet family pig, who was raised by hand since it was a piglet. For the pig to turn on the father and bite him was strange, but then, a few days later, the pig turned and bit the mother, who cared for it from birth. The people felt this was an evil omen and were wondering what it meant."

My wife and I both knew Martha, the young Christian daughter, very well. She had told my wife that her family was pressuring her to marry a man who was not a committed Christian. She was unhappy and was praying that God would do something to change their minds. But Martha's elder brother was also putting pressure on her to get married, because the bride-price that would come to the family would help him to pay the bride-price he needed for his wife. One depended on the other, and Martha was caught in the middle. Gandi told me that the pig in question was going to be given to the bridegroom's family once Martha married him.

Gandi looked at me earnestly, "What do I tell these people? They are wondering why the pig bit Martha's parents." I said, "Let me think and pray about it. I have never been asked this sort of question before." Gandi asked me to let him know as soon as possible.

I remember kneeling down and praying, "God can you please tell me the theological significance of pig bites because I have no idea." As I waited on my knees, God said, "If I can speak through a donkey, can't I speak through a pig?"

I opened my Bible and re-read the story of Balaam. He was determined to go through with his plan, and God was trying to stop him, but he would not listen until the donkey squashed his foot and lay down in the path. I saw parallels. The family was determined to marry Martha to someone she didn't want to marry. They would not listen, and she was praying fervently for God to intervene. Perhaps God had spoken through the pig, which would be a crucial part of the marriage

> ceremony? I mentioned this idea to Gandi, who thought it made sense. So he went up to the village and talked with the men.
>
> Early the next morning, there were twenty men from the village sitting on my front lawn. They said, "Tell us about the donkey and the pig." I told the story of Balaam and then drew parallels to Martha's situation. I said, "God is saying to you, like he said to Balaam, 'This is not the right path. Do not go down here. Stop and change direction.'" They listened politely and discussed things amongst themselves. Then a spokesman said, "It is too late to change. We have made our decision and we cannot go back. We will go through with the wedding whether Martha approves or not."
>
> Martha continued to pray fervently for God to intervene. In fact, the stress Martha was suffering almost took her life before Martha's family and the tribal elders changed their mind. Finally, they called off the marriage. Martha was overjoyed and made a full recovery. About two years later, she married a pastor, and they have served the Lord together faithfully for more than twenty years and are still very effective in ministry in Papua New Guinea.

22:36–41 Balaam and Barak Speak

Chapters 23 and 24 will concern themselves with the actual operation of Balaam's attempted curses of the Israelites. Here, in these six verses, which conclude the lengthy introductory section, Balaam finally reaches Balak. Understandably, Balak wants to know what took the prophet so long. Interestingly, he expresses his frustration in economic terms, asking, "Am I really not able to reward you?" (v. 37). With this question, Balak betrays his primary motivation: he expects Balaam to give him his money's worth. Though the context certainly does not warrant a full critique about the use of money, Balak's statement – and Balaam's cautionary response – may indicate something along these lines. Believing that money is the primary motivator for Balaam, Balak assures the prophet that he can – and will – honor him well for his services.

Yet Balaam cautions that Balak might be disappointed, because Balaam can only say what God allows him to say. With this statement – which is consistent with what God tells Balaam throughout the story – Balaam overturns Balak's supreme confidence in the reward he's offered the prophet. If Balaam's motivation were strictly monetary, then perhaps he could say what would please his employer. The payoff – pun intended – of this exchange between

Balak and Balaam does not come until the end of the episode, when Balak finally gives up in disgust – but the seeds are sown here.

23:1–15 Balaam's First Oracle and Balak's Response

Balaam now sets to his work. He and Balak offer sacrifices of one ram and one bull on each of seven altars. Throughout the ANE, sacrifices like this served as a way to summon the gods – or to get them to pay attention to the petitioner's request. A quick search of the OT reveals several examples of this phenomenon: the offering of a sacrifice followed by a visit or word from God. Noah offers a sacrifice to God, and after the aroma pleases God, God promises never again to destroy the earth in a flood (Gen 8:20–21). In 2 Samuel 24:25, David builds an altar and offers sacrifices; then God answers his prayer and removes a plague from Israel. In 1 Kings 18:32, Elijah builds an altar to God before praying that the fire will come down. Even though Balaam is not, strictly speaking, a prophet representing Israel's God, God inserts himself into the conversation by being the first deity to speak to Balaam – as noted above. Thus, Israel's God becomes the recipient of Balak and Balaam's sacrifices. As also noted above, Israel's God is involved in the activity from the beginning, which should give Balak pause, as this surely reveals the impending failure of his intentions. But Balak pays no attention to the signs.

Understandably, the Hebrew writers want to portray the enemy king as a fool who thinks his money will get him whatever he wants. Thus, Balak consistently fails to perceive the signs, even as they continue to pile up – so much so that the reader begins to wonder how the king could be so foolish.

Three of Balaam's oracles (see below) increase the words of blessing for Israel before turning toward words of judgment on their enemies. By contrast, the prophet's first oracle does not really pronounce anything. Instead, this first oracle says more about Balaam and God than about Israel. Balaam tells Balak that he can see Israel from the "rocky peaks" (v. 9; also 22:41) and, having seen them, he finds himself unable to curse them. Indeed, he cannot curse those whom God has not cursed. On the one hand, as previously noted, this word is consistent with what Balaam has been saying all along – he can only say what God has told him to say. On the other hand, this statement seems to be an innovation, because up to this point in the story, God has not said anything to Balaam about the Israelites. The combination of these two sentiments – that Balaam can only say what God tells him to say, and that God has never cursed or denounced the Israelites – serves to build up the tension in the narrative. The story hooks the readers, making them want to know not only what will happen to the Israelites, but whether and how long Balak will continue in a vein of activity that the readers know from the start will fail. Thus, Balaam's first message brings Balak disappointment.

From Balak's reaction to Balaam's first oracle, it is clear that the Moabite king will not back down. Though he might not have put it in these terms, it seems that even if Balak were standing at the gates of hell, he would not back down. He angrily tells Balaam that he believes his money should get him what he wants, with no questions asked. He clearly fails to appreciate Balaam's admonition that he can only say what God puts into his mouth (v. 12; see also 22:18, 20, 35, 38). An English pun made from the words of verse 11 expresses well the heart of Balak's words: simply replace, "I *brought* you here to curse my enemies," with, "I *bought* you here to curse my enemies." As it turns out, Hebrew also spells the equivalents of these two words similarly. The word for "curse" here (*qabab*) appears thirteen times in the Hebrew Bible, with eight of those in the Book of Balaam (22:11, 17; 23:8, 11, 13, 25, 27; 24:10). The word for "buy" is *qanah*. While the pun in Hebrew is not as close as it is in English, and while the writers of Numbers do not make this connection, it remains a possible interpretation, especially given Balak's attitude toward both the Israelites and his hired (and disappointing) prophet Balaam.

23:16–30 Balaam's Second Oracle and Balak's Response

Whereas Balaam's first oracle seems to say more about the prophet than anyone else, the second oracle seems to focus more directly on God and God's nature. In verse 21, "Jacob" and "Israel" appear in parallel expressions, indicating that these two terms are synonymous. In addition, the text indicates increasing anxiety on the part of Balak. In verse 17, Balak asks the prophet what the Lord has said (which he does not do after Balaam's first oracle). Perhaps he expects God's word to change, and indeed, the content of Balaam's second oracle seems to respond rather directly to such an expectation. For in describing the character of God, Balaam maintains that God cannot change, even if Balak might foolishly expect him to do so.

The metaphor used to explain God's unchangeability sounds an interesting note. With a bit of rhetorical flourish, Balaam (or the writers) equate being a man with being a liar and being a human being with being changeable. The point is not that humans are inherently untrustworthy, but rather that God is inherently trustworthy. Because God does not (and cannot) change, then Balak should not expect the word which God gives Balaam to change. After this statement, which almost functions as an introduction to the second oracle, Balaam turns his concern to Israel, proclaiming that they will have no misery (vv. 21, 23–24) and briefly recounting what God has already done for them (v. 25).

While Balak's insistent concern about the content of Balaam's oracle betrays his increasing anxiety, his response at the end of the oracle betrays his increasing frustration. Whereas God does not change the content of Balaam's oracle, Balak does change his mind – for rather than asking Balaam to curse the Israelites, he asks him not to say anything about them at all. In verse 26, Balaam reminds Balak that he can only say what God wants him to say. Now, however, the statement delivers an even stronger word in favor of Jacob/Israel (as noted above, these two terms are synonyms). Yet Balak still tries to get Balaam to get God to do what he wants God to do (v. 27).

24:1–14 Balaam's Third Oracle and Balak's Response

A change comes over Balaam in this section. Though he does "not resort to divination as at other times" (v. 1), it strains credibility to suggest that he has converted to the worship of Israel's God. We will revisit this idea below. In keeping with the trend noted above, each oracle provides a successively stronger statement in favor of Jacob/Israel. At present, however, one may notice the strong similarities between this text and the Tell Deir 'Alla inscription mentioned above. The first line of that inscription reads, "The misfortunes of the Book of Balaam, son of Beor. A divine seer was he."[5] The translation of verse 3, "the prophecy of one whose eye sees clearly," seems a clear equivalent of "a divine seer was he," though it tends in a monotheistic direction.

The remainder of Balaam's third oracle consists of praising Israel. Verse 8a in this chapter ("God brought them out of Egypt; they have the strength of a wild ox") copies 23:22 exactly. Interestingly, Balaam does not say the holy name of God here, but perhaps this contributes to the emerging stance of monotheism, which colors Numbers and the Pentateuch as a whole. Verse 9 recalls the promise given to Abram back in Genesis 12:3: "I [God] will bless those who bless you, and whoever curses you I will curse." Though the translation is similar here, the Hebrew word for "curse" is different.

As with the first two oracles, the content of Balaam's third oracle causes Balak to become angry. He has had enough: three times he has asked Balaam to curse Israel, but the prophet has done nothing but bless them. The prophet

---

5. J. Hoftijzer and G. van der Kooij, trans., "Deir 'Alla Inscription," *Livius,* accessed January 29, 2016, http://www.livius.org/sources/content/deir-alla-inscription.

says what he has said before, repeating 22:18. In the previous context, Balaam refuses to do anything for Balak, because he can only do what God allows him to do. Now, after Balaam speaks what God allows him to speak, Balak refuses to pay him. The commentary notes above that Balak demands to get his money's worth. I cannot help but see an indirect critique here about how money is used – and too often abused – even in the religious sphere.

The critique is indirect because it occurs within a narrative. A straightforward, surface-level reading of the text yields little more than a nice story about how God cares for Israel even through the agency of a non-Israelite prophet. One must be careful not to confuse the issues at play in this text, especially since the Israelites have not been directly involved. Indeed, it is clear from the text that the Israelites do not even know what is going on between Balak and Balaam. So any "lesson" to be derived from this text is not a generic theological statement about the grace of God – for all Scripture evidences the grace of God. Rather, the text seems to sound a warning: do not presume upon God; do not put God to the test. The Israelites themselves repeatedly put God to the test because of the abundance of their poverty.

Indeed, sometimes God is working for us even in ways we cannot see. A recently published devotional speaks to the same theme: "Lord, you have done great things for us, many of which we have hardly noticed. You are Lord over the past, sovereign in the present, and victorious in the future. Even in our trials, we celebrate you. Amen."[6] In other words, as the old saying goes, the Lord works in mysterious ways, and once we think we have God figured out, we should be prepared to be surprised.

However, Balak's wealth seems more harmful, because it affords him more choices than the Israelites. He thinks his wealth will win over Balaam – and God – to his cause, and when it does not, he refuses to pay on the promise he made to the prophet. Many Scriptures speak against the breaking of promises. For example, Ecclesiastes 5:4–5 tells us that it is better to keep one's mouth shut than to offer a vow to God and not fulfill it. In addition, the Minor Prophets have many harsh words to say about the rich and their tendency to exploit things for their own gain while hurting the poor (see, for just two examples, Amos 2:6 and James 2:3).

Admittedly, Balak is not an Israelite, and so he is not, on one level, accountable to Israel's God. However, Balak experiences the power of Israel's

---

6. Shane Claiborne, Jonathan Wilson-Hartgrove, and Enuma Oroko, "May 31," in *Common Prayer: A Liturgy for Ordinary Radicals* (Grand Rapids: Zondervan, 2010), 299.

God when he tries to use God to call down a curse upon his enemies, the Israelites. In the end, Israel's God thwarts Balak's plans, and he is shown to be a fool – just like everyone who believes that their riches can satisfy God, bring glory to themselves, or enable their control of institutions or persons to whom they give their resources. Even more troubling is those who believe that their financial resources are evidence of God's blessing and can get them into heaven. Jesus was unbendingly clear on this point: "Again I tell you, it is easier for a camel to go through the eye of a needle than for someone who is rich to enter the kingdom of God" (Matt 19:24).

24:15–24 Balaam's Fourth Oracle

The NIV breaks Balaam's fourth oracle into four separate sayings: the fourth (vv. 15–29), fifth (v. 20), sixth (vv. 21–22), and seventh (vv. 23–24) oracles. This seems unnecessarily complex. Instead, it is much simpler to consider this as one prophetic saying with four targets. Other English translations (e.g. NRSV) follow this simpler approach. An examination of the form of this oracle provides further evidence for considering these four statements as one prophecy. First, the typical phrase, "The prophecy of Balaam son of Beor," only occurs in verse 15 of this section. This phrase introduces the third oracle of Balaam earlier in this chapter (v. 3). The first oracle (23:7) and the second oracle (23:18) both begin with the phrase, "he [Balaam] spoke his message." True enough, what the NIV calls the fifth through the seventh messages of Balaam begin with this abbreviated phrase (see v. 15, 20, 21, and 23), but these statements lack the intervening exchanges between Balak and Balaam (see 23:11–12, 25–26 and 24:10–14).

Thus the fourth and final message of Balaam is a prophetic oracle with four different targets. The first targets are Moab and Edom, who are traditional enemies of Israel. The Minor Prophet Obadiah, the shortest book in the OT, is also concerned with the Edomites. Moab's distasteful origin – at least the Israelites' view of it – is explained in Genesis 19, but the book of Ruth has a much more favorable view of one particular Moabite, the ancestor of King David (Ruth 4).

The second target in Balaam's fourth oracle is Amalek, another long-standing enemy of Israel. In fact, King Agag of the Amalekites – and the mercy that the Israelite King Saul shows to Agag – proves to be Saul's undoing (see 1 Sam 15).

The third target in Balaam's fourth oracle are the Kenites. The most famous Kenite is Heber, whose wife, Jael, enters the Deuteronomistic history in a fantastically violent manner (Judg 4). She kills Sisera, the commander of a Canaanite army, by driving a tent peg through his skull as he sleeps. This later text is more positive, but the ambiguity toward the Kenites might perhaps give evidence of shifting alliances and relationships. Informed readers would expect such changes in relationships between people groups, not least because they happen all the time in the modern world among nation-states and among groups within particular countries.

Finally, the fourth target in Balaam's oracle are the Cypriots, sailors who will come to destroy from Cyprus. This final statement is interesting because it carries some ambiguity. First, the Cypriots will be raised up to destroy others, Ashur and Eber. However, they will have no reason to be haughty because their victory will be short-lived. They destroy only to be themselves destroyed. Similar statements are found elsewhere in the OT. Take, for example, Jeremiah's prophecies about Babylon (the city) and Babylonia (the nation and empire). On the one hand, God gives Judah into the hand of Nebuchadnezzar, King of Babylon (Jer 32:28; 43:10). On the other hand, the destruction of Babylon itself is predicted in the lengthiest of Jeremiah's oracles against the nations (Jer 50–51).

24:25 Conclusion

The long Book of Balaam ends rather abruptly. Balak gives up protesting that he is not getting his money's worth out of Balaam. Balaam, for his part, steadfastly insists that he can only say what God tells him to say, and thus he is not beholden to Balak or to anyone else who might hire his services. The narrator comments simply that Balak and Balaam go their separate ways. Balak's frustration is obvious, but the quiet parting of stubborn prophet and disappointed king lends a significant bit of comedy to this scene. As noted previously, these three chapters demonstrate that God can use a non-Israelite (even one who has no scruples about speaking oracles in the name of other gods in exchange for the appropriate fee) to accomplish God's purposes. Thus, even though the story interrupts the wider story of Israel's journey with God in the wilderness, it hints in a direction that the prophets will later make explicit: the God of Israel is the God of the whole world.

25:1–18 A SIN, A SPEAR, AND A SCOURGE

The 1970s and 1980s witnessed the creation of many movies known as "slasher flicks," which prominently featured the deaths of several characters. This genre of films spread into Asia. Many of these films became series, with the deaths of the characters increasing both in frequency and intensity. One of these series, *Friday the 13th*, plays upon the particular superstitions associated with that date on the calendar. The second film in the franchise, which was released in 1981, includes a scene of two characters meeting their end in a similar manner to Numbers 25:7–8.

Upon deeper investigation, the connection between a horror movie and the Bible is not as trivial as it might first appear. Film theory has established itself as a field of inquiry within the humanities, and so a comparative study of biblical texts and films can yield fruitful results. Shying away from popular culture as "sinful" – even if much of popular culture *is* sinful and exploitative – may make the church increasingly irrelevant rather than purifying the church's theological expression.

In fact, some film theorists speculate that horror movies often use religious symbols and motifs in much the same way as they function within religion itself. Put simply, religious rituals and artifacts often help human characters defeat supernatural foes. This feature of horror movies leads film theorists Flesher and Torry to write that horror films "depend on our willingness to accept a prescientific world in which supernatural forces are encountered and in which the only reliable way to deal with them is combat with methods, religious and magical, that prove more powerful than the tools employed by modern, rational culture."[7] Flesher and Torry emphasize that horror movies are the most conservative of all movie genres, precisely because science and rational thought do not help the protagonists defeat the monster. Demonic characters, such as the monster in *Friday the 13th*, often find inspiration in biblical or other religious texts. In the movie, the couple whom the monster kills with the spear dies while engaging in illegitimate sexual relations – just like the Israelite man and Midianite woman in Numbers 25. Yet in the biblical narrative, the killer is a priest rather than a demon.

Although both the film and the biblical text include the executions of persons involved in illegitimate sexual activity, they eventually part ways. In the logic of Numbers 25, the adultery that the Israelite men commit with the Midianite women carries with it a particular form of idolatry. This theme will sound again in the criticisms of King Solomon who, having married hundreds

---

7. Paul V. M. Flesher and Robert Torry, *Film and Religion: An Introduction* (Nashville: Abingdon, 2007), 177.

of foreign wives, builds shrines to their gods and by so doing leads Israel away from the worship of the true God (see 1 Kgs 11).

In Numbers 25, Phineas, the grandson of Aaron, takes it upon himself to remove the sin from the people. He kills both the man (Zimri, son of Salu, of the tribe of Simeon) and the woman (Kozbi, daughter of Zur, a Midianite tribal chief) – though their names are not revealed until verses 14–15. God rewards Phineas for this service by making "a covenant of peace" with him and his descendants. The phrase "covenant of peace" occurs only three other times in the OT (Isa 54:10; Ezek 34:25; 37:26). In all four instances, the term indicates an eternal covenant that God makes with a partner (Ezek 37:26 says this explicitly). The Numbers instance is unique for two reasons. First, in each of the other three instances, God makes the covenant with Israel as a whole. Second, in the other three instances, God makes the covenant of peace without specific reference to anything the covenant partner does. By contrast, the covenant of peace in Numbers – which is eternal – is made in response to Phineas' work. Moreover, for his service in turning away God's wrath, God awards him the hereditary priesthood, even though God already gave this to Aaron and his descendants after the incident with the miraculous budding of his staff (chs. 17–18). Here, we encounter the many differing traditions that make up the rich tapestry of Israel's national saga.

In literary terms, verses 16–18 foreshadow the revenge that Moses and the Israelites will take against the Midianites in chapter 31. With a twinge of irony, one reads in the later text that Phineas, the priest, goes to the war, whereas in chapter 25, he takes it upon himself to punish the Israelite who commits adultery with the Midianite woman. Indeed, the Midianites will play a significant role in Israel's national saga, both by oppressing the Israelites (the story of Gideon in Judg 6–8) and by losing wars to them (Num 31). This development gives the reader pause, especially when one considers the fact that Moses' wife, Zipporah, comes from Midian – not the "Cushite wife" who begin Aaron and Miriam's claims against Moses in chapter 12 (see Exod 3:1, where Moses' father-in-law is described as a priest of Midian).

26:1–65 THE SECOND CENSUS

As noted in the introduction, the book of Numbers likely gets its name from the censuses of the people. Both of these censuses are taken to count the number of Israelites who can serve in the army. As will be seen, the final numbers betray a significant discrepancy, lending credence to the earlier suggestion that these numbers are most likely idealized. Though the discrepancy is a rather small percentage of the total, it does present a problem, especially for those whose theory of biblical inspiration is rigidly on the side of verbal dictation. A wiser solution would be to set aside such rigid notions and allow for historical-critical investigation, which explains multiple sources for the same event or a series of similar events through duplication in the sources of the Pentateuch.

26:1–51 List of the Tribes by Their Clans

In the Hebrew text, the first three words of 26:1, "After the plague" (NIV), fall in verse 19 of chapter 25. However, because the phrase in this verse clearly belongs to the succeeding chapter, the NIV follows most English translations and places this in 26:1. The phrase serves to mark the time at which the LORD's instructions come to Moses, and it is a standard narrative device used to move the story forward. Another example occurs in Genesis 22:1, which begins the story of the near-sacrifice of Isaac. That text begins with the phrase, "Sometime later . . ." – that is, after the previous events in Genesis – "God tested Abraham."

As to the census itself, a comparison with the census in chapter 1 reveals some differences. The possible explanations for these differences range: on the one hand, this may indeed be a second census; on the other hand, a common explanation points to the differing traditions lying behind Numbers. At the beginning, both censuses seek to count the number of persons who, at twenty years of age and older, may serve in the army.

There are more differences between this list and the one in chapter 1 in the details of the count. First, the census in chapter 26 does not identify the leaders of the tribes as assistants in making this count. Only Eleazar the priest helps Moses (v. 63). The commentary to chapter 1 notes the importance of using these assistants, since errors can enter a count even with such help. Of course, this does not necessarily mean that Moses does all of the counting himself.

Second, the numbers resulting from the count of each tribe also show rather significant differences from chapter 1. The statement of verse 4, "These were the Israelites who came out of Egypt," suggests the traditional scholarly explanation for the doubled census, which is that the differing accounts come from different literary and oral traditions within Israel's national saga.

Both tribal counts list the Israelite soldiers by their clans. Chapter 26 mentions the names of the clan leaders, whereas chapter 1 mentions the overall head of the tribes. The totals from the individual clans do not merit mention, and cosmetic difference somewhat pales in importance compared to the numbers themselves.

The Reubenites have 43,730 in chapter 26 and 46,500 in chapter 1, which makes the new count lower by 2,770, or about 6 percent.

The Simeonites have 22,200 in chapter 26 and 59,300 in chapter 1, which makes the new count lower by 37,100, or an amazing 63 percent. The text explains this difference by referring to the Korahite rebellion in chapter 16, which says that only that 250 died!

The Gadites have 40,500 in chapter 26 and 45,650 in chapter 1, which makes the new count lower by 5,150, or 11 percent.

The Judahites have 76,500 in chapter 26 and 74,600 in chapter 1. For the first time, this makes the new count higher by 1,900, or 3 percent. Interestingly, the census includes Er and Onan in the list, who "died in Canaan." This differs markedly from the declaration in verse 4 that the people counted here came out of Egypt. Thus, one wonders why the list mentions Er and Onan at all, since both died without progeny (see Gen 38).

The Issacharites have 64,300 in chapter 26 and 54,400 in chapter 1, which makes the new count higher by 9,900, or 18 percent.

The Zebulunites have 60,500 in chapter 26 and 57,400 in chapter 1, which makes the new count higher by 3,100, or 5 percent.

The Manassites have 52,700 in chapter 26 and 32,200 in chapter 1, which makes the new count higher by 20,500, or 64 percent. One finds within the Manassites the character of Zelophehad, who merits special mention. The daughters of Zelophehad will come to Moses later with a claim that they should receive an inheritance so that their father's name will not pass out of memory in Israel. In their genealogical record, the Chroniclers give a similar almost parenthetical note about Zelophehad (see 1 Chr 7:15). In my commentary on Chronicles, I make the following observations about the legal precedent set by these daughters: "So long as the daughters married within their clan, the name of their father would not be forgotten. And so it was noted, for the Chroniclers, though doubtlessly drawing on their source material, did not fail to mention Zelophehad, who had only daughters, and thus was in danger of failing ever to be mentioned again in Israel" (see more about this claim in the commentary on 27:1–11 and 36:1–12 below).[8]

---

8. Modine, *1–2 Chronicles*, 70. Note, however, that 1 Chronicles 7:15 says only that "Zelophehad had daughters," leaving out that he has only daughters and that this fact constitutes a particular problem in need of legal redress.

The Ephraimites have 32,500 in chapter 26 and 40,500 in chapter 1. Once again, the new count is lower, this time by 8,000, or 20 percent. Interestingly, chapter 26 reverses the order of Joseph's clans, which may reflect the story in Genesis 48 of Jacob blessing his twelve sons and two of his grandsons, Ephraim and Manasseh, Joseph's eldest sons. In the Genesis narrative, Jacob puts his right hand on the head of the younger Ephraim and his left hand on the older Manasseh, which irritates Joseph, who tries to move his father's hands (vv. 13–18). But Jacob refuses and says that even though Manasseh will become a great people, Ephraim, his younger brother, shall be even greater (vv. 19–20). Thus Numbers 1 reflects the correct order of the two patriarchs' births, whereas chapter 26 reflects Jacob's reversal. In fact, the name "Ephraim" served as a symbol for the northern tribes of Israel after the division of the kingdoms under Jeroboam in the north and Rehoboam in the south. The prophet Hosea reflects this usage when he quotes God, saying, "When Israel was a child, I loved him . . . It was I who taught Ephraim to walk" (Hos 11:1, 3).

The Benjaminites have 45,600 in chapter 26 and 35,400 in chapter 1, which makes the new count higher by 10,200, or 29 percent.

The Danites, in only one clan, have 64,400 in chapter 26 and 62,700 in chapter 1, which makes the new count higher by 1,700, or 3 percent.

The Asherites have 53,400 in chapter 26 and 41,500 in chapter 1, which makes the new count higher by 11,900, or 3 percent.

Finally, the Naphtalites have 45,400 in chapter 26 and 53,400 in chapter 1, which makes the new count lower by 8000, or 15 percent.

The total of all the tribes is 601,730 in chapter 26 and 603,550 in chapter 1, which makes the overall count lower by 1,820, or 0.3 percent. Everything noted about the accuracy of these numbers in chapter 1 bears repeating here. Hanging orthodoxy upon details such as this courts disaster and incredulity. A much better strategy of interpretation for the numbers in Numbers places them within the proper framework of Israel's national saga. Thus, the specific count has little relevance, except as a contribution to the religious value of the text: namely, the overarching claim of God's deliverance of Israel from the land of slavery into the good and broad land flowing with milk and honey (see Exod 3:8).

26:52–56 Apportionment of Land

Whereas the census of the army in chapter 1 leads into the arrangement of the tribes for the march, the text in chapter 26 looks forward to the division of the land as an inheritance for the tribes. Of course, the book of

Numbers – regardless of when its underlying texts were written and how long they circulated as oral stories – comes together some centuries after the events it relates. So even though the present passage assumes a great deal – most notably, the success of the conquest – both the readers and the writers (whoever they were) have more knowledge of what is going to happen than the characters in the narrative.

God's instructions for dividing the land are quite logical. Larger amounts of land go to larger groups, and smaller amounts of land to smaller groups. In verse 54, God suggests that the land will go by lot "according to the number of those listed." This seems to refer to those who have just been counted, yet God commands Moses to count the soldiers – not the total number of people. Nevertheless, Moses takes the census in order to determine the population in preparation for dividing up the land. Thus this census looks forward into the books of Joshua and Judges as well as later material within Numbers, especially the legal machinations necessary to aid the daughters of Zelophehad (see chs. 27 and 36).

26:57–62 No Land Assignment for the Levites

Continuing the comparison with the census taken in chapter 1, one sees a similarity in that the Levites do not receive an inheritance among the Israelite tribes. Although the census in chapter 26 has an ambiguous purpose – counting soldiers early on, then talking about the division of the land later – the Levites again prove to be an exception. Whereas Moses counts men twenty years of age and older among the other tribes, he counts Levites who are one month of age and older. The commentary notes at various other points the differences in the age requirements for Levites (see, for example, 3:14–20; 4:21–28; 4:34–35; 8:23–26).

Before arriving at the number 23,000 for the Levites, the text takes special care to note the genealogy of Aaron, Moses, and Miriam. Interestingly, the three leaders do not appear in birth order, for Miriam is older than Moses. In addition, the text refers to Nadab and Abihu, who were killed by God for offering "unauthorized fire." As noted in the commentary on Numbers 3:1–4, Leviticus 10:1–2 describe this sin by Aaron's sons and its punishment. Neither Leviticus 10 nor Numbers 26 devote much space to the description of this sin, which indicates that the priestly writers behind the two books apparently accepted the righteousness of this judgment (see Ps 51:4). In addition, the genealogies here reference another book in the Pentateuch, Genesis – as with the parenthetical comment noted above regarding the deaths of Er and Onan, the sons of Judah (26:19). Such divisions may have come along rather late in the development of Israel's literary saga; nevertheless, for those reading the final form of the text, they hold certain significance.

According to Miller and Hayes, the four groups mentioned in verse 58 "may or may not have originally been regarded as Levites."[9] Two of the names here correspond to town names in the southern part of Judah: Libnah (with the Libnites) and Hebron (the Hebronites). Hebron, in fact, serves as the first capital of David's growing kingdom while he engages in his civil war with the House of Saul (see 2 Sam 5:5; 1 Chr 29:27). The Mushites and the Korahites appear elsewhere in the biblical tradition, the latter in the context of a rebellion that threatens to wipe them out. They do not go completely extinct, however, as testified by the authorship of several of the Psalms (e.g. Pss 42, 44–49, 84–85, 88). The Mushites, according to Miller and Hayes, may have had a more direct connection to Moses.

26:63–65 Conclusion

The conclusion to the second census makes a startling claim: none of the Israelites counted here also numbered "among those counted by Moses and Aaron the priest when they counted the Israelites in the Desert of Sinai" (v. 64). This statement cannot be taken seriously, for if true, it would seem to double the number of Israelites who journeyed with God in the desert. As noted throughout the commentary, however, any doubt regarding the accuracy of the numbers in Numbers does not call into question the ultimate function of the story as Israel's saga, a story defining national identity. As part of such a story, these three verses look ahead to the next chapter in the saga, along with the previous discussion of the division of the land (see above on vv. 52–56).

The principal contribution of this text to the ongoing narrative is the introduction of Caleb and Joshua (v. 65). As noted above, 13:1–14:10 tells the story of how Caleb and Joshua (who is called Hoshea in the earlier story) try, unsuccessfully, to convince the other spies and the rest of the people that the land is ripe for the taking. They receive a reward from God for their faithfulness, but the reward is truly bittersweet: though they may be happy for themselves, they must grieve that their compatriots – including Moses (see 27:12–14) – will not get there with them.

---

9. Miller and Hayes, *History of Ancient Israel*, 106.

Numbers 21:4–36:13

27:1–11 THE DAUGHTERS OF ZELOPHEHAD, PART ONE

At several points in the commentary (most recently in 26:33), we learn that Zelophehad had only daughters. All of those previous hints find their resolution here and in the final chapter of Numbers (ch. 36). Certainly, ancient Israelite society was patriarchal, as the story of Zelophehad's daughters illustrates very well. The parenthetical note in 26:33 (which is reiterated in 1 Chr 7:15, as noted above) sets up the extraordinary legal decision that these circumstances call upon Moses to make.

Zelophehad's daughters approach Moses and lay out the preliminary matters of their case in an interesting fashion. On the one hand, they claim that their father did not participate in the rebellion led by the Korahites (see chs. 16–17). On the other hand, they accuse their father of sin. They do not explicitly link Zelophehad's sins with the fact that he only has daughters. Though the patriarchal context would seem to dictate such a link, perhaps the daughters do not make this link because that would identify them as a curse from God rather than a blessing. Psalm 127:3–5 indicates that children (NIV) are a blessing from the LORD. The Hebrew there says "sons," and though it could refer to children of both genders, the simile of arrows in a warrior's quiver (v. 4) employs a clear phallic symbol, which suggests sons as a greater blessing. Moreover, the oft-repeated note that Zelophehad had only daughters tends in this direction as well.

After the daughters make their case, Moses consults with God. In the ANE context, lawgivers such as Hammurabi in Babylonia and Moses in Israel often appear as the direct representatives of a deity. Though one could say that God gives the law – for God, in fact, serves as the ultimate source of the ruling – the tradition regards the human leader, who stands in this important representative position, as the one who makes the law. This particular case appears to be a perfect example of what biblical scholarship has come to describe as "casuistic law," or a law that employs conditional statements.[10] These laws have a form like this: If such and such happens, do this; if such and such does not happen, do this instead. Thus, the case here runs in this way: first, if a man has no sons, but only daughters, then give the inheritance to the daughters; second, if he does not have any children, then give the inheritance to his brothers; third, if he does not have any brothers, then give the inheritance to his uncles; fourth, if he has no sons, no daughters, no brothers, and no uncles, the inheritance

---

10. See Alt, "The Origins of Israelite Law," 101–171.

remains within the clan. All of this takes place so that the name of the dead man will not fade away in Israel, as Zelophehad's daughters plead (v. 4).

27:12–23 MOSES LOOKS TO THE FUTURE

In the final two sections of chapter 27, Moses looks toward the future of the children of Israel. The commentary above notes that chapter 20 witnesses the removal of all three of the leaders who brought the Israelites out of Egypt: Miriam dies at the beginning of the chapter (v. 1); Aaron dies at the end (vv. 22–29); in the middle, Moses commits the sin that precludes his own journey into the Promised Land (vv. 9–13). Here, that judgment finally comes to realization. With Moses removed, the community requires a new leader. The second of the two sub-units here describes the selection of the new generation of leadership in the person of Joshua, son of Nun, who will lead the children of Israel over the Jordan. It will fall to Moses, in a manner of speaking, to ordain him for this responsibility.

27:12–14 You Shall Not Go There

The African-American civil rights leader, Dr. Martin Luther King Jr., who was assassinated in the early evening of April 4, 1968 in Memphis, Tennessee, compared his position as a leader resisting the power of the white establishment with Moses leading his people to the edge of Canaan, but not being able to cross over. In a sermon entitled, "I Have Been to the Mountaintop," which King delivered less than twenty-four hours before he died, he seems in hindsight almost to have predicted his death. As King's biographer Stephen B. Oates claims: "Many who heard the 'Mountaintop' speech were convinced that King had a premonition of death."[11] Yet the particular image of Moses being denied entry into the Promised Land appears in King's preaching both near the beginning as well as at the end of his public career. Richard Lischer notes a key change of phrase between two iterations of this motif in King's preaching: "The prophecy with which he concluded 'The Birth' in 1957 he repeated almost verbatim the night before he was assassinated. In April 1957 he said, 'Moses might not get to see Canaan.' In April 1968, with his destiny bearing down on him, he said, '*I* may not get there with you.'"[12] Many Asians

---

11. Stephen B. Oates, *Let the Trumpet Sound: The Life of Martin Luther King Jr.* (New York: Penguin Mentor, 1985), 468.
12. Richard Lisher, *The Preacher King: Martin Luther King Jr. and the Word That Moved America*, Kindle Edition (New York: Oxford University Press, 1995), 211–212.

living in similarly oppressive circumstances could take inspiration from the way Dr. King used this text in his preaching.

In terms of the text itself, the introduction above (and elsewhere in the commentary) notes the power shift away from the first-generation Israelite leaders, which takes place in chapter 20. In 20:12–13, God tells Aaron and Moses that they will not go into Canaan because of their sin at the waters of Meribah. Later, in Numbers 27:14, the narrator's parenthetical comment gives this place a slightly different name: Meribah Kadesh. This difference does not appear large, since in chapter 20, the narrator mentions Kadesh in connection with Meribah, noting that the Israelites camped there after Miriam's death (see v. 1) and also that Moses sent messengers from there to the king of Edom just after the incident with the rock (see v. 14). Yet the two-word phrase, "Meribah Kadesh," appears only here and at Deuteronomy 32:51 in the Pentateuch. Two references to this place, both within the context of boundary markers, occur in Ezekiel – one at 47:19 and the other at 48:28. Both of these come within the context of the idealized restoration of the land, thus establishing positive connotations over against the negative ones connected to Meribah here (see, for example, Ps 81:7 and 95:8).

27:15–23 Appointment of Joshua

At the end of the second census of the army in chapter 26, verse 65 says that only "Caleb son of Jepunneh and Joshua son of Nun" of the Exodus generation are left to enter into the Promised Land. Earlier, in 13:8, among the list of the spies, Joshua's name appears with the alternate spelling "Hoshea." Later in that same chapter (13:16), the narrator reports that Moses gives him the name Joshua. "Hoshea," which means something like, "he will save," will also be the name of the first (in canonical, though not chronological, order) of the Minor Prophets.

The name Joshua, which means more specifically, "the LORD will save," will appear again in the Aramaic name of Jesus, Yeshua. In fact, the Greek NT (Luke 3:29, Acts 7:45, and Heb 4:8) spells Joshua in precisely the same way as it spells Jesus. In spite of this connection between Jesus' name and Joshua's name (see especially Matt 1:21), it makes little sense to discredit the name Jesus for the Second Person of the Trinity in favor of the supposedly more original "Yeshua." A student once informed me about a pastor who frequently ranted about this issue, arguing that use of the name "Jesus" was sinful, because "Yeshua" was the Son of God's real name. Sometimes it is best simply to disengage from an argument, especially when your dialogue partner will neither offer evidence for her position nor listen respectfully to alternative positions.

This section of chapter 27 details Joshua's appointment to leadership. From the first two verses of the passage, it becomes clear that Moses properly defers the decision to God. A parallel text in Deuteronomy 31:1–8 tells the story a bit differently. There, Moses tells the Israelites what God has decided about who shall become their leader (Deut 31:3). Here, the text details Joshua's ordination ritual, so to speak. One should not make too much of these differences, nor of the fact that later in the saga, the book of Joshua does not record a similar story about Joshua passing on leadership to someone else.

A much better strategy for interpreting this text flows directly out of the statement in verse 20, where God commands Moses to give Joshua some of his authority "so the whole Israelite community will obey him." This recalls Moses' statement in 11:29, "I wish that all the LORD's people were prophets and that the LORD would put his spirit on them." Ironically, Joshua son of Nun, here appointed as Moses' successor and given a measure of his spirit, alerts Moses in chapter 11 to the prophesying activities of Eldad and Medad and asks Moses to "restrain them" (v. 28). The commentary on that passage mentions the intertextual traces that this idea shares with Joel 2, Mark 9, and 1 Corinthians 12. The commentary also notes that, theologically, a reduction in the spirit of God given to Moses does not represent a reduction after all. In the present context, God tells Moses to give Joshua some of Moses' own spirit, so that he will have credibility with the people (v. 20). With this statement, we find at least two more intertextual traces. Looking backward, when God calls Moses to lead the Israelites out of Egypt, Moses is concerned with his own weaknesses, though God counters all his objections (see Exod 3:11–4:17). Looking forward, when Joshua assumes the mantle of leadership in Joshua 1, the people affirm God's choice by saying, "Just as we fully obeyed Moses, so we will obey you" (Josh 1:17).[13]

The final verses of chapter 27 detail how Moses is to ordain Joshua (vv. 21–23). The text emphasizes the role of the priest in commissioning the leader. This principle operates throughout Israel's history as recorded in the Bible: the responsibility of ordaining the political leader falls upon the spiritual leader. Though this does not come through explicitly in the period of the judges, it certainly pertains once Israel takes on a monarchy, especially with the prophet/priest Samuel, who anoints the first two legitimate kings of Israel. The text

---

13. For in Num 27, Deut 31, and Josh 1, this transition has always been God's choice.

also notes that the "whole assembly" witnesses Joshua's commission (v. 22). While at various times the commentary warns against a too-easy leap toward application, this particular point has relevance for continued practice in setting apart leaders in the church: the people must be present and must, in a way, give their assent to the appointment of the leaders who are set over them. In a contemporary ordination ritual, the one who appoints the new leader does not necessarily need to step away. Similarly, after Eleazar ordains Joshua, the priest continues on in his priestly role. Both will share the spiritual and political/military leadership, though the latter will rise to prominence with the continuation of the saga in the book of Joshua. Just as Moses ordains Eleazar to succeed Aaron upon his death, so now Eleazar ordains Joshua to succeed Moses, even though Moses has not yet departed the scene.

28:1–29:40 RULES FOR OFFERINGS

This bit of legal material concerns rules for the various offerings that Israelites will make either in the tabernacle or, later, in the Temple. The book of Leviticus has a similar list of offerings in chapters 1 through 7. While the list there contains only five different offerings, there are eight here. This probably reflects nothing of significance other than the slight differences in tradition that one might expect in such a diverse phenomenon as ancient Israelite worship. The commentary alludes to the existence of such diversity within the community, which is reflected, for example, in the disputes over leadership found in chapters 12, 16, and 17.

Chapters 28 and 29 detail these offerings in a particular and rather logical order. First, the daily burnt offering and the Sabbath offering take place on a regular basis, either every day or at the end of each week. Second, the New Moon Offering takes place at the beginning of each month (ancient Israel, like many countries in Asia, followed a lunar calendar). Finally, the Israelites are to bring the other five offerings once per year at particular times. The ordering here assumes that the new year begins in the fall, as current Jewish practice also dictates. (See, by way of contrast, Exod 12:2, which presumes that the new year begins in the spring by associating Passover with the first month of the year.)

28:1–8 Daily Burnt Offering

God instructs the Israelites to bring the daily burnt offering, as the name implies, every day. This offering consists of: two unblemished lambs, each a year old, one offered at dawn, one at twilight; approximately one and one-half kilograms of flour, mixed together with one liter of oil; approximately 250 milliliters of fermented wine (literally, "strong drink"). Recognizing the great expense of such an offering, the Torah also provides alternatives for poorer worshippers. A poor person can substitute two doves or two pigeons for the lamb (see Lev 5:7; 12:8; 14:21–23).

When Jesus overturns the tables in the Temple, he likely has an exploitative system, where unscrupulous dealers cheat the poor, in mind. Moreover, Jesus intends to overturn the sacrificial system himself. Leroy Andrew Huizenga writes: "the Matthean Jesus' action in the temple seems to be a prophetic action portending the end of the temple-based sacrificial system to be replaced by himself as a sacrifice."[14] Huizenga quotes Jacob Neusner with approval, who notes that this "action will have provoked astonishment, since it will have called the very simple fact that the daily whole-offering effected atonement and brought expiation for sin, and God has so instructed Moses in the Torah."[15]

Though Christianity does not practice a daily burnt offering because Jesus replaces this requirement, we can still glean wisdom by studying the old practices. For indeed, daily connection with God remains important for Christians, and the overturning of an old tradition carries with it a substitution of something new. To put this in biblical terms, the book of Ecclesiastes blows apart all human pretensions to newness: "What has been will be again, and what has been done will be done again; there is nothing new under the sun" (Eccl 1:9). In current Christian practice, whatever replaces the function of the daily offering depends on the particular branch of Christianity that one professes. For many Roman Catholics, daily attendance at mass might serve this function. For Protestants, daily devotions and prayer might do the same.

28:9–10 Sabbath Offering

The commentary for the passage on the lamps or candles used in the tabernacle (8:1–4) notes a Talmudic provision which prohibited use of a seven-branched candlestick (menorah) anywhere but in the Temple. After the Romans destroyed the Temple in 70 AD (incidentally, long before the creation of the Talmud), the menorah became a symbol for Judaism, and in particular the hope for the restoration of the Temple. Menorahs that appear in synagogues throughout the world symbolically reenact this hope. The place of the Torah

---

14. Leroy A. Huizenga, *The New Isaac: Tradition and Intertextuality in the Gospel of Matthew* (Leiden, Netherlands: Brill, 2012), 290.
15. Neusner, "The Absoluteness of Christianity," quoted in Huizenga, *The New Isaac*.

at the center of Jewish worship serves this symbolic role as well: though the sacrificial system ended with the destruction of the Temple, Jews continue to remain faithful to God as they await the consummation of their hopes.

Verse 10 in this passage notes that the Sabbath offering does not completely supersede the daily burnt offerings described in verses 1–8. In other words, at least according to this passage, the daily offering does not end on the seventh day (unlike other works prohibited on the Sabbath). This means that the Torah adds the already costly daily offering to an even costlier Sabbath offering (the Sabbath offering is double the daily offering, which means that on the Sabbath, one would be offering three times the daily offering).

The commentary on the lamps in 8:1–4 also notes the issue about the day of the week on which one observes Sabbath. God commands the Israelites to set aside the seventh day three times in the Torah within various lists of the Ten Commandments (Exod 20, Deut 5, and perhaps Lev 19) along with various other allusions to it (Exod 31:15, for one example). For the present purpose, we will deal with these three main Sabbath commands in the order of what seems to be the most theoretical to the most practical. Here, the terms "theoretical" and "practical" refer to how the particular instance justifies the keeping of Sabbath.

In Leviticus 19:30, one finds a theoretical instruction to keep the Sabbath, founded simply on the identity of God. This occurs in the context of several laws (often misleadingly called "miscellaneous laws" by English translations). Exodus 20:8–11 grounds the Sabbath law within the fabric of creation. This alludes to the first creation story in Genesis 1:1–2:4, particularly God's keeping rest on the seventh day "after all the work he had done in creating" (Gen 2:2b, AT). Deuteronomy 5:12–15 seems to be the most practical, for this passage sets the Sabbath commandment not merely in the context of God's name, nor because of what God has done, but in what the Israelites find themselves able to do because they have been freed from Egypt. In other words, Deuteronomy 5 grounds the commandment to keep the Sabbath in the people's freedom from slavery because of God's liberating action. Jewish rabbi and author Harold S. Kusher writes the following about this most practical basis for keeping Sabbath: "The first reason the Sabbath is special is as a symbol and reminder of our having been freed from slavery in Egypt. Slaves have to work all the time; free men and women can take a day off for their own pursuits . . . That is what we do when we keep the Sabbath as a special day . . . We declare that . . . we are in fact not slaves. We belong to no one but ourselves."[16]

The majority of Christians do not practice Sabbath *per se*, since Christian worship generally takes place on the first day of the week (in English, "Sunday," or in Spanish, "*Domingo*," or "Lord's Day"). The earliest Christians, having come out of Judaism, observed both the Jewish Sabbath (Saturday or, in Tagalog, *Sabado*) and the Christian Lord's Day, especially since the latter functioned as a weekly celebration of the resurrection of Jesus. Incidentally, the grounding of the Sabbath in God's act of liberation (per Deut 5) has the most relevance, since the resurrection of Jesus is God's strongest act of liberation from humanity's greatest enemies, sin and death.

Some Christians, unfortunately, believe that others sin when they worship on Sunday instead of Saturday. This is a grave misunderstanding, for as Rabbi Kushner maintains, the day of the week does not matter so much as the act of setting one day aside for God: only free women and men may accomplish this. Most importantly, only God can bring about the freedom that enables women and men to dedicate one of their days to giving glory to God. How one does this should be determined by the individual in conversation with a faith community, but the practice of keeping Sabbath stands near the heart of the biblical tradition, since God's acts of liberation undoubtedly stand as the most important ways in which we can know God.

28:11–15 New Moon Offerings

Continuing the movement toward less frequent offerings, the text turns to the new moon offerings at the beginning of each month. Judaism, like other religious and cultural traditions originating primarily in the East, has followed a lunar-based calendar for most of its long existence. Christianity, though it has become the predominant Western religion, also follows a lunar calendar in determining when its principal holidays fall in the year. Thus, the date of Easter is connected to the first new moon following the spring equinox.[17]

The fact that the Jewish month always begins on the new moon plays a role in Rabbi Kushner's explication of Jewish living for modern times. He writes: "what are the chances that a solar eclipse will fall on the first day of a

---

16. Harold S. Kushner, *To Life!: A Celebration of Jewish Being and Thinking* (New York: Warner, 1994), 95–96.
17. See below for more regarding connections to Passover, as well as ongoing discussions about fixing the date of Easter to a particular day on the calendar (for example, the second Sunday in April).

Jewish month . . .? Solar eclipses happen when . . . the side of the moon that is turned to us is totally dark. That is a new moon, and the Jewish month would be beginning."[18]

In the text itself, verse 15 explicitly says that the daily offering is not to be suspended on the first day of the month, as with the Sabbath offering. Thus, the large offering given at the beginning of the month (two young bulls, one ram, and seven male lambs – the first time the text specifies male lambs) is to be added to the regular daily offering – and even to the Sabbath offering if the new moon and the Sabbath coincide. Surely, practice would make provision for those too poor to afford such lavish offerings, though one could not claim a poverty that was not real in order to get away from making the offerings. (One may say the same thing; incidentally, for tithes and offerings that Christians bring to church!) A further additional offering takes the form of a lamb, set aside for a sin offering, an idea which will occur again in connection with the Passover ritual (see 28:16–25 below).

The months of the Jewish year do not have names in the Bible, but are simply called first, second, third, and so on.[19] In post-biblical practice, names coming from the Babylonian calendar, adopted by the returning exiles, attached themselves to the months of the Jewish year. Occasionally, the Jewish year has thirteen rather than twelve months in order to compensate for the greater length of the lunar month within the context of the solar year. As noted above, the spring New Year assumed by this chapter of Numbers includes Passover in the first month, even though the New Year celebration itself (and the change in the number of the year) occurs in the fall with the festival of Rosh Hashanah. The names of the months of the Jewish year, with their approximate secular equivalents, are as follows: Nisan (March–April; 30 days), Iyar (April–May; 29 days), Sivan (May–June; 30 days), Tammuz (June–July; 29 days), Av (July–August; 30 days), Elul (August–September; 29 days), Tishri (September–October; 30 days), Cheshvan (October–November; 29 or 30 days), Kislev (November–December; 30 or 29 days), Tevet (December–January, 29 days), Shevat (January–February; 30 days), and Adar (February–March; 29 days). In leap years, an additional month, also called Adar (sometimes Adar I) is added between Shevat and Adar (II).

---

18. Kushner, *To Life!*, 90.
19. In current practice, the Jewish year follows the movement of the earth around the sun, creating a moveable calendar, since approximately 12.4 lunar months occur in one solar year.

28:16–25 Passover

As of this writing, discussions are ongoing between principal leaders of the Roman Catholic, Anglican, and Eastern Orthodox families of churches to fix the celebration of Easter on the second Sunday of April.[20] I am personally unsettled on this question. On the one hand, it would perhaps more strongly indicate that Easter commemorates a historical event – along with other historical events, such as the Philippine Independence on June 12. On the other hand, general agreement on this question is unlikely, since, as the Roman Catholic Second Vatican Council recognized, the Eastern churches – not to mention the Protestants – lack central authority to make such decisions universal.[21] These difficulties aside, the proposals so far have been careful to keep Easter after Jewish Passover. This is an essential theological connection. The Gospel writers unanimously affirm the symbolism of Jesus as the Passover lamb, both as the ultimate act of redemption from sin – mirroring the connection of the first Passover lamb with the liberation from Egypt – and also as a proclamation of Jesus as the final sacrifice for sin.

In the Torah, when the Passover is established, God tells Moses and Aaron that the month in which this miracle occurred should become the first month of the year for the Israelites (see Exod 12:2). Even considering the apparent difference between the spring and autumn New Year (see above), counting the month in which Passover occurs as the first month of the year makes an important theological point. The Israelites' new life as a free people begins with the first and most important act of God on their behalf. One must remember that the events that the Passover ritual commemorates constitute twin miracles. First, God spared the Israelites' children during the visit of the angel of death, for the angel of death "passed over" the houses of the Israelites (Exod

---

20. The Second Vatican Council of the Roman Catholic Church, among others, proposed such a fixed date for Easter. First, in the "Constitution on the Sacred Liturgy," the Fathers wrote that the Council "would not object if the feast of Easter were assigned to a particular Sunday of the Gregorian Calendar, provided that those whom it may concern give their consent, especially the brethren who are not in communion with the Apostolic See" (Walter M. Abbott and Joseph Gallager, eds., *The Documents of Vatican II* [New York: Guild Press, 1966], 177). As an aside, one should not miss the final clause of this sentence, which reveals the far more positive view of official Catholic teaching regarding Protestants than many Protestants, particularly evangelicals, have regarding the Catholics. Perhaps we could learn something. In another document, the "Decree on the Eastern Churches," the fathers mention the possibility of a fixed date in passing: "Until such time as all Christians desirably concur on a fixed day for the celebration of Easter . . . it is left to the Patriarchs or supreme authority of a place to reach a unanimous agreement . . . on a single Sunday for the observance of Easter" (ibid., 382).
21. Ibid., 382, n. 43.

12:13). Second, God brought about the liberation of the entire community from slavery in Egypt.

This stands as the principal reason that the sacrifice of Jesus is connected to Passover: not only did it occur at the same time of the year, but it also marked both continuity and discontinuity with how God had previously acted toward Israel. As for continuity, the connection between Holy Week and Passover makes the same point about liberation being the most important act of God. As for discontinuity, Holy Week and Easter bring about, for Christians, a new way of thinking about God. The breaking of the once close relationship between Judaism and Christianity – for all of the first generation and most of the second generation of Christians were also Jews – makes this new understanding necessary. As Christianity became primarily a Gentile religion, some Christians no longer celebrated Passover, at least in the same way as the earliest Christians. However, that original connection needs to continue, especially since Jesus died during the time of the Passover.[22]

As previously noted, the other offerings do not end even during special times like Passover (see v. 23). Indeed, the initial contents of the Passover offering (two bulls, one ram, and seven male lambs) duplicate that which the Israelites offer at the beginning of each month. In addition, three-tenths of an ephah of flour accompanies the bulls, two-tenths the ram, and one-tenth with each of the lambs. The total amount of flour thus amounts to one and one-half ephot (the plural of ephah). As a final note on the celebration of the Passover, God commands the Israelites to observe the seventh day of the Passover (which would have been a Sabbath) and not to do any work on that day. In modern-day Jewish practice, the Passover offers a time to reflect on what God has done for the people in the past, an important ritual that occurs in many religious traditions.

28:26–31 First Fruits

The offering of first fruits coincides with the Festival of Weeks, also known as Pentecost, which falls in the calendar fifty days after Passover. In fact, this calendar location gives the holiday (in Hebrew *shavuout*, or "weeks") the name Pentecost. Thus, the six verses describing this offering hold tremendous

---

22. I have spent a great deal of time thinking about this, and my opinion has shifted even during the writing of this commentary. When I submitted the first draft, I was against the idea of fixing the date of Easter. As I was editing the first draft and studying the question again, however, I noted that the proposed fixed date of Easter will always occur after Passover, and sometimes during Passover. This means that what I have called an "essential theological connection" will not be severed.

potential for intertextual investigation. First, one may look to the ritual detailed in Deuteronomy 26, which includes instructions for a lengthy historical recital of what God has done for Israel in the past. Remembering God's prior good acts on behalf of the people plays a large role in the biblical tradition.

Second, the offering of first fruits in the context of Pentecost also connects to the book of Ruth. The internal setting for the main events of this book is Bethlehem during the time of the barley harvest (Ruth 1:22). This literary setting causes many Jewish communities to read the book of Ruth during the Pentecost celebration. Furthermore, one notices a thematic link between Numbers 28:26–31, Deuteronomy 26:1–11, and Ruth in that all three celebrate the provision of God in bringing people through adverse circumstances.

All of the sacrifices in Numbers, as argued above, demonstrate the Israelites' command over their time and their subsequent ability to devote time to God: thus in this text, the Israelites cannot do any work on the day of the first fruits offering. In addition, as also noted above, the regular burnt offering given every day does not stop when it comes time for the first fruits offering. Thus, the special offering does not replace the regular obligation placed on all the Israelites. The inclusion of a goat "to make atonement for you" (v. 30) recalls Yom Kippur, or the Day of Atonement (see below), on which the high priest makes a similar offering on behalf of all the people.

A final intertextual connection with this text reaches into the NT and one particularly momentous day of Pentecost (see Acts 2). True enough, the experience of the apostles speaking in the languages of all the visitors to Jerusalem about the good things of God does not have a particular relationship to the Feast of Weeks/Pentecost or the offering of first fruits beyond a temporal setting. However, the thematic connection of God providing a new way of life comes through quite strongly. The miracle of the visitors' hearing – for it is a miracle of hearing rather than a miracle of speech – communicates that God has the ability to do the impossible – or what appears to humans to be impossible – in order to accomplish God's overriding purposes.

29:1–6 Rosh Hashanah

People often refer to Rosh Hashanah, or the Jewish New Year, as the feast of trumpets, partly because of the instruction to sound trumpets in 29:1. As noted above, the list of offerings in chapters 28 and 29 assumes a new year that begins in the fall, in accordance with modern practice, even though some say that the secular New Year and the Jewish New Year both belong in the calendar. The number of the year changes with Rosh Hashanah. Rosh

Hashanah also begins the period known as the High Holy Days, a ten-day set of observances, prayer, and repentance that culminates in Yom Kippur, the holiest day of the Jewish year.

As we have noted in all of these offerings, at no time did the Israelites, according to this text, receive a release from the obligation of the daily offerings. Moreover, since Rosh Hashanah occurs at the beginning of the month, the text carefully notes that the daily offerings and the new moon offerings do not stop on Rosh Hashanah, so adding them all together would be quite expensive. Each obligation remains distinct, so that there can be no question about which offering satisfies which obligation, even though many of the obligations require a similar amount of sacrifice. The whole complex of offerings presents a picture that would have made sense to an Israelite. Hence any analogies and comparisons to offerings and obligations for other religious systems should be made with a measure of humility and uncertainty.

29:7–11 Yom Kippur

Coming ten days after Rosh Hashanah, Yom Kippur is without doubt the most solemn holy day of the year. Elsewhere in the Pentateuch, Leviticus 16 gives great detail about what should occur on this day. The details in the present text, by comparison, seem quite sparse. Though the contents of both Leviticus and Numbers largely stem from the so-called Priestly source, a comparison between the two accounts of the Day of Atonement (the English meaning of Yom Kippur) still yields important insights.

Both pastors and laypeople must recognize that the Bible – both the individual books and the collection as a whole – came together over many years (centuries, in the case of the OT) and was used, reused, altered, and preserved by countless thousands of people. The Bible began as oral stories, passed down through the generations for a thousand years or more, before finally being committed to writing, perhaps as early as the time of the United Monarchy (tenth century BC). When they were finally written down, some variations from the oral period were likely preserved in the different writings. One could say that one of these versions explains the other; or one could say – and this is the option I prefer – that the differences between them should be celebrated as evidence that God is able to work even through diverse human writings to accomplish his purposes. One should not expect every writing in the Bible to agree on every point. If agreement were the central concern, then why were both accounts of the Day of Atonement kept? In the NT, we would need to ask the same question about the four Gospels. Having different writings that disagree with each other from time to time does not harm the idea of God's inspiration of the Bible; in fact, it enhances it!

First, Leviticus 16 sets Yom Kippur in a definite narrative context, with God giving the instructions for this ritual "after the death of the two sons of Aaron when they approached the Lord" (Lev 16:1). In Leviticus 10, Nadab and Abihu meet their deaths at the Lord's hand for offering "unauthorized fire." Numbers 3:4 and 26:61, in the context of genealogical records, repeat this confusing phrase without offering any explanation. Numbers 29:7–11 leaves this story out, perhaps because it is difficult to understand.[23] Indeed, the overarching context for the list of offerings in Numbers only says that the Lord commands Moses to command the Israelites to offer these specific – and expensive – offerings at these specific times (see 28:1).

Second, Leviticus 16 notes an unusual command given to Aaron: he must not come into the most holy place at any time he wishes (v. 2); this may or may not mean that entrance is allowed only on the Day of Atonement. This injunction comes with the threat of death (v. 2). Now Aaron, as the Leviticus text reminds us, has just lost two of his sons, whom God killed apparently because "they approached the Lord" (v. 1). One can just imagine the fear Aaron must have felt upon hearing these words of Moses. This story seems to be yet another odd part of the OT that the NT writers felt they needed to explain away by noting that, just as Jesus was dying, the curtain separating the most holy place from the rest of the Temple was torn in two (see Matt 27:51, Mark 15:38, Luke 23:45, and especially the theological reflection in Heb 10:20). The curtain being torn away signaled not only that everyone would have access to God, but also that God could be accessed at any time. Again, Numbers 29:7–11 leaves all of these details to one side. If the Numbers text came later than the Leviticus text (not an assured possibility), then the summary version might have, at least in part, served to eliminate some of the more horrifying implications of Leviticus 16:1–2.

Third, Numbers 29 says nothing about the high priest serving as the representative for all the people (by way of comparison, see Lev 16:32–33). The high priest plays a central role in the Leviticus 16 version, not least because

---

23. This is a speculation on my part. Numbers 29 could have been written either before or after Numbers 3 and 26, since the biblical texts were not necessarily written in the order we have them, but were arranged by an editor. If Numbers 29 was not written last, then the bit about the unauthorized fire was not left out simply because it was confusing, but for another reason entirely. More likely, these three genealogies are more-or-less independent traditions, which the editors have brought together and arranged in just this way for an overarching purpose.

the instructions came to the high priest, Aaron, and, through him, to all his successors. Because Leviticus 16 concerns itself with what Aaron should do, it spends a great deal of time describing precisely what Aaron should wear, how he should take a bath before putting on his ritual clothing, how many animals he should bring for sin offerings (and for whom), and so on. Numbers 29, as noted above, simply stipulates the offerings that worshippers (who apparently do not need the assistance of a high priest) should bring. Finally, Numbers 29:11 reminds the Israelites that the required offerings on Yom Kippur do not suspend the required offerings they are to bring to the holy place every day. However, in a twist not yet seen in chapters 28 and 29, tradition designed the calendar so that Yom Kippur never falls either on the day before Sabbath or on the Sabbath itself. This custom prevents two successive days on which one cannot prepare food or bury the dead. Thus, the other two regularly scheduled offerings – the New Moon offerings and the Sabbath offerings – will never coincide with the Day of Atonement. These further cement the character of this day as one like no other.

The fourth and final difference between the Leviticus 16 and Numbers 29 versions of Yom Kippur laws concerns the scapegoat. While verse 11 of the Numbers passage simply says that the Israelites must include a goat for a sin offering, Leviticus spends a great deal of time describing what should be done to the goat (vv. 20–22). Incidentally, the Israelites bring two goats forward in Leviticus (vv. 6–10), while only one in Numbers (v. 11). In Leviticus, the high priest slaughters one of these goats (vv. 15–17), apparently the same one offered in Numbers 29:11, and then sends a live one out to Azazel (vv. 20–22). The NIV follows the Septuagint and translates this phrase "as a scapegoat" (Lev 16:10). Azazel may have been some kind of desert-dwelling demon, though no extra-biblical Jewish evidence exists to help us decide. Numbers 29 avoids this problem not only by deleting the reference to the scapegoat, but also by stipulating the presence of only one goat, slaughtered for a sin offering. This interpretation assumes that the shorter text of Numbers 29 came later, which is usually not the case. However, this reading remains plausible in light of the Septuagint's difficulty in understanding "Azazel" in Leviticus 16; deleting all reference to the confusing ritual may have seemed an easier option.

29:12–40 Sukkot

The Hebrew word *sukkot* may be translated in various ways in English: booths, tabernacles, or tents. The distinguishing feature of this holiday involves the practice of erecting temporary shelters near one's home. Israelite families live in these shelters during the days of the festival. This practice symbolically serves to reenact the experience of the people living in the desert. Doing this on a yearly basis helps the Israelites throughout successive generations to remember their journey with God in the desert, the story of which is told in the book of Numbers.

In light of this, the current text says nothing about this characteristic practice. Parallel versions of this festival exist in Leviticus 23:33–43 and Deuteronomy 16:13–17. Only Leviticus 23:42 specifically mentions the practice of living in booths, though all three versions emphasize rejoicing before the Lord (Lev 23:40; Num 29:12; Deut 16:14). The Leviticus version, in addition, adds a note about gathering branches to be used in rejoicing before the Lord (v. 40).

Here in Numbers 29, the focus remains on the offerings that the Israelites are to bring on each day of the festival. It is unique among the three versions in the level of detail given to the offerings, although Leviticus and Deuteronomy mention bringing in offerings of produce that has been gathered (Lev 23:39; Deut 16:10, 13, 15). The fact that the festival includes the harvesting of produce further indicates the connection between these offerings and the fruitfulness of the land. The size of the offerings begins with thirteen bulls, two rams, fourteen one-year-old male lambs, with the accompanying drink offerings that have already been detailed for other offerings discussed in this chapter (v. 13). On each of the successive days, the number of bulls to be offered reduces by one until, on the seventh day of the festival, they only offer seven bulls (v. 32). On the eighth and final day of the festival, only one bull is offered (v. 36). During all of this, as we have repeatedly seen, the daily burnt offerings, Sabbath offerings, and New Moon offerings continue. Certainly, at least one Sabbath would come along during the eight-day-long festival, though the New Moon Offering would only be a possibility.

All of the offerings given to God are burned, which solves a practical problem. Simply put: God is in heaven and cows are heavy. Therefore, in order to offer a cow (or sheep or goat or whatever) to God, it must be burned, and the smoke, moving upwards toward heaven, becomes the substance of the offering. Moreover, we have encountered the interesting phrase, "an aroma pleasing to the LORD" (v. 36), before in Numbers. It crops up thirty-nine other times in the Pentateuch as well. Of these, eighteen occur in Numbers, seventeen in Leviticus, three in Exodus, and one in Genesis. Only Deuteronomy does not use this phrase, which is an example of anthropomorphism – describing God in terms usually reserved for humans. In other words, if the sacrifices need to be pleasing for God to smell, God must have a nose. One must remember that this is symbolic and imaginary language, for the text does not say that God *does* have a nose with which to smell pleasing offerings. Rather, it simply describes, in terms humans would understand, one of the values of making sacrifices. God enjoys – indeed, one could say that God takes genuine delight in – the obedience of God's followers. Perhaps doing what God wants should not be seen as an obligation, but as an opportunity to delight in a relationship in which God also delights.

30:1–16 VOWS

A series of instructions on vows occupies chapter 30. Throughout the OT, this subject appears repeatedly. In one instance, the judge Jephthah makes a vow before the Lord, which, as it turns out, has disastrous consequences for his only daughter (Judg 11:29–40). This story leads Gordon D. Fee and Douglas Stuart essentially to charge Jephthah with child abuse. They write that the text presents Jephthah "as rash and self-centered, a man for whom a vow is more important than a daughter."[24] This statement fails, in my opinion, to take proper account of the Middle Eastern/Asian context of the story.[25] Jephthah's vow supports his own ongoing self-interest; he attempts to manipulate God by what he promises, and great suffering comes as a result. However, even though his vow costs him terribly – and, indeed, it represents an even greater cost to his daughter – he cannot turn away from it. Much later, the book of Deuteronomy warns, "If you make a vow to the LORD your God, do not hesitate to fulfill it, for the LORD your God will surely seek it from you, and guilt will come upon you" (Deut 23:21 [MT 22], AT). The sage whose collected teachings form the book of Ecclesiastes echoes this sentiment, indeed in even stronger terms: "Whenever you vow before God, do not hesitate to fulfill it, for God does not enjoy fools. Fulfill what you have vowed" (Eccl 5:4 [MT 3], AT).

The chapter goes on to contrast the vows of women and the vows of men. If a woman made a vow while still living in her father's house, the father could

---

24. Gordon D. Fee and Douglas Stuart, *How to Read the Bible Book by Book: A Guided Tour*, repr. (Manila: OMF Literature, 2002), 75–76.
25. As a Westerner, I came to a revelation in my teaching some years ago simply by looking at a map of Asia. There is no major body of water separating Israel on the extreme Western side of Asia from China on the extreme eastern side of Asia. Though "Asia," in my mind, meant primarily East Asia and Southeast Asia. While, of course, the cultures of ancient Israel and the modern-day Philippines, for example, are quite different, they seem to me to be far more like each other than ancient Israel is to the modern West.

cancel this vow if it were deemed to be rash (vv. 3–5). The text does not consider why fathers can negate daughters' vows but not sons' vows, since both daughters and sons can make foolish vows while young. The principle becomes even more interesting in verses 6–14, where the text says that the woman's husband also has the power to nullify her vows. This seems to denigrate women's religious expression more directly than the previous stipulation. According to verse 15, the husband will incur the guilt of an unfulfilled vow if he waits too long to express his disapproval of his wife's vow. Again, the text does not explain the difference between men and women on this point. It is perhaps too easy to write this off to the patriarchal context of Numbers. If the power to nullify a woman's vow rests with either her father or her husband, this is a point against her religious freedom. Yet on the opposite side, this whole complex of material places a significant limitation on men – who, regardless of their age or mental ability, cannot get out of a vow to the Lord. Moreover, because men are given the ability to nullify women's rash vows, they must fulfill this responsibility carefully, particularly husbands. In sum, those who make vows will do well to heed the warnings of the Ecclesiastes sage: "Do not be quick with your mouth, do not be hasty in your heart to utter anything before God. God is in heaven and you are on earth, so let your words be few" (Eccl 5:2).

31:1–54 REVENGE AGAINST THE MIDIANITES

Chapter 31 details a battle against the Midianites in five scenes, which go back and forth between two narratives: the first concerns the battle (scenes one and four), and the second concerns a sin that the soldiers commit at the end of the battle (scenes two and three). The fifth and final scene connects to both of these narratives. The first scene describes the battle itself, with the primary indicator being that this is God's war of revenge, not Moses' or Israel's (31:1–8). In the second scene, the soldiers commit a sin after the end of the battle and are caught (31:9–12). In the third scene, God judges the sin (31:13–24). In the fourth scene, the soldiers count the spoils taken in battle (31:25–47). In the fifth scene, the soldiers take some of the spoils and make an offering to God, presumably not only to celebrate their victory, but also to atone for the sin which they committed (31:48–54).

This story recalls the adultery that certain Israelite men commit with Midianite women earlier in Numbers (see 25:1–3). The priest Phineas, who is involved in this war against the Midianites (31:6), stops a plague, which has been sent as a punishment from God because of this adultery, by killing an Israelite man and a Midianite woman while they are having sex (25:7–8). Further on in Israel's story (Judg 6), the Midianites will appear again, this time as the oppressors, whom God allows to dominate Israel. In that story, the judge Gideon will rise up as the deliverer.

31:1–8 Description of the Battle

As noted above, the wording of the text makes it clear that this is God's battle. It does not belong either to Moses or Israel. Interpreters must keep this point firmly in mind when reading these texts, since the violence in these stories often turns people away from reading the OT. One should remember the contention of Steve Almond, cited above in a different context, that "we need not endorse the savagery of our holy book to recognize the beauty in its ideas."[26] In the modern world, bald militarism that disguises itself as faithfulness to the biblical mandate has created many problems. Such a militaristic worldview has brought about the deaths of many people – indeed, many more civilians than combatants.

When dealing with passages such as these, it is important to keep twin cautions in mind. First, we should not judge the ancient world by modern sensibilities. Even if the thoughts, ideals, and practices espoused by the biblical text (e.g. the acceptance of slavery) are judged wrong by modern standards, that does not mean that the Bible is wrong for all time; its ideas may well have represented the best thinking of its time.

This is, at heart, another way to state the "redemptive-movement" hermeneutical model proposed by William J. Webb. He describes this model as follows: "I encourage Christians to embrace the redemptive spirit of the text, which at times will mean that we must move beyond the *concrete specificity* of the Bible. Or, we must move beyond the *time-restricted elements* of the Bible. Or, we must be willing to venture beyond simply an *isolated* or *static* understanding of the Bible."[27] Webb's comments on slavery in the ancient world also prove helpful for the present point: "To call the biblical treatment of slaves 'abusive' in terms of the original culture would be anachronistic. Relative to the ancient culture many of these texts were in some measure progressive.

---

26. Almond, "Chanukah Your Hearts Out!", 40–41.
27. William J. Webb, "A Redemptive-Movement Model," in *Four Views on Moving Beyond the Bible to Theology*, ed. Gary T. Meadows, Counterpoints Bible and Theology Series (Grand Rapids: Zondervan, 2009), 215.

Nevertheless, the . . . practices [of slavery] are problematic and in need of movement toward an ultimate ethic."[28]

The second caution to keep in mind is that we should not allow the ancient world to judge what we do in the modern world without careful reflection. (For an example of this, see the topic box entitled "Marriage of Daughters in Nagaland, India" within the commentary for 36:1–12.) Just because the ancient people did or believed something does not mean that modern people should do or believe that same thing. Making such decisions involves clear and careful theological reflection – not only on the Bible, but also on the contemporary world. This means that, in some cases, scriptural teaching should be set aside as not entirely relevant, perhaps even damaging, in the present age.[29] This setting aside of a particular scriptural teaching must be done with great care. Indeed, the NT already provides a model in this regard in the way that Jesus sets aside laws regarding clean and unclean food (see Mark 7:14–23; Acts 10:9–16).

Returning to the text, Numbers 31 operates on the claim that the battle belongs to the Lord because the Lord ordered the battle. This statement is in line with the thought-world of the Bible, and therefore it is valid within the context of that world, even if one might wish to reject such a militarist view today. The fact that the battle belongs to the Lord also helps the interpreter clarify the excessive violence of this battle as indicated by verse 7. Oftentimes, when the Bible – or any other ancient document – claims that every one of the "bad guys" died, this may be an exaggeration of the claim that the "good guys" won the battle. A student from Papua New Guinea informed me in class that in his country, they often report the results of tribal fights in a similarly exaggerated manner. This phrase then speaks of a complete victory, whether or not the claim is true that everybody died. Balaam the prophet also counts among those "killed . . . with the sword" (v. 8). See the third section (31:13–24) for more about the death of this non-Israelite prophet.

---

28. Ibid., 225.
29. I recognize the difficulty this may pose for some evangelical readers. However, one could draw an analogy here to Islam. Islam has a doctrine called "abrogation," according to which a later text in the Holy Qur'an can set aside an earlier text. This doctrine is defined in Qur'an 2:106 and 16:101. One example of this is the prohibition of drinking alcohol by Muslims. An earlier revelation allowed this practice (2:219; 4:43), but a later revelation (5:90) completely banned it.

31:9–12 The Soldiers Sin

After winning the battle, the soldiers divide the spoils, as soldiers did in the ancient world. In this particular instance, the soldiers commit a sin by allowing some of the Midianites to live, specifically the women and children. The present text does not make the sin explicit, but the implicit reference goes back to 25:16–18, where God tells Moses that the Israelites must take total revenge upon the Midianites. That text also conflates the Moabites and Midianites. True enough, the Book of Balaam indicates an alliance of sorts between Moab and Midian, though chapter 25 only mentions the Midianites as those upon whom revenge must be taken for the incident at Baal Peor (see also 31:16 below).

One wonders whether the soldiers deserve blame for the sin Moses accuses them of in verse 15. Since Moses does not tell them that they must kill all of the Midianites, does Moses have the right to be so angry? On first glance, Moses seems to be trying to shift the responsibility for this sin to the soldiers (see v. 15). On closer inspection, however, the text does not say that the soldiers sinned by failing to carry out a command of total annihilation, which does occur, for example, in Joshua 7:1 (see more on this below).

31:13–24 Judgment upon the Sin

An interesting note at the end of the first section above concerns the death of Balaam the prophet (v. 8). This note reaches back to the lengthy Book of Balaam (chs. 22–24) and forward to verse 16 in the current section. Although Balaam does not directly curse the Israelites – having been prevented by the Lord from doing so – verse 16 accuses the slain prophet of having advised the women to entice "the Israelites to be unfaithful to the Lord in the Peor incident." The NT reuses this theme in Revelation 2:14, where following the advice of "Balaam" has led some of the Christians of Pergamum into sin. Thus Balaam, because he is a non-Israelite prophet, and even though God first uses him to bless Israel, ends up serving as a symbol of evil and treachery. The way later biblical texts reuse him in this way speaks not only to the vitality of the biblical traditions but also to the relative importance of Balaam in historical memory, even if the historical memory of the Israelites may not match the external evidence (such as the Deir 'Alla inscription, as discussed above in the introduction to the Book of Balaam, chs. 22–24).

Also, in the present text, neither Moses nor Eleazar directly instruct the Israelite soldiers to kill everyone (the women as well as the men). Yet such a command apparently lies behind Moses' accusatory question in verse 15, especially since the text reports in the previous verse that Moses is angry with the returning soldiers. Without asking the question, Moses already knows the answer. God tells Moses (see 25:16–18) that the offense of the Midianites will one day face vengeance, and the soldiers, having been given the opportunity to exact this revenge, fail to do so. As noted above, chapter 25 maintains some ambiguity regarding the nationality of the women with whom the Israelite men sinned (25:1 says Moabites, but 25:6 mentions a Midianite).

Throughout Israel's story, this will certainly not be the only time that the Israelites fail to execute properly God's commands with regard to either destroying all of the holy things in a place or killing all the members of a particular tribe. Joshua 7 reports the sin of Achan, in which Achan took some of the devoted things from Jericho. This sin causes the Israelites to lose the first battle against the city of Ai, even though Ai is much smaller than the already conquered Jericho. Moving further in the story, God rejects King Saul for, among other things, showing mercy to the Amalekite King Agag (1 Sam 15). In both of these latter cases, explicit instructions are given to the Israelite army (Josh 6:19) and to Saul (1 Sam 15:3). One wonders, then, whether this failure might not belong on Moses' record! Though the text does not speculate on this point, later interpreters have the freedom to do so.

In any event, Moses decides to "purge the evil" from the camp. This phrase, which is not used in Numbers, is a favorite of Deuteronomy (where it is used nine times), and it is also used once in Joshua. Thus Moses issues a new command: kill the boys and every woman who has had sex with a man, but spare virgin girls (vv. 17–18). Interpreters should not miss the simple contradiction between God's command given to Moses in 25:16–18 and what Moses commands the soldiers here. While it is true that the virgin girls could not have been involved in the Baal of Peor incident in chapter 25, this truism whitewashes the contradiction between the two texts. Indeed, the suggestion above that the soldiers should have understood the command for total extermination of the Midianites also falls to a logical error: argument from silence; we simply do not know what the soldiers did or did not understand.

Further, Moses allows the soldiers to keep captured virgins for themselves – for sexual slavery, doubtless – which seems to suppose resistance on the part of the soldiers against this brutal command. As noted above, the text is not interested in such matters. Nevertheless, modern interpreters must be thorough in their investigation, especially when what "the good guys" do causes discomfort. The solution of Marcion – to cut out the OT altogether because of its violence – will not do, but any attempt to "sanitize" the violence and the contradictions that remain in the OT is also insufficient. Rather, modern interpreters should be honest about our awkward and halting attempts to work through the often complicated, confusing, and self-contradictory biblical text.

31:25–47 Counting the Spoils

As noted in the introductory comments to chapter 31, this fourth section returns to the usual way of describing a battle: description of the battle, taking the spoils, counting the spoils. The second and third sections interrupt this pattern by introducing the unstated command that the soldiers should have killed everyone and Moses' anger at their not having done so. Having purified the spoils taken, and having been ordered to kill more Midianites – though, at Moses' insistence, saving the virgins for themselves – the Israelites return to counting up what they have taken from the slain Midianite army.

Interestingly, the soldiers do not count the spoils themselves, as this task falls to "Moses, Eleazar, and the family heads of the community" (v. 26). The soldiers receive half of the spoils for their work, and God orders them to divide the rest among the people. Following this, God instructs each group (soldiers and people) to bring an offering. It seems odd, first, that the assessment is different for the soldiers' portion over against the people's portion and, second, that in neither case does the assessed amount come out to one-tenth. One-tenth is a far more familiar fraction, turning up repeatedly in Numbers (5:15; 15:4; 28:5, 13, 21, 29; 24:4, 10, 15) as well as various other places in the Pentateuch. Here, however, God commands the soldiers (through Moses) that they are to give one out of every five hundred, which works out to an offering of 0.2 percent. Moreover, God commands the people (again through Moses) that they are to give one out of every fifty things taken in spoils as an offering to the Levites, or an offering of 2 percent. Though the standard of the people's giving is much higher than the soldiers', it is still quite low, and nowhere near the "standard" biblical amount of 10 percent. While this note cannot be separated from its historical context for this particular battle and its literary context in Numbers, it raises a significant point for reflection. Though churches and ministers depend on the offerings of the people (just like the priests and Levites throughout Israel's history), a particular percentage may not be as important as a willful and obedient, even joyful, attitude toward giving (see 2 Cor 9:7).

The remaining verses of this passage give, in excruciating detail, the numbers of spoils taken. This information lends the narrative a sort of historical completeness. Yet a further surprise comes in verse 47, which reports that

Moses gives the offerings of the people to the Levites: one out of every fifty, according to God's command. There is no mention of the one in five hundred demanded from the soldiers (see next section).

31:48–54 Offerings of the Soldiers

The leaders of the army – the commanders of thousands and of hundreds (see v. 14) – conduct another count of those under their charge. This time, the narrator spares us the details of the count. The commanders then report to Moses that no one is missing, and the soldiers come forward to bring their atonement offering. As the commentary repeatedly notes, it seems that the soldiers did not know they were supposed to kill all of the people – or they may have had doubts about the wisdom of the order. In any event, at least two different stories come together here. Further evidence for this comes in the shifting details of the soldiers' offerings and what they can keep. Here, the text does not mention whether the 16,750 shekels (420 pounds or 190 kilograms, according to NIV footnote) represent the one-fiftieth portion the soldiers are supposed to bring (v. 28).

The combination of multiple sources reveals itself in verses 53–54, each in a different way. In verse 53, the text notes simply that the soldiers each take some plunder, without specifying what it is. Earlier, Moses says that each one can keep a virgin (v. 18). The text does not mention the gold and other precious items that have been purified (vv. 21–24). One might assume that this will go to the soldiers, excepting the one piece in five hundred that Moses demands as an offering. Such attempts at harmonization, however, suffer for lack of evidence in the text. Second, verse 54 reports that Moses and Eleazar take the offerings as a "memorial for the Israelites before the LORD." This seems to contradict verse 50, where the commanders of the army say they are bringing the offerings to make atonement for themselves. Once again, viewing this as a composite account seems to be the only sensible solution.

32:1–42 THE TRANSJORDANIAN TRIBES

Chapter 32 deals with the two tribes who will live on the eastern side of the Jordan River: the Reubenites and the Gadites. The tribe of Manasseh sometimes numbers among the Transjordanian tribes. Some texts consider Manasseh as two tribes – or, more properly speaking, two half-tribes (see, among others, Num 34:14; Josh 13:7; 1 Chr 6:61–62, 70). In fact, the tribal territory of Manasseh extends over both sides of the Jordan, so some other texts consider Manasseh as one tribe (Josh 17:1, 6, 17; 20:8; 1 Chr 12:19; Rev 7:6). Of these, the most interesting is Joshua 17:17, which ascribes to Joshua the statement that since Ephraim and Manasseh – the two "Joseph" tribes – are so large, they will each have more than one territorial allotment. The present text in Numbers 31 does not include the tribe of Manasseh, but only Reuben and Gad.

The text introduces the story of these two tribes by maintaining that they take great pride in their abundant livestock. Later, in Israel's saga, Deborah's song will chastise the Reubenites, in particular, for staying behind with their flocks rather than joining the summons for battle (see Judg 5:15b–16 and also vv. 6, 23, 30 below). Here, their large flocks lead them to desire to stay on the far side of the Jordan River rather than coming with the rest of the people into the Promised Land. They say, "If we have found favor in your eyes," then let us do what we desire (v. 5). The phrase "find favor in the eyes" refers to having a good reputation in the eyes of another. Alongside the present text, the phrase occurs in the context of a request thirteen other times (Gen 18:3; 19:19; 30:27; 33:10; 47:29; 50:4; Exod 34:9; Num 11:15; Judg 6:17; 1 Sam 20:3; 20:29; 27:5; 2 Sam 14:22). The last in this series, 2 Samuel 14:22, is not a request, but rather a response to the granting of a request. Joab realizes that he has found favor in the eyes of King David, because the king grants his request.

When someone makes a request, especially a request for some item (such as land), the one who considers the request may approach it from two angles: the available supply of the requested item and the relationship with the requestor. To illustrate the former, consider the following hypothetical situation: you want to bake a cake, the recipe calls for two eggs, and you just happen to have precisely that many. Now imagine I come along and ask you for one of your eggs so that I might make a sandwich. You now face a decision: if you give me the egg I have asked for and let me eat my sandwich, you will not be able to make your cake, and you may go hungry. In many Asian societies, the cultural rules are such that you would give me the egg without even thinking about it. In Western societies, however, I would likely complain that I could not fulfill your request because of what it would do to me. This situation effectively describes the concept of limited good, which operated in ancient societies like Israel. Ronald A. Simkins defines this concept when he writes: "According to the peasant view of the world, all the good things in life exist in fixed quantities and in short supply and their distribution are largely outside the peasant's control."[30]

The present situation works out differently. Here, and in all the other cases in which the phrase "If I/we/your servant has found favor in your eyes" appears, the requestee grants or refuses the request based on the relationship with the requestor. Thus, the assumption of the Transjordanian Tribes is that Moses will grant their request if the personal relationship between them and Moses is such that Moses sees fit to do so. Moses does not face a shortage of land in this instance; on the contrary, the land is abundant and good (in the common biblical phrase, "flowing with milk and honey"). Thus, Moses will not face a shortage of land to be distributed amongst the other ten tribes if he grants this request (remember the Levites do not receive an inheritance). The decision, then, is a matter of preference and relationship.

Moses first reacts to the request harshly, casting some doubt about whether the Reubenites and the Gadites have, indeed, found favor in his eyes. He begins by questioning their loyalty to the other tribes (v. 6). Although the land in the nine areas detailed by the requestors in verse 3 has already been subdued (v. 4), much work still lies before the remaining Israelite tribes. The books of Joshua and Judges will detail this accomplishment, sometimes in disagreement with one another. Moses begins by suggesting that the Transjordanian tribes want to stay where they are because they plan to shirk their responsibility to the other Israelites (v. 6). This statement implies that the conquest must involve all of the Israelites in order to succeed. Verse 30, however, negates this assertion (see below).

Moses' objection becomes more serious in the next few verses (vv. 6–15), for he accuses the tribes of following in the same sins as the Exodus generation. Specifically, he says that they are refusing to go into the land because of fear. One wonders whether this text has a composite nature, since the Transjordanian tribes have not made any suggestion that they want to stay out of the Promised Land for this reason. True enough, they do say, "Do not make us cross the Jordan," but they may have meant that they do not want to settle there – not that they do not want to help the other Israelites take the land. At the very least, Moses seems to overreact, for he says that the Transjordanian tribes' refusal will bring the wrath of God down upon all the Israelites (vv. 14–15). This argument seems unsteady, for back in chapter 13:25–14:11, when

---

30. Roland A. Simkins, "Limited Good in Genesis 23," in *Teaching the Bible: Practical Strategies for Classroom Instruction,* eds. Mark Roncace and Patrick Gray, Resources for Biblical Study 49 (Atlanta: Society of Biblical Literature, 2005).

the initial reports of the spies come back, the people as a whole decide not to go in. In other words, Moses has no justification for his accusation against the Transjordanian tribes.

The Transjordanian tribes do not reference Moses' accusation in their defense speech in verses 16–19, perhaps because it is baseless. (Indeed, the text would still make sense if verses 6–15 were taken out and the tribes' request ran from verses 1–5 and then 16–19.) Here, the tribes insist that God has given this area to them as an inheritance. They only ask to build pens for their livestock and fortified cities for their women and children before joining the rest of the tribes. They conclude their speech by affirming that they will not come back until all of the tribes have settled in their own allotments on the western side of the Jordan River.

If the objection of Moses in verses 6–15 is genuine, then it seems that good relations ultimately prevail between Moses and the Transjordanian tribes, for the leader grants their request. If the objection was added later, as noted above, one arrives at the same conclusion. Regardless, Moses gives his approval with a condition, detailed in verses 20–24, which uses typical covenant language: while the historical prologue is missing, the text includes the benefits that the subordinate party will receive (freedom from further obligation, v. 22) as well as a threat for non-compliance (discovery of their sin by God, v. 23). Moses does not spell out exactly what God might do in order to punish them for their sins.

The remaining eighteen verses of this chapter detail the Transjordanian tribes' acceptance of Moses' terms (vv. 25–27), to which they already committed themselves in verses 16–19. Since they already committed themselves to this task, it may be that Moses' speech in verses 20–24 was added later. Moses gives instructions concerning the tribes to Eleazar and others (vv. 27–30), with the odd assertion that, should they fail to fulfill their obligation, "they must accept their possession with you in Canaan" (v. 30). This note throws into question the earlier suggestion, which is implicit in verse 6 (above), that the Israelites must all join in the battle or else abandon hope for success. Verses 31–32 indicate the acceptance, again, of the Reubenites and Gadites. Finally, verses 33–42 give the narrator's report of Moses' assignment of these areas on the eastern side of the Jordan to these two tribes. Once again, the composite nature of the narrative becomes clear through the repetition of the various elements.

33:1–49 RECAPITULATING THE JOURNEY

From time to time in the OT, especially in the books that include long narratives of major historical events, the narrators or editors go back and tell the story again. Sometimes these retellings are in a summary form, and sometimes they tell the story completely differently. The books of Kings and Chronicles stand as the preeminent examples of two different accounts that are substantially different from one another. With such discrepancies, we need to consider the intent of the documents. The intent of the documents may or may not be consistent with what the authors, editors, and compilers had in mind (even insofar as later interpreters can recapture this). For once a document, either ancient or modern, comes to completion, it takes on a life of its own, existing alongside and entirely separate from its creator(s). If they are still alive, the creators may see their texts taken in new interpretative directions. The Italian semioticist, Umberto Eco (d. 2016), writes: "Nothing is of greater consolation to the author of a novel than the discovery of readings he had not conceived but which are then prompted by his readers."[31]

One may consider now two principal examples of this phenomenon. The first is the retelling of Genesis to Kings in 1–2 Chronicles, which is within the same document. With regard to this retelling, I maintain the following in my commentary on Chronicles: "the Chroniclers' use of the Deuteronomists' work need not have been any sort of reworking or copying. The Chroniclers could have, instead, written an entirely different historical work, but while not failing to consult previous sources."[32] The nature of the Chroniclers' work prevents what one might call an "internal retelling," or a restatement of the same story with different details.

The second example, which is quite different, is Jeremiah's two versions of the story of the fall of Jerusalem. Jeremiah 52 retells the story of the fall of Jerusalem to the Babylonian army. This represents the final vindication of what the prophet has been saying throughout his career, though he probably is not especially happy about that. Literarily, this comes after the curious phrase, "the words of Jeremiah are up to here" (51:64). Moreover, Jeremiah 52 stands as the last of three such stories. Other, perhaps earlier, versions are found in 2 Kings 25 and Jeremiah 39. I suggest that these differences are like variations

---

31. Umberto Eco, "Postscript to *The Name of the Rose*," in *The Name of the Rose,* reprint (Orlando: Harcourt Brace & Co., 1994), 506.
32. Modine, *1–2 Chronicles*, 29.

on a musical theme in a symphony.[33] Thus the retelling of Jeremiah 52 has both internal and external elements, with additional details regarding the numbers of the Babylonian exiles and a third deportation in the twenty-third year of King Nebuchadnezzar (582 BC).

The retelling of the journey in Numbers 33:1–49 is more like the example from Jeremiah than the example from Chronicles. Like Chronicles, however, which summarizes thousands (millions?) of years of history in the form of a vast genealogy (1 Chr 1–9), the present chapter summarizes much more lengthy history found in the books of Exodus and Numbers. Leviticus is an outlier here, since there is very little in the way of narrative – and no journey narratives – in that book.

The journey told here takes place in forty-two stages. The great early Christian biblical exegete, Origen of Alexandria, went on a flight of allegorical fancy with this. In his Homily 27, he compares the forty-two stages of the journey to the forty-two generations listed in the Gospel of Matthew for Jesus' genealogy. Thus, for Origen, the forty-two stages are applicable to various stages in the life of the believer. While this interpretation fits in well with the allegorizing typical of early Christian exegesis, it is not helpful for modern interpreters, and it should be avoided in preaching, as it may lead to a congregant to a fair bit of confusion.

For the most part, each stage in the journey takes up one verse. A few exceptions to this appear in the chapter. The first of these, verses 1–4, introduces the whole summary. The second exception comes in verses 38–39, which retell the death of Aaron on Mount Hor (see above on 20:22–29). Interestingly, the summary makes no mention of the death of Miriam, which in the larger narrative merits only one verse (20:1). However, here one reads the added detail of Aaron's age, which chapter 20 does not include. A third exception comes right after the death of Aaron in verse 40, which notes the news of the Israelites' arrival coming to the Canaanite King of Arad (21:1–3). The final exception comes at the end, in verses 48–49, two verses that detail the Israelites' arrival in the plains of Moab, looking across the Jordan River to Jericho, which will be the first stop of their journey into, and conquest of, the Promised Land in the book of Joshua.

Outside these exceptions, the summary may be treated, if the pun be allowed, in summary form. That is, two large questions seem worthy of

---

33. Alex Varughese and Mitchel Modine, *Jeremiah 27–52: A Commentary in the Wesleyan Tradition* (Kansas City: Beacon Hill, 2010), 305.

treatment. On the one hand, even though the summary of the journey appears rather precise, attempting to reconstruct the details of the Israelites' journey through the wilderness will prove unsuccessful and unnecessary. At various other points in the commentary, we have noted that the precision of Numbers seems deceptive. One must bear in mind that the nature of this material is a national saga and an identity-forming story, not unlike the stories of Homer. The most important theological point to remember when reading these stories, and particularly this summary, is that the journey through the desert is primarily a journey *with God* – not a journey from this place to that place and then from that place to this other place.

33:50–35:34 INSTRUCTIONS FOR PROMISED LAND ENTRY

The remainder of chapter 33 and the entirety of chapters 34–35 contain instructions for the Israelites upon their entry into the Promised Land. This section of Numbers prefigures the book of Deuteronomy in significant ways, since Deuteronomy presents itself as a series of four speeches delivered by Moses to the people just before they enter the Promised Land. Significantly, Moses himself will not go into the land. We noticed this back in chapter 27. Yet it is helpful to note it again because in these speeches, Moses is giving instructions to the people, and so his influence will continue in Israel even though he himself is not physically present. This idea is proclaimed strongly at the end of the book of Deuteronomy, which states that Moses enjoyed a particular relationship to God, even seeing God face to face (34:10–12).

33:50–56 You Must Dispossess the Canaanites

The Israelites arrive at their final destination prior to crossing the Jordan and engage in the conquest of the Promised Land. The commentary notes earlier that the plains of Moab will form the internal setting for the speeches in the book of Deuteronomy. This setting thus ties the end of Numbers together with the beginning of Deuteronomy. However, problems remain with reconstructing the external setting, since Moses' involvement with the events described in the Pentateuch appears to make the narrative historically untenable. The critical consensus, as noted above, regarding the lengthy and complicated production of the Pentateuch as an overarching literary work need not dissuade the reader from noticing the careful splicing between the different parts of Israel's masterful national saga.

God says, through Moses, that the Israelites must do a number of things. First, they must drive out all the other inhabitants of the land (v. 52a). Second, they must destroy all of the remnants of the Canaanite religion (v. 52b). Third, they must take possession of the land and settle in it (v. 53). Fourth, they must divide the land according to their tribal inheritances (v. 54). The final verses sound a warning: if they fail to do what God tells them to do, the Canaanites will bother them throughout their days, and God will do to the Israelites what God plans to do to the Canaanites (vv. 55–56).

The first of these statements – that the Israelites must drive the Canaanites out of the land and destroy all their idols (v. 52a) – sounds quite odd when compared to other statements about the Canaanites in the Pentateuch. For example, Leviticus 20:23 indicates that the Israelites must "not follow the customs of the nations I am going to drive out before you" (see also Lev 18:24; 2 Sam 7:23). All three of these passages use the Hebrew word *shalach*, meaning to send, send out, or drive out. Verses 52–53 in Numbers use a different word than these other passages, *yarash*, which has the dual meanings of possess and dispossess (in other words, "take" and "take from"). This full form, with a second masculine plural ending, occurs elsewhere in the MT only at Joshua 8:7 and Ezra 9:12. The first of these carries the idea of taking something (in that case, the city of Ai), while the second carries the idea of leaving something as a possession for one's children. The key point here is that the Israelites are dispossessing the Canaanites and then possessing the land. In contrast, the passages that use *shalach* indicate, for the most part, that the sending out or driving out is the action of God. This speaks again to the different emphases advanced by the different materials that make up the Pentateuch.

Moreover, many Asian readers – in particular, Palestinians – run into difficulty with this material because they identify with the Canaanites in the story. In countries that experienced European colonization, the indigenous populations who lost their land understand quite well what the Canaanites might have felt. In Israel/Palestine, this feeling may be rooted in a misidentification of ancient Israel with modern Israel, yet this is not the only explanation. For the experience of dispossessed persons identifying with the Canaanites who were robbed of their land happens also in the West among First Nations members. In the West, there is no chance of the colonizers being confused with ancient Israel, even though some of the rhetoric produced at the time did invoke the imagery of the children of Israel heading into the Promised Land to describe how European settlers felt upon coming to America. Modern and postmodern readers should be sensitive to the different ways in which experience leads diverse communities to read the Bible.

The second instruction – removing/destroying all the remnants of Canaanite religion (v. 52b) – is an often-encountered command in the Pentateuch. In fact, the Deuteronomy version of this command in 12:3 forms part of the basis for the command against taking the name of the Lord in vain (the third commandment, according to Protestant and Jewish countings). As a reading of Israel's national saga bears out, however, the Israelites fail to carry out this commandment completely. The Pentateuch as a whole, which comes into its final form around the time of the Babylonian Exile, thus gives this command again, implying that the exodus and conquest generations failed in this task.

The third and fourth instructions – to take possession of the land and to divide it amongst the tribes (vv. 53–54) – go together. We note above the dual significance of the term *yarash*, which appears in verse 53 in the sense of possessing, whereas it has the sense of taking in verse 52a. The division of the land into tribal portions in verse 54 also proves interesting. On the one hand, it presupposes a successful conquest: the text does not say, "Fight the Canaanites for the land, sustain some losses, enjoy moderate to increasing success, and finally after a long struggle declare victory." Instead, it assumes certain victory in the war for conquest. Later parts of the saga (especially the book of Judges) detail how the Israelites' entry into the Promised Land is neither as certain nor as swift as the present text assumes. This reality, coupled with abundant archaeological evidence of the simultaneous existence of Israelite settlements in the central hill country and Canaanite cities in the plains, has led many to question the historicity of the conquest narratives. Though this investigation is beyond the scope of a Numbers commentary, informed teachers and pastors should be aware of it.[34]

---

34. The three main alternative theories to the biblical narrative are a peaceful infiltration, a peasant revolt, and a gradual withdrawal. The peaceful infiltration model was developed in 1925 by Albrecht Alt, whose work we have explored earlier with regard to OT law. The great German scholar Martin Noth further explored this theory. The peasant revolt model was popularized by George Mendenhall in a 1962 article. This theory changed the direction of the Hebrews' movement: they were already inside Canaan when they established their separate identity. Norman Gottwald expanded on this idea, giving it a neo-Marxist slant. The third alternative, which encompasses a number of slightly different though related theories, begins from the premise that the biblical record is not completely historically reliable. The main idea is that the emergence of Israel was not so much an event but a gradual evolution. The main question in this discussion is when Israel emerged as an ethnic as well as a political identity. An external source recovered by archaeologists, which is called the Merneptah Stela after the Egyptian Pharaoh who it set up, refers to Israel as an ethnic identity some time before 1203 BC, when Pharaoh Merneptah died. The bibliography provides some assistance for interested readers to investigate this further.

Verse 54 specifically mentions a principle that comes into play later – namely, that the size of a given tribe should dictate the size of land given to it. In the commentary on chapter 32 above, we note that some texts consider the tribe of Manasseh as two half-tribes, each of which settles on a different side of the Jordan. Others consider Manasseh as one whole tribe, and Joshua 17:17–18 specifically grants a large area of land to the tribes of Ephraim and Manasseh because they are so large.

The final two verses of this text (vv. 55–56) alert the Israelites to some penalties for non-compliance. Specifically, God warns that he will do to the Israelites what he plans to do the Canaanites! This recalls Jeremiah's vision of the potter's house (Jer 18), where God tells the prophet that God is able to change God's mind about the good or ill designed for a particular nation if that nation changes its ways. The sentiment here also recalls Leviticus 18:24–28, which warns the Israelites that if they follow the ways of the other nations, the land "will vomit you out just as it vomited out the nations which were before you" (v. 28).

34:1–15 Boundaries

Reading this text, the interpreter must again come to terms with the difference between the internal setting (literary) and external setting (the place and time of the writing). The commentary above (see 28:26–31) defines the concept of an internal setting regarding the book of Ruth. The internal setting in a story includes the aspects of space and time, and in this particular text, the question about time generates some interest. With the Lord speaking through Moses, this text anticipates the subduing of the natives who already live in the land (see the previous passage). The external setting looks forward to a return from exile, which, according to the books of Ezra and Nehemiah, requires something of a second conquest, even if this time it is more ideological than military. In either case, the description of the national borders in Numbers 34:1–13 seems strange. Though the borders listed are similar to the long-standing borders of the land of Canaan, this text seems to imply that the Israelites should not go out of these borders in order to create a larger empire for themselves.

If this inference is correct, the sentiment appears to be different based on a consideration of the internal or the external setting. As an aside, one does not need to opt for one or the other; the genius of the text is that it allows for a consideration of both. If one considers the internal setting, defining these rather rigid national boundaries puts a kind of check on any natural ambition the Israelites might have to go about empire building. In a way, this could be read as a kind of statement against King Solomon, who (more than any other Israelite king) works to expand the borders of the Israelite sphere of influence beyond the borders of the land of Canaan.

On the other hand, a consideration of the external setting leads to a rather different reading. For the returnees (i.e. the descendants of those who went into exile) might have come back to the land with a defeated mindset. In this case, they might have been glad to get this much in terms of land. Actually, Judah (Yehud) as a Persian province was considerably smaller than it is described here. In that light, a desire for the restoration of the original borders might be behind this text. Significantly, these boundaries are never again controlled by Israel, and so this hope recedes into the distant future, becoming by the time of Jesus a key element of Messianic hope (see Acts 1:6).

Verses 13–15 describe how Moses commands the Israelites to divide the land, based on the previous twelve verses in which God describes the boundaries. The external setting fades from significance here, since the tribal distinctions, perhaps even as far back as the monarchy, cease to function as more than geographical boundaries. Verse 14 recalls chapter 32, where Moses commands the leaders under him to force the tribes of Reuben and Gad to accept inheritances on the western side of the Jordan if they fail to carry out their obligations to help the Israelites with the conquest (v. 30). Yet here, a different tradition asserts itself, for the text says that "the families of the tribe of Reuben, the tribe of Gad and the half-tribe of Manasseh have received their inheritance." Thus, this chapter betrays a different tradition than the one underlying chapter 32. For, on the one hand, this text includes the half-tribe of Manasseh (see 32:1–42 above); on the other hand, no obligation lies upon the Reubenites and the Gadites to fight and help their fellow Israelites take the Promised Land. As this commentary states repeatedly, these different texts imply different textual traditions. The different textual traditions, in turn, bear witness to a diverse and creative literary and oral tradition within ancient Israel.

34:16–29 Appointment of Leaders

In Numbers 32:13, Moses informs the Reubenites and Gadites – who ask to remain and settle on the eastern side of the Jordan – that the Lord was angry with the whole Exodus generation (see also Deut 1:35; 2:14; Judg 2:10). So God declared that all of them (including Miriam, Moses, and Aaron, the leaders) would perish in the wilderness and that only Caleb and Joshua, the two spies who brought back a good report, would be able to enter the

Promised Land. The present text describes the appointment of new leaders for the tribes. In two different places, chapters 2 and 7, the text identifies the leaders who bring the tribes out of Egypt, and the commentary notes that the two lists are identical.

This chapter also lists the tribes in a different order than the birth order of the patriarchs. Judah still occupies first position, owing to their ancestor's elevation to a place of prominence. Below, when the commentary returns to the daughters of Zelophehad (ch. 36), we shall discuss this phenomenon. The tribes that appear in chapter 34 include those who are settling on the western side of the Jordan (thus Reuben and Gad are excluded). In addition, the list here moves in a general south-to-north direction in terms of tribal territory. This stands in contrast to chapters 2 and 7, where the tribes are listed more or less in birth order. The order in chapter 34 runs: Simeon, Benjamin, Dan, Manasseh, Ephraim, Zebulun, Issachar, Asher, and Naphtali. Here, as in chapter 32, the tribe of Manasseh counts as a whole tribe (32:33 is an exception). Rather than divide them in half and give each one a separate territory, the text considers both the Cisjordanian and Transjordanian Manassites together (see Josh 17:17). A final note to consider is that Joshua is not included in the list of the leaders of the tribes. That is, Moses will appoint him in due time as the leader of all the Israelites, but he does not lead a tribe as well (see Num 27:15–23; Deut 31:1–8, 14–23). These three different texts each come from a different Pentateuchal source (P, D, and E respectively), and they do not refer to each other, again showing the deft, if somewhat haphazard, way in which the Pentateuch was put together from its disparate sources.

35:1–8 Towns for the Levites

Since the Levites do not receive an inheritance along with the other tribes (see Num 18:23, 26:22, and various other references), God tells Moses in this passage to set aside towns for the Levites within the other tribal territories. The later history of 1 Chronicles preserves one version of the list of the cities which the Israelites assigned to the Levites (6:54–81). The Chroniclers seem to have adapted their material directly from Joshua 21:4–39.[35] While Numbers 35 does not provide a similar list of cities, the idea that the pasturelands around each city should provide for the physical needs of the Levites appears in both texts (Num 35:3–4; 1 Chron 6:64). The uneven number of cities contributed

---

35. Modine, *1–2 Chronicles*, 68.

by each of the tribes has to do with the relative size of the tribes, and this is reflected again in the list in 1 Chronicles 6.

Numbers 35 alone stipulates that the pasturelands belonging to each city should extend one thousand cubits (approximately 450 meters) in every direction from "the town in the center" (v. 5). The plan envisions a square plot of two thousand cubits (900 meters) on each side, with the city walls forming a square inside this one with one thousand cubits (450 meters) on each side. The distance from the city walls to the border of the pasturelands is thus five hundred cubits (225 meters) at any point.

The dimensions of these cities are without a doubt idealized, and one should not be overly concerned with the specific numbers. The more important point is that, since God gives the Levites spiritual responsibility in lieu of territorial inheritance, God also provides for their physical needs. The book of Deuteronomy is filled with commands to care for the Levites who are living in the Israelites' towns. While this seems to reflect a slightly different tradition than the one in Numbers 35, the provision is the same. Because the Levites do not have a tribal inheritance of their own, and because they have such an important responsibility, the Israelites must dedicate some of the resources that God has given them in order to care for the Levites.

Thus, even today, caring for the physical needs of pastors and other ministers is a moral responsibility for those whom the ministers are caring for spiritually. Most churches do not have a membership fee, *per se*, and no one should expect small churches, especially when filled with poor people, to be able to handle all of these expenses. In such cases, support should fall on the larger community or denominational structure to which the local church belongs. This is one of the most important functions of denominational structure, though perhaps it is not as important as doctrinal integrity. It is a great tragedy when those upon whom the call of God has fallen cannot afford to feed their families. No one expects pastors to become wealthy – and indeed, it is a problem if pastors do become wealthy – but pastors and other ministers who have dedicated their lives to the service of God should receive salary and benefits sufficient to provide a reasonable standard of living. We are, in short, not meant to be in this alone.

35:9–15 Cities of Refuge

Along with the towns set aside for the Levites to live in, God commands the Israelites to set apart six cities as "cities of refuge." The forty-eight towns the Israelites are to give the Levites include these cities of refuge (v. 6). This section of Numbers 35 stipulates the purpose of these cities of refuge. The fact that verse 6 mentions the cities of refuge without defining them, and that verse 11 defines the cities without referring to the previous command, may indicate the convergence of two different textual traditions. In any event, the cities of refuge exist for the safety of anyone who kills someone without intending to do so. This connects with the principle that a town or a shrine associated with a particular deity falls under the protection of that deity. Hence, if someone flees to a Levitical city, he or she can claim sanctuary within that city.

Leviticus requires atonement even for "unintentional" sin (Lev 5:15). The simplest act of atonement for killing a person would be for the killer to be killed. Even in modern times, many traditional societies follow this practice. However, ancient Israelite society, like many other ancient societies, made a distinction between murder and accidental killing. Modern legal theory has developed a number of levels to describe the severity of an act of killing – from self-defense and justifiable homicide to premeditated murder. Something like this lies behind the idea of the cities of refuge.

Verse 12 stipulates that the accused can live to stand trial if he or she makes it to the city of refuge. In practice, the killer could live in the city of refuge without fear of a revenge killing until the death of the current high priest, at which point he or she could leave the city of refuge without further fear of retribution (see vv. 25, 28). Violations of this practice – such as entering and killing someone who fled there, or revenge killings after the death of the high priest – were considered new murder offenses and were dealt with accordingly (see v. 32 below). A trial before the assembly could find one guilty (v. 12), even if one believed oneself to have killed the person accidentally (see v. 24).

The placement of three cities of refuge on either side of the Jordan provided for two things (v. 14). On the one hand, multiple cities of refuge ensured that a person who needed to flee to such a place would have a reasonable chance of getting there. On the other hand, the limitation of six cities of refuge meant that the suspect fleeing an unintentional killing had to expend effort to save his or her life.

35:16–29 Settling Murder Cases

In this passage, the focus changes from unintentional killing to murder with various weapons. The ordering of this material appears somewhat confusing, because the texts describing the cities of refuge (vv. 6, 9–14) concern unintentional killings, which are discussed further in verses 22–28 (and yet again in v. 32 below). Perhaps the definitions of murder should have come first.

Nevertheless, one may discern certain cohesiveness in the material. These laws define murder as: (1) any intentional act involving an iron, stone, or wood implement; or (2) premeditated murder, with previous malice, regardless of the manner in which it is accomplished. As noted above, modern societies make similar distinctions as well. The limiting of possible murder weapons to iron, wood, and stone owes to the historical context: iron was the hardest substance known to exist at that time, then stone, then wood. Bronze, also used for tools, weapons, etc., had been supplanted by iron since the latter had far more durability.

It is interesting that the one responsible for carrying out the death sentence should be a family member of the victim. Modern societies in which the death penalty is legal lay this responsibility on the government, making revenge killing by a family member or by someone else connected to the victim an additional crime, punishable according to its own severity. Whatever one thinks of the state employing death as a means of punishment for crime, most would agree that revenge killing is a greater evil. Exodus 21:23–25 defines the law of retribution (also known by the Latin phrase *lex talionis*), restricting revenge to an equivalent amount of damage. The present passage, being concerned only with murder, stays on the level of retribution by the family, though the beginnings of the legal restrictions familiar to modern societies have their roots here. The principle of legal restriction in this text is the cities of refuge.

The question, however, remains: how would the society determine whether the one responsible for the killing is guilty of murder? Such a person is never "innocent," since his or her action did in fact cause the death of another; the level of intention defines the severity of the crime. The cities of refuge come into play again (vv. 6, 9–15). Specifically, verse 12 maintains that the person who has killed someone unintentionally (compare vv. 22–23) may remain alive until the community has had a chance to sort through the issues and assign the severity of guilt and the punishment to be enforced (see above). The "assembly," a body usually made up of the elders of the town, judge whether the accused is guilty of murder (v. 24).

Interestingly, the one accused of murder and found not guilty must go back to the city of refuge (v. 25). On first glance, this appears to be a punishment; someone who killed another by accident cannot go back to his or her home and continue to live there, as in modern societies. Instead, such a person must remain in the city of refuge until the death of the high priest. Only after such a time may the accused return home (v. 28). On a deeper level, however, this protects the accused from the avenger of blood, who cannot enter the city of refuge to exact revenge (see v. 12). Thus, the confinement to the city of refuge preserved the life of the unintentional killer (vv. 26–27).

Later on, as legal theory developed and the right of revenge came out of the hands of the family and was reserved for the government, further changes took place. First, when modern societies determine that a murder is unintentional and thus declares the accused "not guilty," he or she returns to life as normal. Second, and because of the first change, the city of refuge ceases to function, since its necessity is taken away by the criminalization of revenge killing. In other words, many modern societies include the desire for revenge as one of the factors that make a killer guilty of murder. As societies have continued to develop, they have sought to reduce violence among its members – though many societies still have a long way to go.

35:30–34 Judicial Laws

The last five verses of chapter 35 give four more laws regarding murder. Thus, the final form of this passage appears to be a kind of compendium of murder laws. The first law directs that someone may face the death penalty only on "the testimony of witnesses" (v. 30). This particular text does not specify how many witnesses a capital murder case requires, but only that it must be more than one. One gets the sense that this is a later addition, perhaps in order to limit the number of people suffering the death penalty. Thus in later years – at any rate, prior to Numbers coming to its final form – ongoing legal discussion within Israel revealed some level of discomfort with this ultimate punishment.

Hebrew has three different forms of nouns to describe how many of something one has: the singular, the dual, and the plural. The singular is used for one thing only, while the dual is used to describe things that naturally occur in pairs (ears, eyes, hands, feet, etc). The plural is used for more than one thing (two as well as more than two). The vocalized form of the word used for "witnesses" in verse 30 is plural, not dual. Had the text used the dual form, then one could infer a direct statement regarding two – and only two – witnesses to a murder. However, witnesses are not like ears or hands in that they normally occur in pairs. Other texts, such as Deuteronomy 17:6 (dual form for two) and 19:15 (plural form for two), stipulate that two or three witnesses are necessary to sustain a capital murder charge.

The second and third of these laws stipulate that one may not offer a ransom in exchange for the penalty one must face (vv. 31–32). In the case of a capital murder, the guilty party must die (v. 31). One must remember that the text comes from an ancient society, and that society came to these conclusions about murder and guilt. In other words, this text is descriptive of ancient Israel only and is not prescriptive for modern societies. In fact, taking ancient holy texts and their legal material as exclusively prescriptive has led to many difficulties and, in extreme cases, the fracturing of modern societies and even bloodshed. The Bible, like the Qur'an, has material that offends modern sensibilities and should give us pause.

Similarly, those who kill unintentionally cannot find release from their punishment by paying a fine either (v. 32). As noted above, the one who flees to a city of refuge has to stay there until the death of the high priest (v. 25). This person cannot go out of the city of refuge without facing the threat of death. For even if someone is judged not guilty of murder, the blood avenger can kill the accused if he or she leaves the friendly confines of the city of refuge (vv. 26–27).

Though friendly, the walls of the city of refuge were still confines, and being exiled to a city of refuge might have lasted many years – especially if the high priest was a young, healthy man. Thus, people might have tried to buy their way out of "jail." As noted above, and in the same way as the laws having to do with capital punishment in the previous verse, one must recognize that these laws applied to ancient Israel alone, and that cities of refuge were made obsolete when the government took over the right to impose the death penalty.

It surely offends modern sensibilities that one declared "not guilty" should have to spend anywhere from a day to twenty-five years or more in a kind of prison. This practice likely separated people from their families and certainly destroyed their prospects of making a living. Depending on the population of the city of refuge, an exile might have lived a very lonely existence. Certainly, he or she lacked extended kinship relations, which had so much importance in the ancient world (and continue to be important in Asia). However, having the government punish offenders does not eliminate all problems either. For example, how many people spend years in jail, having been put there by corrupted or mistaken witnesses, only to be exonerated by better evidence?

The final two verses bring together all the laws on killing, including the establishment of the cities of refuge (vv. 33–34). The overriding principle here is the need to preserve the land from pollution. The only way to make atonement for bloodshed is by bloodshed. Again, later interpreters (as evidenced in this chapter) had difficulty dealing with the stark insistence on the death penalty in this text. However, one must remember that, like the cities of refuge, the land itself lives under the protection of the deity. In a sense, all of the Promised Land is the dwelling of God. This, after all, is the point of the moveable tabernacle.

Later on in Israel's saga (see especially, 2 Sam 7), King David laments that the Ark of the Covenant – perhaps the principal symbol of God's presence with the people – remains in a tent while he himself dwells in a fancy palace. On the one hand, the (aborted) attempt of David to build a temple for God represents a noble gesture on the king's part to bring honor to the deity. On the other hand, it represents an attempt to domesticate God, to confine God to a particular space. In this latter sense, the fact that the worship of the Lord is only limited to the Jerusalem temple for about forty years at the end of Judah's existence is a good thing – not the sin the Deuteronomists make it out to be. The sense of the abiding presence of God with the Israelites is thus strengthened by the idea that the stain of bloodshed can only be gotten out of the carpet, so to speak, by adding to it the blood of the one who caused the stain in the first place. Again, this is a descriptive text, not a prescriptive one. Viewing it in this manner not only saves us from a load of discomfort, but it also gives us an amazing vantage point to examine the deep structures of ancient Israelite society.

36:1–12 THE DAUGHTERS OF ZELOPHEHAD, PART TWO

The final chapter of the book of Numbers includes a kind of coda to the story of Zelophehad's daughters. Earlier, the daughters appear in chapter 27, attempting to preserve their father's memory among the Israelites. They say that Zelophehad's name threatens to fade into oblivion, since he died with only daughters, no sons. Numbers 26:33, in the context of a genealogical record, also notes the apparent tragedy of Zelophehad within the patriarchal environment that characterized Israelite society – as well as most of the ancient near Eastern world.

The commentary calls this later text "Part Two" of the story of Zelophehad's daughters because it occurs second in the literary order of the book and because it refers back to the first text (36:2). In terms of content, however, it appears rather different from the earlier story for a number of reasons, as we shall see. From these differences, we may surmise that these are independent versions of the narrative of Zelophehad's daughters, both of which made it into the final form of Numbers, though we cannot definitively say at which point the editors included them. It remains unclear which of the two versions came before the other, a point that will find significance in the first difference discussed here.

Furthermore, looking into the book of Joshua, one finds yet a third version of the story of Zelophehad's daughters (see Josh 17:3–4).

The first difference between chapters 27 and 36 comes in the order in which the daughters appear. When the biblical text preserves a record of sons, it usually presents them in birth order, since the rights of the firstborn son precede all the others. An exception to this rule comes in 1 Chronicles 5:1, which indicates that although Reuben was Jacob's firstborn son, he disqualified himself from that lofty position by sleeping with his father's concubine, Bilhah. By contrast, the birth order of multiple daughters seems not to hold as much interest, since, for the most part, daughters never share in the inheritance of their father. However, the case of Zelophehad's daughters comes up as a glaring exception to this general rule, as we will see below when the patriarchal structure reasserts itself.

In chapter 27, the daughters appear in the following order: Mahlah, Noah, Hoglah, Milkah, and Tirzah (v. 1). In chapter 36, the daughters appear in the following order: Mahlah, Tirzah, Hoglah, Milkah, and Noah (v. 11). Neither story of Zelophehad's daughters specifies that the order in which the daughters appear has anything to do with their birth order. One suspects that the two issues are unrelated, not least because, the order of daughters' births does not seem to be of importance. One exception to this comes in the apparent deceit of Jacob by Laban in first giving him Leah as a wife over the younger – and, by Jacob, more desired – Rachel. Laban justifies this action by the custom of not marrying off the younger before the older (see Gen 29:26). If we assume that the daughters' birth orders did make a difference, we should suppose either that: (1) Noah did something especially bad to have lost her status (as in the case of Reuben); or (2) Tirzah showed herself to be particularly virtuous, so as to be promoted. Although Tirzah does not see her position rise all the way to first place, perhaps she has worked to convince her sisters to accept the stipulation offered by their male relatives (see below). To restate, the text has no evidence, direct or indirect, in favor or in opposition, regarding this possibility. Nevertheless, the fact that Joshua 17:3 preserves the same order as Numbers 27:1 might serve as corroborating evidence (see below).

On a technical level, Israel Yeivin cites these two versions of the daughters of Zelophehad as an example of textual notes made by the Masoretes. He writes: "Notes of this sort deal with combinations of words in which confusion would be easy."³⁶ This probably had much to do with the memorization of the biblical text, in particular the Torah. Yeivin cites all three of the texts coming under investigation here: Numbers 27:1; 36:11; Joshua 17:3. Although the Masoretic notes do not allow speculation about how or why such changes occurred, they do provide evidence that the change was thought to be significant, at least on some level.

The second difference between chapters 27 and 36 concerns the identity of those who make known the details of the case of Zelophehad's daughters. One could describe this as Zelophehad's case, since he is the one who died without daughters (see 27:8ff., where Moses through God describes the case in terms of the son-less father). In the version we have here, the description that seems most appropriate is "the case of Zelophehad," since the family heads of the clan of Gilead, of the tribe of Manasseh, come and present the case. Yet in chapter 27, the daughters themselves approach. The latter scenario finds a parallel in Joshua 17:3-4, which involves the division of the land following its conquest by Joshua and the Israelites. Interestingly, the Joshua 17 text makes no mention of the legal scenarios developed in Numbers 27, or of the particular restriction placed on the daughters here in chapter 36 (see more on this below).

Third, the two versions of this story in Numbers and the third account in Joshua each report different recipients of the information regarding the case and different locations for its delivery. In Numbers 27, the daughters come "before Moses, Eleazar the priest, the leaders and the whole assembly at the entrance to the tent of meeting" (v. 2). In Numbers 36, the clan leaders come and speak "before Moses and the leaders, the heads of the Israelite families" (v. 1). Chapter 36 reports no specific location, and the priest is noticeably absent. In Joshua 17, the daughters approach on their own initiative, this time "to Eleazar the priest, Joshua son of Nun, and the leaders" (v. 4). Though Joshua 17 reports no specific location, the text names Eleazar the priest before Joshua, which may hold some significance about the relative place of spiritual and political leadership, especially since such debates continued into monarchical times and, even more significantly, into the post-exilic situation and the Jewish diaspora.

Fourth, the content of the speeches varies widely between the three accounts. In Numbers 27, as noted, the daughters speak for themselves, mentioning that Zelophehad was not part of the rebellion instigated by the Korahites,

---

36. Israel Yeivin, *Introduction to the Tiberian Masorah*, trans. and ed. E. J. Revell, Masoretic Studies 5 (Atlanta: Society of Biblical Literature, 1985), 69-70.

although he did in fact "die for his own sin" (vv. 3–4). Numbers 36 does not mention the refusal of Zelophehad to participate in the Korahite rebellion (v. 2). The tribal elders give a more extensive speech, but this adds further stipulations to the case (see below) rather than laying out the basic scenario. Joshua 17 reports that the daughters say, "the LORD commanded Moses to give us an inheritance among our relatives" (v. 4). This statement reveals Joshua 17 as a supplemental text to both versions in Numbers, though it has closer affinity to Numbers 27, since the daughters approach the leaders on their own behalf.

Fifth, each of the three versions reports slightly different responses from God. Joshua 17 preserves the shortest text, with no response from God; the narrator simply says that Joshua acts in accordance with the instructions of Moses (v. 4). In Numbers 27, Moses, working under God's influence, sets out several scenarios about where the inheritance should go (vv. 7–11). In Numbers 36, however, the male tribal leaders make something of an appeal based on the previous legal decision set down by Moses (v. 2). They express concern that "the inheritance of our brother Zelophehad . . . will be taken away from our ancestral inheritance" if his daughters should marry outside the clan (v. 3). And so they attempt to preserve the integrity of the inheritance within the clan by preventing Zelophehad's daughters to marry outside the clan (v. 4).

From a feminist perspective, this appears to take the inheritance away from the daughters and invalidate the previous decision. Moreover, the male tribal leaders show little concern for the well-being of the daughters themselves. Noting that these men suddenly seem to realize what a great power play Zelophehad's daughters have accomplished, Sakenfeld acknowledges the narrator's complicity in effectively silencing them. She writes: "The story concludes with an account of the women's compliance with this regulation, so that the entire book ends with an illustration of the narrator's overarching theme of the perfect faithfulness of the second generation."[37] Not only this, but the names of the daughters, which appear at the beginning in 27:1, do not appear until near the end of the text in 36:11 – a detail that speaks strongly in favor of an attempt by the dominant patriarchal structure to reassert itself.

In summary, while chapter 36 does refer back to the decision in chapter 27, an analysis of the differences between the two accounts makes it clear that the men step in to reassert control over these powerful women who issue the challenge on behalf of their dead father. The prevailing custom assumed that women could not inherit; the daughters of Zelophehad constituted a special

---

37. Sakenfeld, *Women's Bible Commentary*, 55.

case, mainly because they took the initiative to request special dispensation from Moses and from God. Thus, as noted in the commentary to chapter 27, they refuse to count themselves as evidence of a curse upon their father (as Ps 127:3–5 seems to imply). Moreover, they take great care to assure that their dead father will not suffer the ignominy of having his name erased in Israel just because he had no sons (27:4). However, the men in chapter 36 do not share this concern and seem to care only for the property, for material gain. In other words, they seem unconcerned about showing compassion for their dead brother Zelophehad as well as the young women, who are gifts of God (as implied by the NIV's translation of Psalm 127) just as much as sons.

MARRIAGE OF DAUGHTERS IN NAGALAND, INDIA

Sometimes when we read the Bible with care, we run up against a contradiction between the biblical text and a particular feature of our society. This seems to be a particular concern for evangelicals, who, for the most part, try to follow the Bible as God's Word. This becomes even more difficult if we try to follow the Bible literally, as A. J. Jacobs discovered in his attempt to live in this way for one year. Jacobs writes, "To follow the Bible literally – at face value, at its word, according to its plain meaning – isn't just a daunting proposition. It's a dangerous one."[1] At the end of his journey, Jacobs concludes: "The Bible may not have been dictated by God, it may have had a messy and complicated birth, one filled with political agendas and outdated ideas – but that doesn't mean the Bible can't be beautiful and sacred."[2]

This reality was brought home to me through a conversation with a couple engaged to be married from Nagaland, in northeast India. After reading through Numbers 27 and 36 – the two versions of the story of Zelophehad's daughters – they were dismayed. The woman informed me that her culture would prevent her from marrying inside her clan, as 36:6 orders the daughters of Zelophehad. In Nagaland, to marry within her clan would cause this woman, in her words, to be "excommunicated." In other words, she may be considered a harlot or as guilty of incest. In both ancient Israel and modern Nagaland, the question centers on the issue of property inheritance. However, it also carries implications for how these different cultures interpret and apply the Bible within their own contexts.

I recognize that such questions of contextual interpretation may create problems, particularly for evangelicals. Nevertheless, the Bible needs to be carefully read and interpreted, not least because of the distance between its writing and its reception in modern societies.

---

1. A. J. Jacobs, *The Year of Living Biblically: One Man's Humble Quest to Follow the Bible as Literally as Possible* (New York: Simon & Schuster, 2007), 9.
2. Ibid., 316. The disagreements that evangelicals may find with Jacobs' statement lie beyond the scope of the present project.

Numbers 21:4–36:13

36:13 THE ENDING THAT DOES NOT END

Many of the biblical books end rather abruptly. I have written commentaries on Jeremiah and Chronicles, and the same phenomenon operates in both of these books. The final passage of Jeremiah (52:31–34) describes the elevation of King Jehoiachin in exile (as does 2 Kgs 25:27–30, with disagreement in one minor detail). Though this sounds a note of hope, it is muted since Jehoiachin remains in exile. Similarly, 2 Chronicles ends on a hopeful note, with the Persian King Cyrus declaring that any Jews who desire to return home may do so (36:22–23). However, there is no indication, at least in Chronicles, that they do so. In both of these cases, I gave the final texts the title, "The Ending that Does Not End."[38]

It seems appropriate to give this title to the last verse of the book of Numbers as well. True enough, the abrupt statement of verse 13 may function as the conclusion to the story of the case of Zelophehad's daughters. However, this seems unsatisfactory, since the verse sounds more like an introduction than a conclusion. Similar statements occur in Genesis 2:4a and Exodus 1:1, the former of which is usually considered the conclusion to the "first creation story." Hence, the text leaves the reader wanting more. Of course, there is indeed more to come in the book of Deuteronomy, so this verse could be seen as an introduction to that book. However, Deuteronomy will have its own introduction, which also occurs in the same form: "These are the words Moses spoke to all Israel in the wilderness east of the Jordan" (1:1). After such a long journey with God through the wilderness, it is difficult to explain why the ending is so abrupt. All the major sections of the Torah end outside the Promised Land, indicating that there is yet a future for the people of God, though most of them fail to see it realized in their lifetimes (see Heb 11:39).[39]

---

38. Varughese and Modine, *Jeremiah*, 314; Modine, *1–2 Chronicles*, 213.
39. Federico Villanueva, my editor, shared with me in a private communication how this reminds him of the Filipino song, *"Malayo pa ang Umaga"* (Morning Is Still Far): "We wait for the promise, and we hope in the promise, even though it seems far away in the midst of our suffering."

BIBLIOGRAPHY

Almond, Steve. "Chanukah Your Hearts Out!" In *How to Spell Chanukah,* edited by Emily Franklin, 39–42. Chapel Hill: Algonquin Books, 2007.

Alt, Albrecht. "The Origins of Israelite Law." In *Essays in Old Testament History and Religion,* 101–171. New York: Doubleday, 1967.

Bach, Alice. "Good to the Last Drop: Viewing the Sotah (Numbers 5:11–31) as the Glass Half Empty and Wondering How to View It Half Full." In *Women in the Hebrew Bible: A Reader,* edited by Alice Bach, 503–522. New York: Routledge, 1999.

"Be Thou My Vision." Translated by Mary E. Byrne. In *Sing to the Lord,* no. 460, stanza 3. Reprint. Kansas City: Lillenas Publishing, 1993.

Boer, Roland. "The Law of the Jealous Man." In *Voyages in Uncharted Waters: Essays on the Theory and Practice of Biblical Interpretation,* edited by Wesley J. Bergen and Armin Siedlecki, 87–95. Sheffield, UK: Sheffield Phoenix Press, 2006.

Bokser, Ben Zion. *The Jewish Mystical Tradition.* New York: Pilgrim Press, 1981.

Brenner, Athalya. *A Feminist Companion to the Latter Prophets.* Sheffield, UK: Sheffield Academic Press, 1995.

Brown, Brian Arthur. "A Diagram of Sources of the Pentateuch." Accessed February 1, 2017. http://www.brianarthurbrown.com/files/A%20Diagram%20of%20 Sources%20of%20the%20Pentateuch.pdf.

Claiborne, Shane, Jonathan Wilson-Hartgrove, and Enuma Oroko. *Common Prayer: A Liturgy for Ordinary Radicals.* Grand Rapids: Zondervan, 2010.

Cline, Eric H. *From Eden to Exile: Unraveling Mysteries of the Bible.* Washington, DC: National Geographic Society, 2006.

Davies, Eryl W. *Numbers.* New Century Bible Commentary. Grand Rapids: Eerdmans, 1995.

Diamond, James S. *Stringing the Pearls: How to Read the Weekly Torah Portion.* New York: Jewish Publication Society, 2008.

Dospěl, Marek. "Who Tells the Truth – the Bible or Archaeology?" *Biblical Archaeology Society* (May 15, 2017). Accessed May 16, 2017. http://www.biblicalarchaeology.org/daily/archaeology-today/biblical-archaeology-topics/truth-bible-or-archaeology.

Douglas, Mary. *Purity and Danger: An Analysis of the Concepts of Pollution and Taboo.* Reprint. London: Routledge & Paul, 2001.

Dozeman, Thomas B., Thomas Romer, and Konrad Schmid, eds. *Pentateuch, Hexateuch, or Enneateuch: Identifying Literary Works in Genesis through Kings,* vol. 8, Ancient Israel and Its Literature series. Atlanta: Society of Biblical Literature, 2011.

Eco, Umberto. "Postscript to *The Name of the Rose*." In *The Name of the Rose*, 503–536. Reprint. Orlando: Harcourt Brace & Co., 1994.

Fee, Gordon D., and Doulas Stuart. *How to Read the Bible Book by Book: A Guided Tour*. Reprint. Manila: OMF Literature, 2002.

Feinstein, Eve Levavi. "The 'Bitter Waters' of Numbers 5:11–31." *Vetus Testamentum* 62, no. 3 (2012): 300–306.

Festinger, Leon. *A Theory of Cognitive Dissonance*. Stanford: Stanford University Press, 1957.

Flesher, Paul V. M., and Robert Torry. *Film and Religion: An Introduction*. Nashville: Abingdon, 2007.

Gladwell, Malcolm. *David and Goliath: Underdogs, Misfits, and the Art of Battling Giants*. Kindle Edition. New York: Little, Brown & Co., 2013.

Gottwald, Norman K. "Early Israel and the Canaanite Socio-Economic System." In *Palestine in Transition: The Emergence of Ancient Israel*, edited by David Noel Freedman and David Frank Graf, 25–38. Sheffield, UK: Almond Press, 1983.

———. *The Hebrew Bible: A Socio-Literary Introduction*. Philadelphia: Fortress, 1987.

Greengus, Samuel. "Biblical and ANE Law." In *Anchor Bible Dictionary*, vol. 4, edited by David Noel Freedman, 242–252. New York: Anchor Doubleday, 1992.

Hoftijzer, J., and G. van der Kooij, trans. "Deir 'Alla Inscription." *Livius*. Accessed January 29, 2016. http://www.livius.org/sources/content/deir-alla-inscription/.

Huizenga, Leroy A. *The New Isaac: Tradition and Intertextuality in the Gospel of Matthew*. Leiden, Netherlands: Brill, 2012.

Jacobs, A. J. *The Year of Living Biblically: One Man's Humble Quest to Follow the Bible as Literally as Possible*. New York: Simon & Schuster, 2007.

Kushner, Harold S. *To Life!: A Celebration of Jewish Being and Thinking*. New York: Warner, 1994.

Lischer, Richard. *The Preacher King: Martin Luther King Jr. and the Word That Moved America*. Kindle Edition. New York: Oxford University Press, 1995.

McCarter, P. Kyle. *Textual Criticism: Recovering the Text of the Hebrew Bible*. Philadelphia: Fortress, 1986.

McDaniel, Jay, and J. Aaron Simmons. "So Many Faces: God, Humans, and Animals." In *Divinanimality: Animal Theory, Creaturely Theology*, edited by Stephen D. Moore, 223–240. New York: Fordham University Press, 2014.

Mendenhall, George E. "The Hebrew Conquest of Palestine." *Biblical Archaeologist* 25, no. 3 (September 1962): 66–87.

Miller, J. Maxwell, and John H. Hayes. *A History of Ancient Israel and Judah*. 2nd edition. Louisville: Westminster John Knox, 2006.

Modine, Mitchel. *1–2 Chronicles: A Commentary in the Wesleyan Tradition*. Kansas City: Beacon Hill, 2014.

Bibliography

———. "Zelophehad Had." Paper Presented at research seminar, Asia-Pacific Nazarene Theological Seminary, Taytay, Rizal, April 17, 2017.

Neusner, Jacob. "The Absoluteness of Christianity and the Uniqueness of Judaism: Why Salvation Is Not of the Jews." *Interpretation* 43, no. 1 (1989): 18–31.

Noth, Martin. *The History of Israel*. New York: Harper, 1958.

Oates, Stephen B. *Let the Trumpet Sound: The Life of Martin Luther King, Jr.* New York: Penguin Mentor, 1985.

Ogden, William A. "Look and Live." In *Sing to the Lord*, no. 372. Reprint. Kansas City: Lillenas, 1993.

Olson, Dennis T. "Nazirite." In *The Oxford Companion to the Bible*, edited by Bruce M. Metzger and Michael D. Coogan, 552. Oxford: Oxford University Press, 1993.

Pixley, Jorge. *Biblical Israel: A People's History*. Minneapolis: Fortress, 1992.

Podhoretz, Norman. *The Prophets: Who They Were, What They Are*. New York: Free Press, 2002.

Rauschenbusch, Walter. *The Social Principles of Jesus*. New York: International Committee of Young Men's Christian Associations, 1916.

Sakenfeld, Katharine Doob. "Numbers." In *Women's Bible Commentary*. Exp. edition. Edited by Carol A. Newsom and Sharon H. Ringe. Louisville: Westminster John Knox, 1998.

Shea, William H. "The Inscribed Tablets from Tell Deir 'Alla (Part II). *Andrews University Seminary Studies* 27, no. 2 (1989): 97–119.

Shurpin, Yehuda. "For Real, How Rare Is a Red Heifer?" *Questions & Answers* 16 (March 16, 2017). Accessed April 24, 2017. http://www.chabad.org/library/article_cdo/aid/3613245/jewish/For-Real-How-Rare-Is-a-Red-Heifer.htm#footnote1a3613245.

Simkins, Ronald A. "Limited Good in Genesis 23." In *Teaching the Bible: Practical Strategies for Classroom Instruction*, edited by Mark Roncase and Patrick Gray, 100–101. Resources for Biblical Study series, no. 49. Atlanta: Society of Biblical Literature, 2005.

Varughese, Alex, and Mitchel Modine. *Jeremiah: A Commentary in the Wesleyan Tradition*. Kansas City: Beacon Hill, 2010.

Webb, William J. "A Redemptive-Movement Model." In *Four Views on Moving Beyond the Bible to Theology*, edited by Gary T. Meadows, 215–248. Counterpoints Bible and Theology Series. Grand Rapids: Zondervan, 2009.

Yeivin, Israel. *Introduction to the Tiberian Masorah*. Translated and edited by E. J. Revell. Masoretic Studies Series, no. 5. Atlanta: Society of Biblical Literature, 1985.

Asia Theological Association
54 Scout Madriñan St. Quezon City 1103, Philippines
Email: ataasia@gmail.com Telefax: (632) 410 0312

OUR MISSION
The Asia Theological Association (ATA) is a body of theological institutions, committed to evangelical faith and scholarship, networking together to serve the Church in equipping the people of God for the mission of the Lord Jesus Christ.

OUR COMMITMENT
The ATA is committed to serving its members in the development of evangelical, biblical theology by strengthening interaction, enhancing scholarship, promoting academic excellence, fostering spiritual and ministerial formation and mobilizing resources to fulfill God's global mission within diverse Asian cultures.

OUR TASK
Affirming our mission and commitment, ATA seeks to:

- **Strengthen** interaction through inter-institutional fellowship and programs, regional and continental activities, faculty and student exchange programs.
- **Enhance** scholarship through consultations, workshops, seminars, publications, and research fellowships.
- **Promote** academic excellence through accreditation standards, faculty and curriculum development.
- **Foster** spiritual and ministerial formation by providing mentor models, encouraging the development of ministerial skills and a Christian ethos.
- **Mobilize** resources through library development, information technology and infra-structural development.

To learn more about ATA, visit www.ataasia.com   or   Facebook /AsiaTheologicalAssociation

Langham Literature and its imprints are a ministry of Langham Partnership.

Langham Partnership is a global fellowship working in pursuit of the vision God entrusted to its founder John Stott –

> *to facilitate the growth of the church in maturity and Christ-likeness through raising the standards of biblical preaching and teaching.*

Our vision is to see churches in the majority world equipped for mission and growing to maturity in Christ through the ministry of pastors and leaders who believe, teach and live by the Word of God.

Our mission is to strengthen the ministry of the Word of God through:
- nurturing national movements for biblical preaching
- fostering the creation and distribution of evangelical literature
- enhancing evangelical theological education

especially in countries where churches are under-resourced.

Our ministry

Langham Preaching partners with national leaders to nurture indigenous biblical preaching movements for pastors and lay preachers all around the world. With the support of a team of trainers from many countries, a multi-level programme of seminars provides practical training, and is followed by a programme for training local facilitators. Local preachers' groups and national and regional networks ensure continuity and ongoing development, seeking to build vigorous movements committed to Bible exposition.

Langham Literature provides majority world preachers, scholars and seminary libraries with evangelical books and electronic resources through publishing and distribution, grants and discounts. The programme also fosters the creation of indigenous evangelical books in many languages, through writer's grants, strengthening local evangelical publishing houses, and investment in major regional literature projects, such as one volume Bible commentaries like *The Africa Bible Commentary* and *The South Asia Bible Commentary*.

Langham Scholars provides financial support for evangelical doctoral students from the majority world so that, when they return home, they may train pastors and other Christian leaders with sound, biblical and theological teaching. This programme equips those who equip others. Langham Scholars also works in partnership with majority world seminaries in strengthening evangelical theological education. A growing number of Langham Scholars study in high quality doctoral programmes in the majority world itself. As well as teaching the next generation of pastors, graduated Langham Scholars exercise significant influence through their writing and leadership.

To learn more about Langham Partnership and the work we do visit **langham.org**

www.ingramcontent.com/pod-product-compliance
Lightning Source LLC
Chambersburg PA
CBHW070534170426
43200CB00011B/2423